WE WALK THE PATH TOGETHER

We Walk the Path Together

Learning from Thich Nhat Hanh and Meister Eckhart

Brian J. Pierce, OP

ORBIS BOOKS

Maryknoll, New York 10545

Second Printing, November 2006

Founded in 1970, Orbis Books endeavors to publish works that enlighten the mind, nourish the spirit, and challenge the conscience. The publishing arm of the Maryknoll Fathers and Brothers, Orbis seeks to explore the global dimensions of the Christian faith and mission, to invite dialogue with diverse cultures and religious traditions, and to serve the cause of reconciliation and peace. The books published reflect the views of their authors and do not represent the official position of the Maryknoll Society. To learn more about Maryknoll and Orbis Books, please visit our website at www.maryknoll.org.

Library of Congress Cataloging-in-Publication Data

Pierce, Brian J.
    We walk the path together : learning from Thich Nhat Hanh and Meister Eckhart / Brian J. Pierce.
      p. cm.
    ISBN-13: 978-1-57075-613-9
    1. Spirituality—Catholic Church. 2. Eckhart, Meister, d. 1327. 3. Nhât Hòanh, Thích. 4. Catholic Church—Relations—Zen Buddhism. 5. Zen Buddhism—Relations—Christianity. I. Title.
BX2350.65.P55 2005
248—dc22

2005009079

In memory of
Louis R. Every, OP,
and
James D. Campbell, OP

"We hold this treasure in earthen vessels."
—2 Corinthians 4:7

Contents

Foreword

Timothy Radcliffe, OP

When Brian Pierce, OP, asked me to write a foreword to this book, I accepted immediately. Brian is a beloved brother and friend, and I was happy to do this small favor for him. But I was wrong. I was the one who benefited. I read this book with immense pleasure, but increasingly I read it as an irresistible invitation to live differently. By the end of the first chapter I was hooked. He writes amusingly. I can often catch his laughter or smile, and yet he touches issues fundamental to our flourishing.

Brian is inspired by two spiritual masters: Meister Eckhart, a fourteenth-century German Dominican, and Thich Nhat Hanh, a contemporary Vietnamese Buddhist. Brian wishes to open up a debate between these two very different people; one is remote in time and the other belongs to a very different tradition. Such a debate is urgent, since so many Westerners find in Buddhism a serenity and peace that we so desperately need in our hectic lives and that Christianity does not always know how to offer. Yet this openness to Buddhism is hard, since its way of seeing reality is apparently so different from that of the West. When we dialogue with Judaism or Islam, it is a conversation between the children of our father Abraham. How can we begin?

This book begins with magnanimity—literally, having a great soul, that large heartedness that enables one to listen to those who are different from ourselves. This is a virtue that Brian has preeminently. His whole life is the story of someone who dares to open himself to other ways of being and seeing the world, and who lets himself and his assumptions be put into question. This journey began with an openness to other Christian denominations in his family, and then continued with his reluctant learning of Spanish, leading to his love affair with Latin America. Then there has been his discovery of the richness of other religious traditions. He is someone who is always learning new things, a permanent disciple. Whether he is working with Lenca Indians in Honduras or on retreat at a Hindu ashram, Brian has his ears and eyes open for whatever gifts may come his way, humble and alert.

Brian Pierce asserts that he is not an expert and he does not "have a handle on all the subtle theological intricacies." It is true that he does not have a scholar's knowledge of the texts in their original languages, and yet he is, in his own way, a master. He has a sureness of touch and a clarity of mind that carry their own authority. These attributes derive both from his reading of the major texts of many religious traditions and from years of practicing the contemplative life.

Confidence in this authority is necessary, since in this book we are guided through the deep waters of the similarities and differences between the teachings of Meister Eckhart and Thich Nhat Hanh, and other religious teachers of their traditions. Brian is convinced that these traditions share central insights and convictions. Before I read this book I was doubtful, but I am now convinced. The chapter on mindfulness, living in this present moment, is profoundly moving. As someone who leads a hectic life and who is perpetually busy, I discover here a powerful invitation to live in the present moment, free of fretting, and there discover God. As Eckhart wrote, "What is today? Eternity!" At the door of the Deer Park Buddhist Monastery there is a sign that reads, "The Kingdom of God is now or never."

Brian also shows many other ways in which Christianity and Buddhism are close to each other, such as spirituality as an awakening, the opening of our eyes to what is before us. Buddhism summons Christians to rediscover the fundamental discipline of breathing, which Brian shows to lie deep and often unnoticed within our own tradition. Both traditions also give insight into how one must dare to open one's eyes to suffering and be touched by it.

Nor is this book afraid to confront the differences between these faiths. Brian tries to understand the scandal that many Buddhists feel faced by the cross. He is able to mediate here because of a similar scandal that he felt when he first went to Peru and was shocked by the gaudy and bloody crosses and the extravagant devotions of the peasants before them. It is because he is always a disciple, always learning, that he can suggest ways across the abysses. One of the most moving passages in the book is his examination of the different reactions of Christians and Buddhists to the decision of the Cistercian monks to remain behind in Algeria, facing almost certain death from fundamentalists. For the Buddhists this seemed like a scandalous provocation to violence, and yet he tries to find a way of so articulating it in terms of compassion that it may make sense to his Buddhist friends.

The book begins with magnanimity and concludes with equanimity. It begins with the invitation to have a large soul and so ultimately invites us to aspire to a balanced one. It is a journey toward serenity, culminating in the beautiful description of Thomas Merton's death, having been bowled over by the revelation of peace in the horizontal statues of the Buddha at Polonnaruwa in Sri Lanka.

I concluded this book with an immense sense of joy. It is the joy of having passed hours with someone who is a wise friend and whom most readers will feel has become a friend by the time they finish the book. But I also ended with the feeling that there is a journey to be made, quietly and calmly, not rushing along as one sprints for the next plane, but dwelling in each succeeding moment, knowing that the kingdom of God is now or never.

Timothy Radcliffe, OP, is the former Master of the Dominican Order. He presently resides in Oxford, England, where he ministers as an itinerant preacher and a professor of theology.

Acknowledgments

This book has been in process my whole life. All of life's moments (a long series of *present moments* linked together by grace) have in different ways taught me to open up to the Great Mystery that cannot be put into words. For this reason I thank first of all my parents for the gift of life and for showing me God's love made flesh. I thank, as well, my three wonderful brothers, their families, and a lifetime of good friends.

I also want to say thanks to those who have been a light on my path of faith, especially this path of engagement with the world's spiritual traditions. I thank my Dominican brothers and sisters who have encouraged me along the way—especially the friars of the community of St. Martin de Porres in Raleigh, North Carolina, who have allowed me the time to write and who have helped me learn what it means to live the life of a contemplative preacher. I also thank Jim Barnett, OP, Kevin Carroll, OP, and the many lay Dominicans and friends in Honduras who, many years ago, understood and supported my search for a way to integrate contemplative prayer with the call to serve the poor. I am grateful for the ongoing, faithful witness of my contemplative Dominican sisters, who continue to teach me to sing the music of God in the language of silence. And profound thanks to my dear brother and teacher, Timothy Radcliffe, OP, who reveals to me and to so many the face of St. Dominic alive in our world today.

I thank my former provincial, Alberto Rodríguez, OP, for encouraging me to spend a year and a half at the Forest of Peace Ashram in Oklahoma, and for the many "friends of the forest," especially Sr. Pascaline Coff, OSB, Sr. Priscilla Trost, OSB, and Sheila Provencher, all of whom have touched my life in untold ways. My heartfelt thanks also go out to two more of my Dominican brothers: Donald Goergen, OP, a friend and mentor of many years, and a co-pilgrim to India; and to Paul Philibert, OP, both of whom have offered great insight in struggling with and clarifying some of the more difficult theological questions in this book. I thank Dr. Ruben Habito, who models for me a way to live Zen and love God, and whose very life is a bridge of hope spanning East and West. And to my friends Barb Pegg, Bob Doenges, Mel Williams, and Huy and Thu Le, I give thanks for your ideas, your technical support, and your prayerful presence along the way.

More recently I am grateful to Brother Pháp Đe, a lover of the way of both Jesus and the Buddha, and a true Dharma brother during my days spent with Thich Nhat Hanh and his community during the 2004 winter retreat. Deepest thanks also to Son and Anna Le and all who made those days of retreat at Deer Park Monastery an unforgettable grace. And to the Trappist monks at Mepkin Abbey in South Carolina, I thank you for caring for the live oak trees and their ancient secrets, and for holding the silence where pilgrim preachers can rest awhile and jot down a few thoughts for the next leg of the journey.

Finally, I thank Shirley du Boulay for our fortuitous meeting at the tenth anniversary of Bede Griffiths Sangha, and for helping to open the way for the initial contact with my editor, Robert Ellsberg, and the fine staff at Orbis Books. What marvelous things can happen when we do absolutely *nothing* to make them happen! Each step on this journey has been an unfolding of the gratuitousness of God.

Introduction

With a combination of pristine simplicity and the exquisite artistic flare of a good chef, Thich Nhat Hanh ends his book *Going Home: Jesus and Buddha as Brothers* with the following words of wisdom:

> The Buddha and Jesus have to meet every moment in each of us. Each of us in our daily practice needs to touch the spirit of the Buddha and the spirit of Jesus so that they manifest. . . . It is just like cooking. If you love French cooking, it does not mean that you are forbidden to love Chinese cooking. . . . You love the apple; yes, you are authorized to love the apple, but no one prevents you from also loving the mango.[1]

The apple and the mango. Jesus and the Buddha. So different, yet so much common ground between them. Both of these great masters and religious founders entrusted rich legacies and profound spiritual teachings to their respective disciples and traditions. Two such disciples are Meister Eckhart and Thich Nhat Hanh, and it is they who invite us to enter into the dialogue that is the aim of this book.

Meister Eckhart was born in the German town of Hochheim around 1260, and though little is known of his early years, it is known that he entered the Dominican order of the Catholic Church before his twentieth year. Founded as part of the mendicant reform within medieval Christianity, the Dominican order quickly connected with the new wave of mysticism sweeping across much of Europe at the time, especially in the Rhineland area of southern Germany. As a young friar, Brother Eckhart was fortunate to be influenced by two of the great Dominican theologians of the era—Thomas Aquinas and Albert the Great—both of whom were creative pioneers, charting new ground in the fields of Aristotelian philosophy, science, and mystical experience. Eckhart's keen intellectual talent earned him early on the honorific title *Meister*, and this, combined with what seems to have been a natural openness to mystical experience and insight, prepared him for a rich life of teaching and preaching.

A number of the Dominican friars around this time, Eckhart included, had close ties with several of the new, innovative, and mystically inclined spiritual movements that were flourishing across Europe, among which were the Beguines and the Friends of God. Strassburg, where Eckhart was assigned as a preacher for the monasteries of contemplative Dominican nuns (many of whom were ex-Beguines themselves), was one of the centers of the mystical renewal. These new movements encouraged mystical experience, while deemphasizing the need to receive ecclesiastical approval of such experience—a combination that was not looked upon very favorably in some circles of the church hierarchy.[2] Many of Eckhart's sermons survived, however, thanks to the nuns from these monasteries, who not only did a heroic job of transcribing them as the Meister preached but also conserved them at great risk when Eckhart himself was called in to explain his teachings before a theological tribunal. There is a general consensus today that Eckhart both influenced the spiritual life of the nuns *and* was profoundly influenced by these women, whose mystical experiences form much of the material for Eckhart's reflections.

Eckhart's daring journey into the terrain of mystical experience, complete with its theology of paradox and negation, was threatening to certain sectors in the church at the time. Mystical experience often defies logic and therefore is easily misunderstood and quickly labeled as dangerous. Seven centuries later, though, we are grateful to Eckhart for his courageous spiritual journey. He has left us a legacy that can both encourage and guide many spiritual seekers today—especially in a world of growing interreligious dialogue. Thomas Merton, the well-known American monk and activist who died in 1968, said of Eckhart, "He breathed his own endless vitality into the juiceless formulas of orthodox theology with such charm and passion that the common people heard them gladly."[3]

Eckhart's "charm and passion," along with his close association with nuns and with the lay spiritual movements of his day, had the unfortunate effect of fanning the fires of suspicion and accusation that plagued him during the last years of his life.[4] As tensions rose, his more outspoken opponents called for investigations into the orthodoxy of his writings. In the end, fourteen of his sentences were categorized as errant, though contrary to historical gossip, Eckhart himself was never condemned as a heretic.[5] In interreligious circles, Eckhart is often compared to his contemporary, the Japanese Zen master Dogen, for in many ways his style of teaching and preaching, like that of a Zen master, is intended to shock the listener into a radical and more liberating encounter with the gospel message of Jesus.

Thich Nhat Hanh is a spiritual master and mystic of our own times, one who has feasted abundantly at the table of spiritual practice while at the same time sharing generously the fruits of his practice with millions of people across the world. Born and trained as a Buddhist monk in Vietnam, Thich Nhat Hanh was relatively unknown in the West until he was invited to the United States in 1966 by the Fellowship of Reconciliation to speak on the suffering of the Vietnamese people. Because of his political views and his tireless efforts at reconciliation and peace, Thich Nhat Hanh was not allowed to return to his native Vietnam and has dedicated the past forty years of his life to traveling the world, sharing the fundamental spiritual teachings of the Buddha, inspiring many spiritual pilgrims in the practice of mindfulness, and working for peace. He has also helped to found three flourishing monasteries in Europe and the United States, giving new expression to the integration of Buddhist monasticism and social engagement in the West.

It is principally the voices of these two spiritual masters, Thich Nhat Hanh and Meister Eckhart, mixed with the occasional voices of other friends walking along the path, that will serve as the centerpiece for this dialogue. The sources for these reflections come primarily from the three-volume collection, *Meister Eckhart: Sermons and Treatises*, translated and edited by M. O'C. Walshe, and Thich Nhat Hanh's two books on Jesus and Buddha: *Living Buddha, Living Christ* (1995), and *Going Home: Jesus and Buddha as Brothers* (1999). At times the voices will seem very different, almost like two entirely irreconcilable melodies. Experts in the field of interreligious dialogue remind us that this is normal and that there is no need to try to force an artificial harmony with what are uniquely different and beautiful melodies. At other times the voices in this dialogue blend together in exquisite harmony, and it seems to me that all we can do at those moments is stop, close our eyes, breathe deeply, and listen with deep gratitude.

I am not an expert in the field of interreligious dialogue; I am a spiritual seeker, like so many in our world today. I must confess, however, that I am more inclined to celebrate the moments of harmonious communion that draw us together than to emphasize the differences that keep us apart. I am profoundly grateful for the wisdom and teachings of other prophets in this field who have touched my life—people like Fr. Bede Griffiths, His Holiness the Dalai Lama, Thomas Merton, Abhishiktananda, Ruben Habito, and, of course, Thây (I will refer to Thich Nhat Hanh in the remainder of this book as *Thây*, a title of respect that translates roughly as *venerable teacher*, and which is used by his own disciples). I single out with the deepest affection my gratitude to Sr. Pascaline Coff, OSB, who has been a faithful companion during the past several years in discovering the path that leads through the wisdom of the world's great religious traditions to the springs of living water.

These and many other saintly sages and prophets have taken the risk of building a beautiful bridge spanning the gap between East and West, laying the foundation for many of us to touch deeply the riches of our own traditions with the help and the light that shine forth from other spiritual legacies. Through the wisdom of these teachers and their fidelity to their respective traditions, the landscape of interreligious dialogue looks today more like a beautiful garden than like a "dry and weary land where there is no water" (Ps. 63:1).

The reflections that follow in these pages began to germinate when a friend, Sheila Provencher, and I decided to read Thây's book *Going Home: Jesus and Buddha as Brothers* and share our insights and reflections. I was living in Central America at the time, so our cyberspace study of Thây's book served as a bridge that both united us geographically, and also helped us to learn ways to build bridges of understanding between Christians and Buddhists. When the invitation came from Orbis Books to organize my thoughts on these two spiritual masters into a more ordered, publishable format, I found myself faced with several questions: To whom am I speaking? What *language* do I speak in this dialogue? What part of the bridge do I want to help build?

First of all, I come to this privileged world of interreligious dialogue as a disciple of Jesus. It is important for me to state this clearly, for my reflections on Thich Nhat Hanh's writings and the Buddhist tradition always come from the point of view of a Christian, albeit one with a great respect for the wisdom that they embody. I write because I long for many of my Christian sisters and brothers to experience the same joy that I have experienced at encountering our Christian tradition with the fresh insights and concrete spiritual practices that Buddhism offers. My reading of Buddhist spiritual texts and the practice of meditation that I have learned over the years, in great part from the Zen Buddhist tradition, are like underground springs watering the roots of my Christian faith. I believe that I am a better Christian because of this exchange.

I also write to share the love of my own Christian heritage with my Buddhist brothers and sisters. I undertake this venture with a sincere dose of humility. At the beginning of this introduction, Thây spoke of loving both French cooking *and* Chinese cooking. I enjoy cooking, but I am no master chef. My hope is that these reflections will be received as coming from an amateur cook who is trying out a new recipe on friends.

Though I began this project resigned to the fact that, because of the centuries of time separating us, I would never have a chance to meet Meister Eckhart, except through his writings, I have cultivated the hope for many years that one day I might have the chance to meet Thây in person. Those hopes, however, seemed to fade away as often as they looked as though they might actually be fulfilled. Every time I would try to make a retreat or a day of mindfulness with Thây, the whole scheme would crumble before my very eyes. I finally resigned myself to writing this book without that meeting ever happening. I let go of planning for the impossible and decided to get busy and write.

In the autumn of 2003, well into the writing of the book, I received a letter from my Vietnamese friends Son and Anna Le, who surprised me with a gift of two weeks of retreat with Thây and more than three hundred of his monastic and lay disciples during their winter retreat at Deer Park Monastery in Southern California. My dream became a reality, and this time I had nothing whatsoever to do with it (if only I had *let go* years ago)! What a profound and moving experience it was! Meeting Thây and practicing with his monastic community have been a gift that I shall never forget, and in a surprising way, it brought me face to face with Eckhart as well. I realized with great delight that—through the person of Thây—I was sitting at the feet of *both* of these beloved teachers, drinking in their teachings in a very profound way.

I know now, in a way that I would not have been able to know otherwise, that to understand Thây's teachings, one must practice them in a communal context. Reading about a beautiful botanical garden is one thing; seeing and smelling the beauty are a wholly different experience. Thây's teachings on the *practice* of mindfulness cannot be grasped on a merely intellectual level. The phrase "spiritual practice" has taken on a whole new meaning for me since this wondrous encounter. Perhaps what made the retreat even more graced for me personally was the openness on the part of the Buddhist monks, nuns, and laity to enter into a mutual dialogue on the spiritual practices and insights of both of our traditions. I can only hope that this was just the beginning of a long friendship that will last for many years to come.

1

Magnanimity

Learning the Art of Dialogue

The Music of Dialogue

Given that the reflections in this book have first passed through my own heart and mind, it seems only right that I share some of my own journey into the world of interreligious dialogue, for it is precisely against this backdrop that I find myself on the path with these two great spiritual teachers.

I am a Christian of the Roman Catholic tradition and a friar of the Dominican order, the same religious order that Eckhart belonged to seven hundred years ago. After I professed my religious vows in 1983 and set off to begin my theology studies, nothing was farther from my mind than the thought that one day I would be meditating at a Buddhist monastery, living in an ashram, or involved in interreligious dialogue. Life is certainly full of surprises. Though our spiritual traditions are different, the daily life of a Buddhist monk and that of a Dominican friar are not so different, and this only makes the dialogue all the more enticing.

I discovered this delightful truth while living and sharing with the Buddhist monks and nuns at Deer Park Monastery in California. One moment in particular stands out for me. Several hundred of us were gathered with Thây for an evening meditation session in the Ocean of Peace Meditation Hall. After the sounding of the bell, a calming silence settled over the entire assembly. Suddenly the pristine voice of a young monk, chanting a Buddhist *sutra* in Vietnamese, pierced the silence. The ancient chant filled the hall with a beauty that was both simple and profound. I was moved to tears, struck once again by the realization that the great religious and spiritual traditions have so much to offer the world, such a richness of spiritual practice, culture, art, and music. As the young monk chanted from some timeless depths within his heart, I was able to glimpse and appreciate anew my own Dominican tradition, in which the chanting of the Hebrew Psalms is a central part of our daily life. My life, like his, is so rich, so full, so beautiful. We have so much that we can give to one another and to the world. What a shame that history has not always been open to that mutual sharing of gifts. As the young monk contin-

1

ued, it dawned on me that maybe interreligious dialogue begins in that very place where silence and song come together. Maybe it is in chanting our sacred music to one another that we will experience a communion that takes us beyond the limitations that have often kept us separated.

In *Living Buddha, Living Christ,* Thây relates an encounter he had several years ago with children on a beach in Sri Lanka. He writes:

> It had been a long time since I had seen children like that, barefoot children on a very green island with no sign of industrial pollution. . . . The children just ran toward me. We didn't know each other's language, so I put my arms around them—all six of them, and we stood like that for a long time. Suddenly I realized that if I chanted a prayer in the ancient Buddhist language of Pali, they might recognize it, so I began to chant, "Buddham saranam gaachami" ("I take refuge in the Buddha"). They not only recognized it, they continued the chant. Four of them joined their palms and chanted, while the other two stood respectfully. . . . I motioned to the two children who were not chanting to join us. They smiled, placed their palms together and chanted in Pali, "I take refuge in Mother Mary." The music of their prayer did not differ much from the Buddhist one. . . . I felt very much at one with each of them. They had given me a feeling of deep serenity and peace.[1]

"The music of their prayer did not differ much from the Buddhist one." These are profound words. Thây is pointing to something much deeper here than a coincidental encounter with innocent children. Though the words of our chants differ, a common music flows through all of us, through the entire universe. We are more alike than different. We are more one than separate.

In my own Dominican tradition, and in most of the Christian monastic tradition, we gather several times each day to chant the psalms *choir to choir.* What this means is that we face each other in two *choirs,* alternately chanting verses back and forth, side to side. As a young friar, I thought that this back-and-forth routine was merely for practical purposes; it gave us all a chance to catch our breath every couple of verses. But as I have grown into this ancient practice over the years, I have begun to realize that we are actually taking part in a sacred dialogue, sharing the holy Word of God with one another. As one choir chants, the other listens attentively, receiving the sacred words into the silence of the heart. The second choir then returns the gift, and the sacred circle of giving and thanksgiving is completed, only to begin anew. This, it seems to me, is a perfect metaphor of what interreligious dialogue is all about. It is about sharing with one another the music that flows through our respective prayer.

Dialogue is rooted in the music of our ancient traditions. If we are to be true to this fruitful encounter, we must practice attentive and respectful listening, what Thây calls "deep listening." It presupposes a certain amount of vulnerability, for we must be willing to open ourselves up to receive an unfamiliar gift. Dialogue is a mutual giving and receiving, a sharing of our respective insights into the music of the Great Mystery. It is an opening up of ourselves to the unique gift of the other. What would our world be like today if the world religions were truly committed to this kind of sacred exchange? Do we dare dream of the day when world conflicts will be solved through a mutual sharing of our spiritual riches, a commitment to discern together the music that unites us? What would the city of Jerusalem look like today if Jews, Christians, and Muslims gathered each morning for a three-way sharing of sacred music and chant? Unrealistic? Maybe it is time to stretch the boundaries of our imagination a bit.

At two different points during my stay with the community at Deer Park Monastery in early 2004, the monks and nuns invited me to share with them different aspects of our spiritual practice and our communal living. Thây had been using excerpts from the monastic Rule of St. Benedict in his *dharma* talks, and so the monks and nuns were curious to know something about the Dominican rule and way of life, as well. I was pleasantly surprised by the request, for I had gone to Deer Park to learn about *their* way of life and practice, and suddenly I found them respectfully interested in my own spiritual path. We spoke and we listened to each other for several hours on each of the two occasions. In the midst of it all, I experienced a profound sense of being of one heart and mind. During one of the gatherings, I responded to a question by reading and reflecting for a moment on a few verses from the Gospel of John (20:19-23), the account in which Jesus gives himself to the community through the breath of the Spirit. I was deeply touched when one of the Buddhist monks raised his hand and said, "Brother Brian, would you ever consider coming to Plum Village in France to teach us about the Bible?" For a moment I experienced in the depths of my being what a world built on harmony and mutual respect might actually *feel* like. It is truly liberating to experience this communion that transcends boundaries. Interreligious dialogue, I am convinced, must form part of all authentic spiritual practice in our day and age, especially if we take seriously the need to work for a world built on harmony and peace.

As a Dominican friar, I have made a choice to follow in the footsteps of Jesus as a brother in the spiritual family that St. Dominic of Guzmán founded eight centuries ago. For Dominicans, this choice is ritualized, after several years of initial formation, through a public vow, a promise to live as a member of this family for the rest of my life. We Dominicans make only one explicit vow—the vow of obedience. Often misunderstood, the vow of obedience is not a relinquishing of one's freedom. It is, instead, a choice to transcend any illusion of separateness and to live as part of a larger body, to be one voice in a choir of voices. The vow of obedience teaches me to sing my own unique song *not alone* but in harmony with my brothers and sisters. Over the years, I have come to understand this vow as a daily practice, a commitment to a love grounded in mutual attentiveness and respect. Obedience liberates me from the tiny world of the ego.

The former worldwide master/teacher of the Dominican order, Fr. Timothy Radcliffe, frequently reminds us that our vow of obedience as Dominicans is really a vow about learning to listen deeply. It forms us for life in community, he notes, and is based on dialogue and respectful discussion. "The word *obedire*," says Timothy, "comes from [the Latin] *ob-audire*, to listen. The beginning of true obedience is when we dare to let our brother or sister speak and we listen to them."[2] To vow obedience, then, is to promise to live a life of respectful listening. This is the basis of all interreligious dialogue. Thây picks up on this theme in a very moving call for true dialogue:

> In a true dialogue, both sides are willing to change. We have to appreciate that truth can be received from outside of—not only within—our own group. If we do not believe that, entering into dialogue would be a waste of time. If we think we monopolize the truth and we still organize a dialogue, it is not authentic. . . . Dialogue must be practiced on the basis of "non-self." We have to allow what is good, beautiful, and meaningful in the other's tradition to transform us.[3]

This is precisely what happened during our gatherings and informal conversations at Deer Park Monastery. We spoke to one another and we listened to one another. We chanted and allowed our common music to bring us closer together. We discovered the goodness and beauty in each other's traditions. When this kind of dialogue happens, the other person is no longer a stranger; he or she has become a brother or a sister.

Thây often comments on the need for people of all spiritual traditions to touch deeply the roots of their own tradition before opening themselves up to a new tradition. He even goes on to insist that his monastic and lay disciples who come from another spiritual tradition must first befriend and be reconciled with their original spiritual roots before giving themselves fully to the rich spiritual heritage of Buddhism. I find such a teaching wonderfully liberating, respectful, and wise.

Hearing Thây's words, I like to close my eyes and imagine my own spiritual heritage as an ancient and magnificent live oak tree, deeply rooted in many centuries of Judeo-Christian faith and practice, yet branching out and embracing the insights and teachings of the other great spiritual traditions. Deeply rooted, yes, but always growing in new and ever more expansive ways.

Maybe this is what Jesus had in mind when he told the parable of the tiny mustard seed "that someone took and sowed in a field; it is the smallest of all the seeds, but when it has grown it is the greatest of shrubs and becomes a tree, so that the birds of the air come and make nests in its branches" (Matt. 13:31-32). The great trees of the world's religious traditions have provided a place of rest for many beautiful birds of varied colors and song. Together we form a great forest of diversity, but a diversity in which our branches are intertwined and in constant communion. The birds, which hop from branch to branch, sing in many different languages and melodies, but on a mystical level, they all sing one song. When we listen to this music, we are led to a deeper experience of the silent music of the Great Mystery that sings through us all.

Both Eckhart and Thây have taught me much about listening to the music of God in its many manifestations. They both help me grow in my understanding of what it means to be a disciple of Jesus. It was in 1993, in a bookstore in Chiapas, Mexico, that I stumbled on and bought my first of Thich Nhat Hanh's books—in Spanish. The title, which caught my attention immediately, was *Ser Paz* (*Being Peace*). I was living and working in a newly founded Dominican community in Honduras at the time and was very much involved with the aspirations and struggles for peace and justice among the poor of Central America. For several years I had been attempting to bring my spiritual life and my work among the poor into a more harmonious balance, guided by the teachings of Jesus.

At the same time, though, I found myself in a constant inner struggle. It seemed that the more I worked for world peace, the less I experienced inner peace. I think, as I look back now, that what I began to discover in Thây's words—in the music that I heard flowing from his heart—was that it is possible to do more than *work* for peace; I could actually learn to *be* peace. That appealed to me immediately. It seemed to open up to me a deeper insight into Jesus' teachings in his famous Sermon on the Mount: "Blessed are the poor in spirit, for theirs is the kingdom of heaven. . . . Blessed are the peacemakers, for they will be called children of God" (Matt. 5:3-10). Thây helped me realize that I could both *be* peace and *make* peace, living the "blessedness" that Jesus proclaimed right here and now. Ever since that fortuitous encounter, my spiritual journey as a follower of Jesus has been greatly inspired by the teachings of Thich Nhat Hanh.

The music of Meister Eckhart came into my life a few years later. After five years in Honduras, and as part of my attempt to renew certain aspects of my spiritual practice, I asked for permission to spend the larger part of a year in prayer and silence in a small hermitage up in the mountains of Honduras. At the end of that year, I was encouraged by my prior provincial to continue this process at a place where I could more fully study and sink my roots into the rich contemplative tradition of our Dominican order. So in January of 1997 I moved to the Forest of Peace Ashram, an interreligious monastic ashram in Oklahoma. It was there, in a forest of magnificent trees, that the resident community of Benedictine sisters and I, along with some Dominican sisters and lay friends from the area, embarked on a year of communal study and reflection on the writings and sermons of Meister Eckhart. Without being aware of it at the time, I began to experience deeply the phrase that is so integral to the teachings of Thich Nhat Hanh: "I have arrived; I am home." My heart began to sing with the joy of "being home at last" long before my head finally caught on to the tune as well.

It was at the ashram that I experienced the gentleness and simplicity of Thây's words mingling harmoniously with the teachings of Meister Eckhart. Both teachers were showing me how to reach across religious borders to find spiritual nourishment at a time when I needed some fresh water to irrigate what had become a rather dry spiritual terrain. Thây's simple teachings on the practice of mindfulness began to offer me a concrete framework within which to understand the theologically rich and dense sermons of Eckhart.

At first I would hear Eckhart says things like, "God is a word, an unspoken word . . . God is a word that utters itself . . . God is spoken and unspoken,"[4] and I would shake my head and wonder just what he was trying to say. Through the practice of mindfulness and contemplative meditation, I began to "hear" that unspoken word. Thây and the practice of meditation have helped me understand that it is not about having these mysteries *explained* to us; it is about *tasting* the Mystery. Eckhart and Thây have become my brothers, for both help me to remain grounded and rooted in the rich contemplative tradition of my Christian and Dominican spiritual path. Thây has especially helped me to discover how my spiritual practice can be freeing, joyful, and down-to-earth. Thây refers to the Buddha and Jesus as *brothers*. In that spirit, I too give thanks for Eckhart and Thây, my elder brothers, who help me to hear the music of God in the depths of my being, and whose footprints along the way remind me that I do not walk this path alone.

The Practice of Magnanimity

The Dominican order was founded in the early 1200s in southern France—not far from Plum Village.[5] Like his contemporary, St. Francis of Assisi, St. Dominic was committed to living a simple life as a wandering beggar, preaching through word and example the teachings of Jesus. Buddhist monks for many centuries have led similar lives—begging for their daily sustenance while attempting to embody the fullness of the teachings of the Buddha and to pass those teachings on to others. Over the centuries monks and mystics of both traditions have lived out in different ways and places the spiritual legacies left by the Buddha and Jesus.

I was raised in an environment in which tolerance and respect for religious differences was simply a part of life. I am one of four sons of a Catholic mother and a Protestant father. My parents were profoundly respectful of each other's religious beliefs, and without making it an issue, my brothers and I learned this respect almost through osmosis. It was not unusual for my brothers and me to visit the Protestant churches of our friends when we were growing up. Religious tensions did creep into the family scene on the part of some of our relatives, and I did experience—personally—the pain caused by such narrow-mindedness. But even that experience has served a great purpose, showing me the ugly face of intolerance and the value of being committed to the healing journey of understanding and reconciliation.

Openness to another kind of *dialogue* made its way into my life when I began high school and signed up to take German, just as my older brother had done. The German professor was a favorite of the students, because he occasionally took them out to eat at a local German restaurant. Unfortunately (or so it seemed at the time), because of overscheduling, I was transferred against my will into the first-year Spanish class. I was not thrilled at all, especially when I met the Spanish teacher, Mrs. Holland, who seemed to me to be older than God! I decided I would resist the imposition by learning nothing.

That, of course, was just the challenge that Mrs. Holland needed. Within a few days she had me in the palm of her hand. She was a miracle worker in the classroom. Her approach to studying a foreign language was about much more than memorizing words and repeating them on exam day. She opened up our hearts to the culture and history of Spain and Latin America. We contemplated the works of great artists, we listened and danced to Latin music, and we even cooked and ate Spanish and Latin American food. Mrs. Holland led us into the heart and culture of worlds that were not our own. While never using spiritual language, Mrs. Holland introduced me to a way of seeing the world from a spiritual point of view, a *seeing* that opened me up to the mystery and beauty found in *otherness*, in people who were different from myself. She taught me tolerance through the appreciation of diverse cultures and their many expressions of beauty.

It was Mrs. Holland who, in my second year of Spanish (I ended up taking three years of a language that I vowed *never* to learn!), encouraged several of us to apply for a scholarship as foreign exchange students. I had no idea at the time what that meant, but lo and behold, at the end of the school year I was awarded one of the scholarships. Before I even realized what had happened, I found myself, at the age of seventeen, living in Peru for several months—an experience that radically changed my life. My eyes were opened even more to both the exciting world of cultural diversity and the ugliness of political and social tyranny. It was in Peru that I discovered the *other*—the one whose experience and vision of the world is different from my own, and yet who is mysteriously my brother and sister at the same time. Slowly, and often clouded with many unanswered questions, my heart began to open up to the world. This led me to pursue studies in political science and Spanish at the university, imagining at that time that I would eventually embark on a life of diplomacy or international relations.

As my university studies advanced, a new spiritual dimension began to open up as well. My fortuitous meeting and befriending of a community of contemplative Dominican nuns, whose monastery is near the university where I studied in east Texas, was just the spiritual nudge I needed. I am forever grateful to this community of prayerful women, whose entire life is committed to listening to the still, quiet voice of God; it was they who first helped me to fall in love with silence. I spent days and nights in their monastic chapel, watching them peer into the dark silence of God's love. It is *that* silence, which I eventually discovered deep within my own heart, that has nourished each step of my spiritual pilgrimage ever since. With the encouragement of the sisters, and the support of my family and my friends from college, I entered the Dominican order as a novice shortly after graduation. I can smile today and admit honestly that I really had *no idea* what I was doing. It was a leap into the unknown that, to this day, continues to unfold as an unending string of surprises.

I have learned many profound and, at times, difficult lessons over these many years of exchange and dialogue, of speaking new languages and listening to the music enveloped and sometimes hidden in the silence. Slowly, over time, something has happened to me in this process of venturing into languages and cultures and religions other than my own. The world has become larger and smaller at the same time. I have learned to see the world with a whole new set of eyes, and today my ears hear music that was once inaudible. It is not so unlike the spiritual journey of enlightenment, and I have begun to discover a world and a life that were always present, though not always perceived. I have tasted the sweetness of a great river that flows through all of life.

I think the metaphor of a world that grows simultaneously larger and smaller is what happens when we enter into dialogue with persons different from ourselves. On one hand, as the world expands, our hearts are challenged to grow larger, all-inclusive, universal—what mystics call *magnanimity*—living with a great soul and an expansive heart. It is the meaning of the title *Mahatma-Great Soul*, given to Gandhi, a man whose heart and soul grew large enough to embrace the whole world. In a mysterious way, though, just as the heart reaches out to embrace the world, suddenly the world seems to grow very small, intimate enough to be held in a gentle, reverent embrace— the way a mother holds her newborn infant in her arms.

This paradox of magnanimity, this experience of a world that is both expansive and intimately close at the same time, can happen upon us in surprising and unexpected ways, easily catching us off guard—not so unlike falling in love. I remember stumbling through my first Spanish conversations as a student in Peru, frequently ending up with my foot in my mouth! I would feel totally lost and discouraged and then suddenly a single word or sentence, spoken or heard correctly, would transform all these new and strange sounds into an experience of communion with someone who had seemed at first very far away. I understand! "I have arrived; I am home!" A similar experience happened years later as I helplessly struggled through my first Zen *sesshins*—trying to sit still on a meditation cushion, my back aching and my legs feeling as though they were folded for all eternity—only to glimpse for a split second a kind of intimate, universal oneness that I could not explain. The cushion was the world, and I was one with it all.

This wonderful gift, called *magnanimity*, usually catches us off guard when we venture into unknown territory and allow our defenses to relax a bit. It is then that the *other*—the one who is different—shows us how much we are really one. I can say with deep gratitude that I have experienced this opening up of the boundaries of my heart many times in my life. Whether it be meditating and chanting with Hindus in India, praying at shrines of Sufi saints in Pakistan, or on pilgrimage to the Basilica of María de Guadalupe in Mexico, I have tasted the spiritual joy that comes with the gift of magnanimity. This happened frequently during my years of ministry with peasants in Honduras and Mayan Indians in Guatemala. In unexpected ways I would suddenly experience the erasing of boundaries, and almost in a way akin to spiritual transmission, gratuitous bits and pieces of the ancient wisdom of these peoples would find their way into my heart.

I will always treasure a visit to Dharamsala, India, with one of my Dominican brothers, Don Goergen, and the graced meeting we had with His Holiness the Dalai Lama and the monks of his monastery. Just the simple gift of experiencing the Dalai Lama's contagious joy and laughter taught me much about how the human heart, when open to all of life's diverse surprises and unexpected tragedies, can lead one to the universal language of harmony and communion, what the Dalai Lama calls the religion of loving kindness. Magnanimity, I have discovered, is one of life's unplanned-for graces; it teaches us to see and hear and learn things that we never dreamed were possible.

One experience in particular stands out as one of the many that opened my eyes and led my heart to see the common ground shared among all the world's spiritual traditions. I was invited to take part in an indigenous religious ceremony with the Lenca Indians in Honduras several years ago. Mixing ancient Lenca rituals with Christian prayers, the elderly *rezador*, or shaman, performed the ceremony while holding a freshly cut pine bow in his hands. I later approached him and asked about the symbolism behind the frequent use of pine branches in Lenca worship. He looked at me with his wide, dark eyes and said, "Oh, you do not know? Then let me tell you. If you sit quietly beneath a pine tree in the early morning hours, before the sun rises, and listen very attentively, you will hear the pine tree singing to God." That was all he said, yet I was immediately aware that his teaching was important for me. Perhaps it was his mention of *listening quietly* that caught my attention, for silence had been one of my spiritual teachers ever since my college days with the contemplative Dominican nuns.

Not long after that, I ran across some words by Thich Nhat Hanh, which led me to an even deeper understanding of the shaman's words. "Ten years ago, I planted three beautiful Himalayan cedars outside my hermitage, and now, whenever I walk by one of them, I bow, touch its bark with my cheek, and hug it," writes Thây. "As I breathe in and out mindfully, I look up at its branches and beautiful leaves. I receive a lot of peace and sustenance from hugging trees."[6] How is it, I remember thinking, that a Buddhist monk and a Honduran shaman both speak about the spiritual power in trees? Amazing! And then came the final blow that made me stop and really look at these underground currents linking all the world's great spiritual traditions. This time it was a couple verses from the Hebrew Psalms: "Let the heavens be glad, and let the earth rejoice; let the sea roar, and all that fills it; let the field exult, and everything in it. *Then shall all the trees of the forest sing for joy before the Lord*" (96:11-12).

I immediately became a believer. Did not the Lenca shaman also speak about pine trees singing to God? As Eckhart summed it up for me later in one of his sermons, "All things speak God. . . . All creatures would like to echo God in all their works."[7] So I thought to myself: if Lenca indigenous trees and Buddhist trees and Hebrew trees and Christian trees can all sing in harmony, then could it be that we human beings can do the same? The humble teaching of the Honduran shaman slowly opened my eyes to the beauty and challenge of interreligious dialogue. I am sure that he did not have college degrees tacked onto his *curriculum vitae*; he probably did not even know how to read and write. But he had learned to listen to the voice of God in the world around him. He taught me about the Mystery that stands beneath and beyond the world religions.

The Risk of Dialogue

As a beginner in the field of interreligious dialogue, I know that it is always a risk to enter into such sacred ground. Competition and arrogance have often spoiled the trust needed for such a delicate conversation. I especially regret the times that my own Catholic Church has fallen into the trap of near-sightedness and arrogance. Having said that, though, I am grateful to live in this particular slice of human history, for certainly more has been done to further interreligious dialogue in my lifetime than at any other time in history.

I am aware that I do not have a handle on all the subtle theological intricacies that would prevent my stepping on someone's sacred toes in this process of dialogue. However, I choose to take the risk anyway. I believe so deeply in the value of this kind of respectful engagement that I trust that even with the frailty of our human words and experiences, our very desire to speak and listen lovingly to one another will give birth to the understanding and communion for which we all long. Perhaps most of all, I choose the path of dialogue because our world is simply too small and too beautiful to continue building walls that separate us. As one of the documents from a worldwide gathering of Dominicans states, "Dialogue is . . . a necessary mode of existence in a world of difference."[8] Only through dialogue can we glimpse the beauty and deep insights of the world's spiritual traditions.

I also choose to risk journeying along this path of dialogue because Jesus risked in this way as well. On one such occasion, Jesus found himself in a region bordering the non-Jewish towns of Tyre and Sidon (Matt. 15:21-28). A Canaanite woman walked up to Jesus and asked him to cure her daughter, who was possessed by a demon. Jesus' disciples, fearing that the presence of the gentile woman might be offensive to their master, offered to send her away. Jesus took a risk, choosing instead to break the cultural and religious rules of the day and speak with the woman. He explained to the woman that his mission, as far as he could see at that moment, was not to be extended to gentiles, that he had come only to serve "the lost sheep of the House of Israel" (15:24).

The woman listened attentively and respectfully to Jesus. She remained committed to the dialogue, even going so far as to say at one point that she and her daughter would be satisfied with the scraps of Jesus' healing mercy and love. After all, she remarked, "even the dogs eat the scraps that fall from the master's table" (Matt. 15:27). Jesus, deeply moved by the woman's dignity, and recognizing the beauty of her transparent faith, exclaimed, "How great is your faith!" The scripture text goes on to say, "In that moment the daughter was healed" (15:28).

What is of great spiritual value, as one reflects on this story, is that both Jesus and the woman took the risk of entering into mutual dialogue. Jesus did so reluctantly, not sure that he could be of any help to her. Even though his vision was still limited, he did not turn away from the challenge at hand; he did not turn his back on the dialogue. As difficult as it was at first, the dialogue gave birth to understanding, and the understanding led to compassion.

This kind of dialogue is precisely the path to healing that our world needs so urgently today.

To be committed to true dialogue, as this story of Jesus points out so well, begins with our willingness to listen—always with the ears of a beginner, always ready to set aside a previous conviction in order to learn something new. The entire collection of Judeo-Christian scriptures begins with the words, "In the beginning" (Gen. 1:1). It seems to me that if God can live eternally "in the beginning," I can at least try to imitate God with an openness to ongoing beginnings. In the words of Zen Roshi Shunryu Suzuki, "The goal of practice is always to keep our beginner's mind. . . . It is open to everything. In the beginner's mind there are many possibilities; in the expert's mind there are few."[9] My hope is that the pages of this book will be one more *beginning* in a lifetime of *beginnings*.

In the quotation from *Going Home* that begins the introduction, Thây says that we can love the apple *and* the mango; we can delight in French cooking *and* Chinese cooking! We can meditate and work for peace alongside Buddhists and Christians, Muslims and Hindus, indigenous shamans and singing pine trees. Along with the many who have set out along the path of dialogue over the centuries, sharing their apples and mangos, kiwi fruits and oranges, I too place into this basket of universal wisdom the peaches and papayas of my native Texas and my beloved Latin America. Through this sharing may we taste deeply the harmony and peace that dwell in the heart of all sentient beings.

Before continuing our conversation, I would like to share a few quotations that come from my own spiritual home, the Catholic Church and the Dominican order, followed by a very moving invitation to openness and dialogue on the part of Thich Nhat Hanh. I share these words as a way of acknowledging the wisdom of those who believe deeply in the value and practice of interreligious dialogue, but also with the hope that many more people will choose to sit down at this table and feast on the riches of mystical insight harvested over the centuries by our friends from other spiritual traditions. The failures, insensitivities, and obstacles of the past must not stand in our way today.

The passion for openness and dialogue with the world was nowhere more apparent in the Catholic Church in the past several centuries than in the person of Pope John XXIII. It was through his prophetic, universal, and all-inclusive vision that the Second Vatican Council was inaugurated in 1962. Throwing open the windows of the Vatican to let in fresh air is an image that has stayed with Catholics ever since. A man of humble beginnings, Pope John XXIII and the worldwide ecumenical council that he set into motion urged as never before a spirit of humility, respect, and reverence when engaged in dialogue with the religions of the world. This is expressed beautifully in one of the council documents:

The Catholic Church rejects nothing that is true and holy in these religions. She regards with sincere reverence those ways of conduct and of life, those precepts and teachings which, though differing in many aspects from the ones she holds and sets forth, nonetheless reflect a ray of that Truth which enlightens all people . . . The Church, therefore, exhorts her children, that through dialogue and collaboration with the followers of other religions, carried out with prudence and love and in witness to the Christian faith and life, they recognize, preserve and promote the good things, spiritual and moral, as well as the socio-cultural values found among these people.[10]

Forty years later, His Holiness Pope John Paul II wrote the following words, stressing that dialogue is another word for love:

We are all brothers and sisters and, as pilgrims on this earth, although on different paths, we are all on our way to the common Homeland which God, through ways known only to him, does not cease to indicate to us. The main road of mission is sincere dialogue. . . . "Dialogue does not originate from tactical concerns of self-interest" (*Redemptoris Missio* 56), nor is it an end in itself. Dialogue, instead, speaks to others with respect and understanding, stating the principles in which we believe and proclaiming with love the most profound truths of the faith which are joy, hope and the meaning of life. . . . Commitment for attentive and respectful dialogue is a *conditio sine qua non* for authentic witness of God's saving love.[11]

In a talk given recently by one of my Dominican brothers, Chrys McVey, who has spent forty years of his life engaged in Christian–Muslim dialogue in Pakistan, the task of interreligious dialogue is described as the "dangerous and costly step of opening ourselves to the other, of enfolding him or her in the same embrace with which we have been enfolded by God."[12] McVey then goes on to quote from the proceedings of an interfaith gathering of Dominicans held in Bangkok-Bang Na, Thailand, in 2001, reminding us that this "costly step" is very much a part of our eight hundred years of Dominican tradition:

Dialogue with those of other religious traditions is the main challenge at the beginning of this new millennium for our Dominican teaching and preaching. . . . [It] opens a door on an unfamiliar world, whose exact contours we do not yet know. But the journey there will lead us home because we believe it is where we belong.

    The Order was called by Dominic's attentiveness to the needs of people in the changing world of the thirteenth century. Like Dominic, like

the Buddhist monk and the Hindu sannyasi, we are called to take to the
road again, to reclaim our mendicant heritage, for we are all beggars
before the truth, which only waits to surprise us. We pray to be able to
trust the Holy Spirit who maps our journey, for . . . it is the Spirit present in every culture and every religion—long before Christianity
arrived—that makes dialogue possible and necessary.[13]

Finally, words that touch the depths of the human heart from my brother,
the humble Buddhist monk from Vietnam:

On the altar in my hermitage in France are images of Buddha and Jesus,
and every time I light incense, I touch both of them as my spiritual
ancestors. When you touch someone who authentically represents a tradition, you not only touch his or her tradition, you also touch your
own. This quality is essential for dialogue. . . . When those who represent a spiritual tradition embody the essence of their tradition, just the
way they walk, sit, and smile speaks volumes about the tradition. . . . For
dialogue to be fruitful, we need to live deeply our own tradition and, at
the same time, listen deeply to others. Through the practice of deep
looking and deep listening, we become free, able to see the beauty and
values in our own *and* others' tradition.[14]

Encouraged by the words of these great teachers, my hope is that the mingling of our many voices and the sharing of our rich and varied fruits might
show us that, while marvelously different, we are truly one. We walk the path
together.

2

Mindfulness and the Eternal Now

Present Moment, Moment of Peace

There is perhaps no teaching of Thich Nhat Hanh that has more profoundly influenced the spiritual practice of millions of people in the West than his teaching on *mindfulness*. Disarming in its simplicity, it is powerfully liberating when put into practice. "Mindfulness is to become completely alive and live deeply each moment of your daily life. Mindfulness helps you to touch the wonders of life for self-nourishment and healing. It also helps you to embrace and transform your afflictions into joy and freedom."[1] Who does not want to be completely alive in each and every moment of his or her life? Who is not looking for nourishment, healing, joy, and freedom? Thây has been able to translate his own experience of a deeply lived life into words that are easily *reachable* for people in today's world.

Christianity has so much to learn from this profound teaching—not because it does not exist in the Christian tradition but because for too long this kind of liberating, nonjudgmental and practical spiritual teaching has been relegated to a back burner on the stove of Christian teachings, hidden behind the huge, steaming kettle of the Ten Commandments. Thây's teachings on mindfulness serves as a wake-up call for the Christian West, which has so overly emphasized the *thou shalt nots* of moralistic rigidity, that it has failed in many ways to show how leading a mature spiritual life actually leads to a full and joyful life.

This is not to say that the Ten Commandments and the ethical teachings of Jesus do not have a place in our spiritual practice. They certainly do. In the same way that the Judeo-Christian tradition has its ancient moral framework, one that facilitates harmonious living in a complex social environment, so too does Buddhism have its Eightfold Path and the Five Mindfulness Trainings or Precepts. Thây has also done a great service to Buddhism worldwide by revising and modernizing the monastic training precepts known as the *Pratimoksha*, as well as the Ten Novice Precepts, for all those embracing the life of a Buddhist monk or nun.[2] Says Thây, "For our world to have a future, we need basic behavioral guidelines. . . . Practicing precepts or commandments is not a matter of suppression or limiting freedom. [They] offer us a wonderful way to live, and we can practice them with joy."[3]

A spiritual life lived *only* as a set of rules to be followed, however, does not lead to freedom and joy. What Thây has done through his teachings on mindfulness is to ground spiritual teaching in concrete daily practice. This is absolutely vital if we are to live our spiritual lives with a healthy balance. He reminds us that we do not have to conceive of the spiritual life as an accountant's ledger into which are registered withdrawals and deposits, with the hope that someday in the distant future we might be fortunate enough to come out with at least a few pennies still in the bank, and thus be saved by God. We are not banking on some prize of eternal life off in some distant future. It is about living *this* day fully alive. Says Thây, "Life is available only in the present moment. If you are distracted, if your mind is not there with your body, then you miss your appointment with life.... Mindfulness is to be there, alive in the present moment, body and mind united. It is the capacity ... to live deeply every moment of your daily life."[4]

By living deeply we are able to keep our appointment with life. How important is this teaching for us who live life in the busy twenty-first century. St. Irenaeus, one of the early fathers of Christianity, speaks of living life deeply in this way: "The glory of God is the human being fully alive."[5] How simple and yet how profound. The fullness of life is now, here, always present. Spirituality is not something we do on Sunday morning or only in a synagogue or mosque. It is a life lived fully, joyfully, in the here and now. And to be mindful of this fullness, conscious of it in each moment, is to taste life truly. It is the true miracle of life.

> To live in the present moment is a miracle. The miracle is not to walk on water. The miracle is to walk on the green Earth in the present moment, to appreciate the peace and the beauty that are available now. Peace is all around us—in the world and in nature—and within us—in our bodies and our spirits. Once we learn to touch this peace we will be healed and transformed.... We need only to find ways to bring our body and mind back to the present moment so we can touch what is refreshing, healing and wondrous.[6]

Dominican friar Thomas Philippe, reflecting on the spirituality of St. John of the Cross, wrote, "The spiritual person is plunged more and more into the darkness of the present moment.... [God] keeps such a person in the *present moment*, in its poverty and nakedness, for *it is only there* that he or she can be brought into the *presence* of God and commune with *eternity*."[7] This insight is deeply part of the Judeo-Christian tradition, and has been the experience of countless mystics and contemplatives over the centuries. There is *no place* and *no time* outside of the present moment for an encounter with God. Another of the great mystics in the Christian tradition is a seventeenth-century Carmelite named Brother Lawrence. His profound yet simple teaching is that it is possible to dwell in God's all-encompassing presence in each and every moment, to remain focused and attentive, without becoming lost in dispersion—even during his many hours each day cooking in the monastery kitchen. So transformed was Brother Lawrence by this practice, that he could not imagine living without it.

> I cannot understand how religious people can live contented lives without the practice of the presence of God. For myself I withdraw as much as I can to the deepest recesses of my soul. . . . It is not necessary to always be in church to be with God, we can make a private chapel of our heart where we can retire from time to time to commune with Him, peacefully, humbly, lovingly. . . . I keep myself in his presence by simple attentiveness and a loving gaze upon God which I can call the actual presence of God or to put it more clearly, an habitual, silent and secret conversation of the soul with God.[8]

Thây says practically the very same thing in his own words, "Where mindfulness is, there is true presence."[9] Eckhart touches on this theme frequently, saying in one sermon that creatures have no being in and of themselves, "because their being is suspended in God's presence."[10] Again, in his *Talks of Instruction*, the Meister says that the person who has God "is penetrated with divine presence."[11] What Philippe, Brother Lawrence, Thây, and Eckhart are pointing to is the eternal fullness, the presence of God, which is available to us when we live our lives grounded in "the darkness of the present moment," not carried away by worries and concerns that shackle us to the past and the future. This is not to deny the fact that Jews and Christians also share a keen sense of history's gradual unfolding toward a final point of fullness, and that both the eternity of the present moment and the final culmination of history form complementary parts of an integral whole. When we contemplate a beautiful rose, which is partially open today, filling the air with its sweet fragrance, we do not think that it is *less* a rose just because it is still unfolding. It is just a rose—fullness blossoming into fullness.

The same is true with eternity. We live immersed in the eternity of God, and slowly that eternal presence is opening up, revealing to us that which is already in us and around us. We too often misunderstand eternity as an *afterlife*, a life that begins only after death. This is like saying that God is gone for the moment, out to lunch, visiting some distant universe for the time being. This is to miss completely what the scriptures point to as living in the kingdom of God as "life in abundance" (John 10:10) in this moment and in this place. The particular, the present moment, is the doorway to the eternal in the Judeo-Christian tradition.

Jesus said frequently throughout his lifetime, using various words and metaphors, "*This* is the time of fulfillment. The kingdom of God is at hand" (Mark 1:15). The whole mystery of the incarnation, the historical taking on of flesh of God's eternal Word, is about showing God's people that it is in the here and now, in *this* place and *this* moment of history, that we experience living in the presence of God. The kingdom, which is divine life-made-flesh in this time and place, is like yeast silently fermenting the dough, or like a treasure buried deep within the earth. Though it is not always completely visible, it is showing itself as present here and now.

Hanging from the branch of a tree as one approaches the lovely gardens at Deer Park Buddhist Monastery in California is a sign, written in Thây's beautiful calligraphy, which reads, "The Kingdom of God is either now or never." These wise words should be imprinted on the hearts of all those seeking to understand and live the teachings of Jesus. One of Thây's monks, Brother Pháp Đe, remarked one day in a conversation, "Thây is always reminding us that the kingdom of God is available here and now. The question is, are *we* available?" And then, recognizing how easily we fall back into old patterns of thinking, he laughed and said, "Sometimes I hear myself saying, 'That's a great teaching; I'll have to get back to that!'" Of course, as soon as we put this teaching on our "things to do on a rainy day" list, we have lost it forever.

Meister Eckhart says emphatically, "There is but one Now."[12] In other words, *This is it*! For Eckhart, to limit the understanding of eternity as life *after* death is rather strange. When we pray, are we not in the presence of God's eternity, God's fullness? Rather than life after death, it would be better to speak of *life after life*. In other words, the God who is present *now*, and the God who will be present *then* (i.e., after death) is simply *present*—now and always. God is not limited to time and space. It is not that God lives an endless number of years and can be everywhere at the same time. The eternal presence of God is like our very breath. We cannot touch it or measure it, but without it there is no life.

Says Meister Eckhart, "There . . . is no becoming: it is one Now, a becoming without a becoming, newness without renewal, and this becoming is God's being."[13] *No becoming, newness without renewal*: what does this mean? It means that we, along with the entire universe, are blossoming and being renewed so that we can be who we already are. We do not have to *become* something other than what we are. There is *no* becoming. There is just *being*. For Eckhart, it is in living the present moment that we find ourselves plunged into the being of God. God simply *is*, and God's *is-ness* is always a present-tense verb.[14] This insight places us on a common ground with our Buddhist and Hindu sisters and brothers. God's *presence* is always *present*, neither in the past, nor in the future. Says Eckhart, "That which happened on the first day and . . . the last day is there all in the present."[15]

The Buddhist teaching on dwelling fully and mindfully in the present moment is helping Christians to rediscover this dimension in our own tradition. "In Buddhism, we speak of nirvana," says Thây. "In nirvana, which is the ground of being equivalent to God, there is no birth, no death, no coming, no going, no being, no non-being. . . . The fact is that you are nirvana. Nirvana is available to you twenty-four hours a day."[16] Says Zen teacher Ruben Habito, "In calling our attention back to the here and now, Zen practice thus enables us to recover the original impact of that Good News that the Reign of God is already at hand, in our very midst, as we go about the manifold task of living from day to day."[17] Certainly there are different philosophical frameworks underlying our two traditions, but the Buddhist emphasis on having access to the ultimate dimension, the presence of God, in each moment of our lives is vitally important for Christians, and to affirm this truth is to recover ancient insights from our own mystical tradition.

For Eckhart, to be overly concerned with life after death is a spiritually dangerous form of attachment, the result of which is a loss of freedom. It is to miss the God who is here with us right now. "All attachment to any work that involves the loss of freedom to wait on God in the here and now, and to follow him alone in the light wherein He would show you what to do . . . [will cause you] to bear no fruit."[18] These words of Meister Eckhart are as challenging as they are insightful. He is saying that anything that prevents us from living in the present moment—in the here and now—is an obstacle to the spiritual life. *Anything.* In the words of the Hebrew psalmist, "Be still before the Lord, and wait patiently for him. . . . Do not fret—it only leads to evil" (Ps. 37:7-8). This means that fretting about an argument I had yesterday with a neighbor or worrying about whether or not I will still have a job next year is all a worthless venture that separates me from God's presence in the eternal now. Or, to bring it down to the *really* everyday level, eating popcorn, watching television, and talking on a cell phone all at the same time is *not* conducive to a life of spiritual fruitfulness. We are not dwelling in one single moment, but several at the same time. When we find ourselves running around, busy about many things and feeling out of sync with ourselves, we can be quite sure that we are far from home in the spiritual sense. In fact, it would be more honest to say that we are simply "out to lunch." To my reader I say, "Believe me; in this particular category, I do *not* speak as one without authority."

On the wall of the Ocean of Peace Meditation Hall at Deer Park Monastery in California is a large round plaque on which are written two words in Vietnamese: *Vô Sự*, a phrase that roughly translates as something like "business-less." It may also be helpful to hear the phrase as "busy-ness-less." Much of Thây's teaching to his monks and nuns during their winter retreat in 2004 centered on the teachings of Master Lin Chi, whose message about living life free from the busy-ness of looking for things that will give us a sense of happiness and fulfillment, is a great challenge for our modern times. Says Thây, in a summary he wrote on the essence of Lin Chi's teachings, "The business-less person is completely free, is not caught in appearances, is not putting on airs and does not leave any trace behind. . . . In this very moment, this person is at home wherever he or she is and does not need to go in search of anything any longer."[19]

Continuing to comment on the relationship between mindful attention to the present moment and the experience of freedom, Thây adds, "Nirvana is described as peace, stability, freedom. The practice is to realize that peace, stability and freedom are available to us right here and now. . . . We only need to know how to touch them, and we have to have the intention, the determination, to do so."[20] Freedom *is* attainable in the present moment. What good news for those of us longing to grow in inner freedom. But Eckhart, Lin Chi, and Thây all remind us that this freedom comes at a cost. Determination, discipline, and practice all play a role in living more mindfully and more freely in the present moment. Though the contemplative life is often an unexpected irruption of grace into our consciousness, we must recognize that even the *unexpected* surprises in life happen because the ground has in some way or other been properly prepared. This is really the key to Thây's teaching. His insistence on living an intentional practice of mindfulness—in each and every moment of the day—is what forms us for a life of freedom and grace.

Dominican friar Richard Woods, commenting on Eckhart's relevance for contemporary spirituality, also points to the need for discipline if we are to grow in the contemplative life. In other words, we learn how to live in the kingdom of God through a disciplined spiritual practice. Says Woods, "We pray, we read, we meditate . . . in order to acquire a certain cast of mind and heart, an affinity for the divine presence that flames out 'like shining from shook foil' in nature and in the faces and lives of the people we encounter."[21] Woods then goes on to quote Eckhart, who, in a series of talks given to novices, uses the example of learning to write to remind them that the peace and stability and freedom of the contemplative life come with diligent practice:

A person must learn to acquire an inward desert, wherever and with whomever she is. She must learn to break through things and seize God in them. . . . It is just like learning to write: truly, if one is to acquire this art, she must apply herself and practice hard, however heavy and bitter a task it seems to her, and however impossible. If she is prepared to practice diligently and often, she will learn and master the art. . . . Later on, when she has acquired the art, she will be completely free . . . so that God's presence shines for her without any effort.[22]

Nirvana is now. Eternity is now. The kingdom of God is now. From the point of view of the Christian mystical tradition, eternity is not a future time out there in heaven, but instead has to do with the God who is here now, eternally present in this moment, the God whom St. Paul described as the One "in whom we live and move and have our being" (Acts 17:28). "What is today?" asks Eckhart, a question to which he gives his own answer, "Eternity."[23] Every day, every now is eternity, and God exists only in the eternal now. If we follow through with the importance given to history in the Judeo-Christian traditions, we would add that the eternal now is unfolding gradually into its fullest manifestation. St. Paul's Letter to the Ephesians says it this way, "God has made known to us the mystery of his will, according to his good pleasure that he set forth in Christ, as a plan for the fullness of time, to gather up all things in him, things in heaven and things on earth" (Eph. 1:9-10). God's "gathering up all things" is happening now and is happening eternally. Is this not what is meant by "the fullness of time?" St. Paul might have defined eternity as "the *now* that is blossoming into fullness."

What Thich Nhat Hanh and other teachers from the East are doing for the spiritual traditions of the West today is to help us hear the voices of our own mystics again. Thây's teachings on mindfulness are not so much *new* teachings, as they are *fresh*. Many people in the West have discovered new life through them. Though Eckhart did not use the term "mindfulness," he did say, "True possessing of God depends on the mind, and on an inner intellectual [i.e., from the depths of the soul] turning toward and striving for God."[24] This "turning toward God" is possible only, according to Eckhart, by dwelling fully in the present moment, the eternal now. It is this that leads a faithful disciple to a deeper taste of life. He spoke of living life fully in the present moment by calling it a moment of birth, the birth of God's Word in our soul: "God is ever at work in the eternal *now*, and his work is the begetting of his Son."[25] In this eternal now God is speaking a word in the deepest part of our being. By listening attentively to that word, which reveals itself to me here and now, I hear the eternal music of God.

Life in its fullness is available to us now. This is what the mystics teach us. This is what it means to be in relationship with God. Says Thây, "To love your God with all your might, what does it mean? It is this: In your daily life . . . to touch the other dimension of your reality, the ultimate dimension, the dimension of God."[26] In the words of Ruben Habito, "We are able to meet life where it is, right here, in all its mystery and wonder."[27]

Coming Home

One of the simple mindfulness practices that Thây uses in his community of Plum Village and whenever he gives public lectures is that of the bell of mindfulness. "Listen deeply to the sound of the bell. . . . This wonderful sound brings me back to my true home. Our true home is something we all want to go back to. . . . Recognize your home in the here and the now."[28] This is such a wonderful and simple teaching. Living for a time with Thây's community truly brings this simple practice of mindfulness into perspective. Clocks chiming, alarm clocks and telephones ringing, wristwatches beeping—these can all serve as mindfulness bells—chances to come back home to the here and now. I remember many years ago, as a college student, meeting a woman who came across to me as a deeply prayerful and contemplative person. I had never heard of the practice of mindfulness or dwelling in God's presence, but I remember a comment she made about the effect that the aroma of the wax from the candles burning on the altar had on her. Just smelling the wax, she said, put her in touch with God's presence. I remember being moved by her words and becoming aware of that wonderful aroma of burning beeswax many times after that. I think she experienced the kind of contemplative mindfulness that is essential to Thây's teaching.

> When we are mindful, fully living each moment of our daily lives, we may realize that everyone and everything around us is our home. . . . See the trees as your home, the air as your home, the blue sky as your home, and the earth that you tread as your home. This can only be done in the here and now.[29]

If home is everywhere, why, then, is it that so many people feel lost? How do we find our home if we have wandered far from it? For many, the first step *back home* happens the moment one brings into awareness the burning pain of separation—separation from oneself, separation from the world around us, separation from God. This awareness can be very painful, but it can also be a moment of great sweetness, the beginning of a journey home, the first step back to that place deep within us where we are genuinely alive. A lovely poem by David Wagoner brings this experience into focus:

> Stand still. The trees ahead and the bushes behind you
> Are not lost. Wherever you are is called Here,
> And you must treat it as a powerful stranger,
> Must ask permission to know it and be known.
> The forest breathes. Listen. It answers,

I have made this place around you.
If you leave it, you may come back again, saying Here.
No two trees are the same to Raven.
No two branches are the same to Wren.
If what a tree or bush does is lost to you,
You are truly lost. Stand still. The forest knows
Where you are. You must let it find you.[30]

Whatever one's spiritual path, this journey home, this journey to the true Self, is a common, unifying theme in the world's great religious traditions. As Pope John Paul II said in the address quoted in chapter 1, "Although on different paths, we are all on our way to the common Homeland."[31]

Of the parables of Jesus, one of the most beloved is that of the prodigal son, found in the Gospel of Luke (15:11-32). It is most often read as a story of forgiveness, the story of a wayward son who returns home to the open arms of a merciful father. It is certainly that, and it is much more. It was through my own reading of the mystics, East and West, that I came to see it as a parable about *coming home* to the present moment as well. The lost son in the story is far from home and finds himself plunged into suffering and misery. Anyone who has experienced alienation from his or her true self knows the feeling. It is what the Judeo-Christian tradition really means by the term "sin." It is the worst kind of misery, for one is estranged from one's very own heart. Says Trappist monk Thomas Merton, "Sin is our refusal to be what we are, a rejection of our . . . spiritual reality hidden in the mystery of God."[32] The turning point in the parable happens when the son is hungry and no one gives him any food to eat. The text continues, "Coming to his senses he thought . . . 'I shall get up and go to my father' . . . So he got up and went back to his father. While he was still a long way off, his father caught sight of him, and was filled with compassion. He ran to his son, embraced him and kissed him" (Luke 15:17-20).

The father in this parable is a symbol of God, the Ground of our being, our one and only home. When we are far from God, we are also far from our true self, and far from the present moment of fullness. Misery is to be far from home, and only the journey back to our truest and deepest self, what Christians would call "the self loved unconditionally by God" will overcome the misery. Thây recognizes very insightfully that when Christians pray the Nicene Creed and say, "I believe in one God, the Father, the Almighty," what we are doing is stating our "intention to go back to our true home."[33] This is just what the wayward son does in the parable. He begins a long *walking meditation*, a spiritual journey—one mindful step at a time—from the alienation of sin back home to his deepest, truest self. The embrace and kiss of the father in the parable symbolize that joy and peace which are the gifts to all who touch deeply the present moment and find themselves once again "back home." This is true as much for Buddhists as for Christians. We all long for the Homeland that is our truest Self. Thây sums it up this way, showing great respect for both traditions:

> If you are a Christian, you feel that Jesus Christ is your home. It's very comfortable to think of Jesus as your home. If you are a Buddhist, then it's nice to think of the Buddha as your home. Your home is available in the here and now. Christ is there, the Buddha is there. The practice is how to touch them, how to touch your home. You call Christ "the Living Christ," so you cannot believe that Christ is only someone who lived in the past, and is no longer there. He is ever-present. Your practice is how to touch him; he is your home. If you are a Buddhist, you practice very much in the same way. You invoke the name of the Buddha as one of the ways to touch the Buddha, because you know that he is your home. The living Christ, the living Buddha is your home.[34]

One of the most beautiful pieces of poetry in the history of Christian spirituality is a prayer that St. Augustine (354-430 C.E.) wrote in his *Confessions*, looking back on his own experience of having been far from home, far from God, and the inexpressible joy and peace he discovered when he finally found his way back home.

> Late have I loved you, O Beauty, so ancient and so new, late have I loved you! And behold, you were within me and I was outside, and there I sought you, and in my deformity I rushed headlong into the well-formed things that you have made. You were with me, and I was not with you. Those other beauties held me far from you, yet if they had not been in you, they would not have existed at all. You called and cried out to me and broke my deafness; you shone forth upon me and you scattered my blindness; you breathed fragrance, and I drew in my breath and I now pant for you; I tasted and I hunger and thirst; you touched me, and I burned for your peace.[35]

In words reminiscent of Augustine's, Eckhart echoes the contemplative journey back home to the indwelling presence of God in this way: "God is closer to me than I am to myself: my being depends on God's being near me and *present* to me. . . . God is near to us, but we are far from him. God is in, we are out. *God is at home* [in us], we are abroad."[36]

Thây expresses similar sentiments in a beautiful poem, "Looking for Each Other." These lines from the poem blend well with the words of St. Augustine and Eckhart:

I have been looking for you, World Honored one,
Since I was a young child.
With my first breath, I heard your call . . .
For millions of lifetimes,
I've longed to see you,
but didn't know where to look.
Yet, I've always felt your presence
with a mysterious certainty . . .

Looking into the mirror of the moon, suddenly
I saw myself,
and I saw you smiling, Blessed One.[37]

Awakening: God Is with Us

Coming back home to God is another way of speaking of what in Eastern religious experience is commonly called *awakening*. "The word 'Buddha,' comes from the root *buddh*, which means to wake up. The substance that makes a Buddha is awakening. Buddha means 'the one who is awake.'" That is why, continues Thây, when Buddhists greet one another, "we hold our palms together like a lotus flower. . . . We acknowledge the seeds of awakening, Buddhahood, that are within the other person."[38] The one who is fully awake is the one who rests *at home* in the true self, and is fully alive.

Living with wakefulness, or attentiveness, is also a theme that appears, perhaps more subtly, in the teachings of Jesus. It is, in fact, the overall spirit that guides the church's season of Advent, a time set aside to prepare for the annual celebration of Christmas. The liturgy and scriptures of Advent remind us that to live mindfully is to live awake, with eyes wide open to the gift that is coming and that is, in fact, already here, in each and every moment. In the northern hemisphere, Advent occurs in the dark days of winter, such that the birth of Christ corresponds to the winter solstice and the beginning of the days of lingering light. Christmas, then, is a feast that invites us to wake up to the coming dawn of Christ-among-us, to be watchful and hope-filled. In his classic, *Walden*, Henry David Thoreau described this kind of attentive watchfulness for the coming of the light in this way: "Morning is when I'm awake and there is dawn in me. . . . To be awake is to be alive. . . . We must learn to reawaken an infinite expectation of the dawn."[39]

One of the ancient canticles sung each morning by Christian monks, nuns, and members of religious and lay communities celebrates this same miracle of awakening to the new light of morning: "By the tender mercy of our God, the dawn from on high will break upon us, to give light to those who sit in darkness and in the shadow of death, to guide our feet into the way of peace" (Luke 1:78-79). When we live with an awakened heart and mind, our feet know the path that leads to peace. In a piece of poetic prose entitled "Renaissance," Thây points to the spiritual significance of morning:

> This morning I understand that this new day does not resemble any other, that this morning is unique. . . . If we are present in front of life, each morning is a new space, a new time. The sun shines over different vistas, at different moments. Your full awareness is like the moon that bathes in the heart of a hundred rivers. . . . A morning is not a page that you cover with words. . . . A morning is a symphony; for it to be there or not depends on your presence.[40]

The theme of wakefulness also appears in a series of apocalyptic sayings in the Gospel of Matthew. "Keep awake!" Jesus exhorts, "for you do not know on what day your Lord is coming. But understand this: if the owner of the house had known in what part of the night the thief was coming, he would have stayed awake and would not have let his house be broken into. Therefore you also must be ready, for the Son of Man is coming at an unexpected hour" (Matt. 24:42-44). This and other similar texts have often been read in a very narrow and moralistic way, interpreted as a warning of coming doom for all those who are not living free from sin or who do not believe in a particular set of beliefs. In other words, "You better watch out, or else!" Unfortunately, those who read these teachings in this fire-and-brimstone manner miss the point and blind themselves to the liberating truth of Jesus' message. Rather than hearing these words as an invitation to practice mindfulness, to dwell here and now fully and consciously in the presence of God, our eyes wide open to God's surprising intimacy, some choose to use these words to sow fear in the hearts of others.

This is not to say that the Gospel does not include a radical call to a holy life based on the ethical teachings of Jesus. This is certainly part of the Christian vocation. But to be boxed in by a moralistic reading of Jesus' teachings is to impoverish the Good News he came to announce. To hear Jesus' call to "Keep awake!" as a warning of some future drama in which we will find ourselves in a stuffy courtroom before a severe judge whose job is to cast a guilty verdict on those who are found unprepared, is a very poor appreciation of the wisdom and saving love of Jesus.

It is not fear that prepares us for the moment-by-moment encounter with God but love and expectant joy. We *long for* this blessed encounter; it is the fulfillment of what Jesus has promised. In the words of the ancient psalmist, "I wait for the Lord, my soul waits and in God's word I hope; my soul waits for the Lord more than those who watch for the morning. . . . O Israel, hope in the Lord! For with the Lord there is steadfast love" (Ps. 130:5-7). This encounter is not something that happens only in some distant future. God's steadfast love is available right now. We need only to live with our eyes open to this gift, which manifests itself in the little unexpected gifts of daily life: the smile on the face of a child, an embrace from a co-worker, a kiss from a spouse, a letter from a friend. *This* is the thief that comes unexpectedly in the night—to surprise us with the gift of fullness and joy! Are we ready? Are we awake and watching?

Christians believe that to be in the presence of God, resting in God's steadfast love, is what the human heart truly longs for. To experience this love requires that we live our lives awake and attentive. This is what Thây calls being mindful, remaining open in each and every moment to the marvelous realization that we *are* in God's presence—now and always. This does not mean that we always experience this presence in its fullness. Sometimes we are able to touch the presence more deeply than at other times, but that does not mean that we are not standing in this holy presence at all times. Cardinal Basil Hume, OSB, of England once said, "In the best of times, [prayer] is like being with someone you love in a dark room. You don't see the person, but you know that the person is present."[41] Oftentimes it is enough to know that the present moment is filled with a divine presence for us to experience the taste of consolation. It is St. Augustine, again, who says it beautifully in a prayer to God, "You have made us for yourself, and our hearts are restless until they rest in you."[42] To *be awake* is to rest in the presence of God, and to hear our heart exclaim with great joy, "I have arrived; I am home."

Thomas Merton, one of those from the Christian tradition who has contributed greatly to the mystical sharing between East and West, uses the following image to highlight the need to remain awake and watchful in the spiritual life.

> To keep ourselves spiritually alive we must continually renew our faith. We are like pilots of fog-bound steamers, peering into the gloom in front of us, listening for the sounds of other ships, and we can only reach our harbor if we keep alert. The spiritual life is, then, first of all a matter of keeping awake ... always able to respond to the slightest warnings that speak, as though by a hidden instinct, in the depth of the soul that is spiritually alive.[43]

This awakening to the "blessed encounter" with God is portrayed in a foundational story from the Hebrew Book of Exodus, when the prophet Moses encounters God in a burning bush in the desert (3:1-15). So sacred is the encounter that Moses is told to remove the sandals from his feet, "for the place where you stand is holy ground" (3:5). To "come home" is to stand on holy ground—*this* ground, in *this* place, at *this* time—and to know that one is in the presence of Ultimate Reality. When Thây teaches the practice of walking meditation, he invites us to take each and every step as if it were the only thing in the universe that really mattered in this moment. When we walk mindfully, each step is a step taken on *holy* ground, for each step is a step taken in the presence of God.

Moses removes the sandals from his feet and stands on the sacred ground of his true self. The taking off of his sandals symbolizes the letting go of his preconceived ideas and notions about God. He becomes naked, so to speak, before this great Mystery that burns and yet is not consumed. This is the "nakedness and poverty of the present moment" mentioned by Thomas Philippe above. Freed from his dualistic notions of a God that is *up there in heaven*, Moses finds himself standing in the presence of God. When God speaks, Moses knows that he is home and is able to listen deeply to God's voice. His deep listening allows him to respond to the call to serve as a liberating catalyst for his people, who suffer as slaves in Egypt. Standing on firm, solid ground—holy ground—Moses overcomes his fears and embraces the job at hand—no small task for a lowly shepherd who struggles with a humiliating stutter.

As Moses stands there, listening to the voice of God, he expresses concern, and rightly so, that the people of Israel will not pay any attention to him. They have been known to show hardness of heart in the past. So he asks God for some clarification, some credentials: "If I come to the Israelites and say to them, 'The God of your ancestors has sent me to you,' and they ask me, 'What is God's name?' what shall I say to them?" (Exod. 3:13). A very important question, no doubt. God answers Moses with a single word and it is this word or, to be more precise, this Name, that becomes for the people of Israel the foundational mystical experience of their common sacred history. God answers, "Yhwh," the sacred Hebrew word that means "I AM WHO I AM" (Exod. 3:14). *I AM here with you.* God's name is a name that denotes presence in the here and now. To awaken to God is to be *here*, immersed *in God*, the very God in whom "we live and move and have our being" (Acts 17:28).

This revelation to Moses and the people of Israel inaugurates a profoundly intimate and symbolic relationship between God and humanity. It is as if God said to Moses, "Repeat after me, Moses: '*I am.*'" Moses repeats the Holy Name to himself: "I am." That is all. Moses hears God's name and his own truest name in that one and only word. "Be still, and know that *I am God*" (Ps. 46:10). Through the stillness and naked simplicity of the present moment, the holy word becomes a mantra within the depths of Moses, slowly carving out within him a vast spaciousness. We can almost hear him say, "It is no longer I, but the sacred 'I am' resonating within me" (cf. Gal 2:20).

When Moses goes to speak to the people of Israel, and they ask him who sent him on this mission, he simply says, "I am." And when the people look upon the face of Moses, all they see is *I am*. They see the resplendent glory of God shining forth from within the spacious expanse of Moses' heart, illuminating his entire face like a burning fire (Exod. 34:29). His entire being simply echoes out *I am*. He has been transformed. The distance between God and himself has been swallowed up for all eternity. All that is left is *I am*. All subsequent mystical insights in the Judeo-Christian tradition stem from this one basic experience. In the end, once the veil that makes us appear to be separate from God and one another falls from our face, all that is left is one great *I am*.

God is Holy Presence. God is the presence that presences itself within us and within the entire universe. When we come home to our deepest, truest self, we come home to the One who whispers *I am* with our every breath. Many centuries after Moses, the prophet Isaiah proclaimed that the Messiah, the anointed one of God, would come. According to the prophecy, the Messiah would be called *Immanuel*, literally, "God with us" (Isa. 7:14). This name later became associated with Jesus, who, for the disciples who gathered around him, was the incarnate manifestation of "God with us" (Matt. 1:23).

So for Jews and Christians alike, God's very name denotes *being home* in the Holy Presence, being in intimate, nondual communion with the great Mystery we call God. When we are home, we are standing on holy ground. Shortly before his death, Jesus reassured his disciples that they would always be able to come home to God simply by remembering, that is, bringing into mindfulness, his words: "Those who love me will keep my word, and my Father will love them, and we will come to them and make our home with them" (John 14:23). Home is that place within our heart of hearts where God dwells with us in the *now* of all eternity.

It is no surprise, then, as one looks more closely at the world's religions, that most all of them have developed some kind of devotional practice around the prayerful recitation of the holy name of God, Allah, the Buddha, Jesus, or some sacred deity or *avatara*.[44] Hinduism's *Namajapa* is one such practice. The Russian Orthodox tradition has an ancient practice called "the Jesus Prayer," which consists of a slow, mindful repetition of the name of Jesus. Thây comments on this practice, "The name of Jesus brings the energy of God, namely the Holy Spirit, into your own being. . . . Buddhists of the Pure Land tradition practice similarly. They know what is essential is to maintain true concentration while reciting the name of Buddha."[45] Muslims recite the ninety-nine names of Allah using a string of beads similar to a Catholic rosary. Though with different words and in different ways, this mantric practice of reciting a holy name serves a similar purpose for all of the world's spiritual traditions. In each of them the meditative repetition of the holy name awakens the practitioner to an inner journey, a *coming home* to the indwelling presence of God, to the Great Mystery, the ultimate dimension that is beyond all others and encompasses all others.

Awakening as Seeing

Anthony DeMello, an Indian and a Catholic priest, often drew from the rich wisdom of his culture's Hindu tradition in his teachings. In this particular story, he captures the spirit of expectant wakefulness in a delightful exchange between guru and disciple.

> The disciple queried, "Master, is there anything I can do to make myself enlightened?" The Master responded wisely, "Do as little as you can to make the sun rise in the morning." The restless disciple continued, "But, Master, of what use then are the spiritual exercises you prescribe?" The Master answered, "To make sure you are not asleep when the sun rises."[46]

The theme of wakefulness often accompanies teachings on seeing the light of God. "The divine light rises in the soul and makes morning," says Eckhart in one of his sermons.[47] He goes on to say that as the day of our spiritual journey progresses, we need less and less light from outward sources, until at last, at the evening feast, "the spark of the soul comprehends the divine light . . . and cleaves entirely to [it]."[48] It is precisely the practice of mindfulness and wakefulness that keeps our eyes open to see the light of God that is always present. Unfortunately, because of spiritual blindness, we do not always perceive it. Eckhart touches on this theme again in his series of talks to novices.

> In all his acts and in all things a [person] should consciously use his reason, having in all things a *perceptive awareness* of himself and his inward being, and *in all things* seize God. . . . For indeed, people who are expectant like that are *watchful*, they look around them to see where he whom they expect is coming from. . . . This requires much diligence, demanding a total effort of our senses and powers of mind.[49]

Eckhart defines mindfulness as perceptive awareness, the practice of which allows one to seize God in all things. Like the teachers of other traditions, Eckhart underlines the necessity of living with eyes wide open and the powers of the mind concentrated—watchful, looking around to see the surprise hidden in the present moment. Thây speaks in a similar vein, reminding his disciples that in each and every moment we are to "practice looking deeply."[50] This, says Thây, leads to understanding. "Understanding is the process of looking deeply. Meditation means to look deeply at things, to touch things deeply."[51] It is noteworthy that Thây does not just say "looking," but "looking *deeply.*" It is quite a moving experience to see Thây walking along slowly, and then suddenly he stops and bends down, gently touching the petals of a flower, looking deeply and lovingly at the flower. The onlooker cannot but understand in a flash what "looking deeply" means. As Eckhart noted, this kind of looking demands "a total effort of our senses and powers of mind." In a similar vein, Richard Woods calls contemplation "an unflinching and loving look at Reality as divine"—what Eckhart calls "seeing God in all things and all things in God."[52]

The Christian Gospels address this theme of living with one's eyes open so as not to miss the visit of God in the here and now. Those who are caught asleep miss the great moment of encounter; they do not *see God.* Heaven is described in traditional Christian theology as the *beatific vision,* seeing God face to face. If we are asleep, we cannot *see* God, and not to see God is to miss out on the kingdom that is God's gift to us. One of the great Flemish mystics, born about thirty years after Eckhart, was Jan van Ruusbroec. In his writings, which are reminiscent of Eckhart and the other Rhineland mystics of the age, Ruusbroec places great emphasis on spiritual seeing; in fact he calls it the *one word* that God speaks—not a word that God speaks to us from outside of ourselves but a word spoken from the very depths of our being.

> Our heavenly Father wishes us to see, for he is the Father of light (cf. Jas. 1:17). Accordingly, in the depths of our spirit he eternally, ceaselessly, and without intermediary utters a single, fathomless word, and only that word. In this word he gives utterance to himself and all things. This word, which is none other than "See," is the generation and birth of the Son, the eternal light, in whom all blessedness is seen and known.[53]

Ruusbroec sums up the whole outpouring of divine life from the Father into the Son with the one word: *see.* To not see is to live in darkness, in a life of unending suffering. This is why the Buddha called ignorance the root of all suffering. To be ignorant of the divine light dwelling within us is to be in darkness, asleep. It is to live our lives separated from the conscious awareness of our inner union with God. We suffer because we are in the loving arms of God and do not know it. There is a song chanted in Zen halls in Japan, called *Zazen Wasan,* or "The Song of Zazen," composed by Master Hakuin (1685-1768). Written as a song of praise, it also serves as a call to wake up and see that very truth that is staring us in the face and yet which our own blindness hides from us. Says Hakuin, "Not realizing that Truth is so close, beings seek it far away—alas! It is like one who, while being in the midst of water, cries out for thirst. It is like the child of a rich household who gets lost in a poor village. We endlessly circle the six worlds. The cause of our sorrow is ego delusion."[54] Buddhist and Christian mystics alike want to heal us from our spiritual sorrow and blindness. Says Ruusbroec, "Our heavenly Father wishes us to see," because God's greatest delight is for us to be aware of our union with the divine nature. St. Irenaeus says, "As those who see light are in the light sharing in its brilliance, so those who see God are in God sharing his glory, and that glory gives them life. To see God is to share in life."[55]

Thây points out that it is sleepiness and sluggishness of spirit that keep us away from dwelling in our true home in the present moment. It is the result of allowing ourselves to be "overcome by dispersion and forgetfulness, the opposite of mindfulness." When this happens, says Thây, one no longer dwells in the house of *Tathagata* (literally, "the one who has gone to suchness").[56] He goes on to quote a thirteenth-century Vietnamese king, Tran Thai Tong, who is critical of those who fall into the temptation of habitual mental dispersion: "You are invited to stay in the house of the Tathagata, but your habit energy makes you sleep at night among the reeds."[57]

We all know the struggle with those habit energies of dispersion, forgetfulness, and worry that entice us to fall asleep at the very moment in which we are called to spiritual awakening. This seems to be a fairly common human weakness, and one finds teachings on this topic in almost all the spiritual traditions. Jesus exhorts his disciples to free themselves from the many worries that disperse one's energies and lead one away from basic trust. In its place he invites us to open wide our eyes and "seek first the kingdom."

> Therefore I tell you, do not worry about your life, what you will eat, or about your body, what you will wear. Is not life more than food and the body more than clothing? Look at the birds in the sky; they do not sow or reap, they gather nothing into barns, yet your heavenly Father feeds them. . . . Seek first the kingdom of God and his righteousness, and all these things will be given you besides. Do not worry about tomorrow; tomorrow will take care of itself. (Matt. 6:25-26, 33-34)

"Do not worry about tomorrow." Is this not a challenge to live in the freedom of the present moment, to be mindful of the presence and providence of God in the here and now? Is this not what Thây means when he says that dispersion and forgetfulness are the opposite of mindfulness? Is this not what Eckhart alludes to when he warns against those attachments which rob us of the freedom to wait on God in this very moment and this very place? To live this moment of time with our eyes wide open—fully awake—is the key that unlocks the door to spiritual freedom.

In the Gospel of Matthew, Jesus tells a parable that invites us into this attentive watchfulness. The parable is about ten bridesmaids who stay up late into the night, waiting for the coming of the bridegroom. Five of them stay put, waiting, while the other five wander far from home, worrying about the dwindling supply of oil for their lamps. They are not present when the bridegroom arrives. The parable is summarized at the end with this admonition, "*Keep your eyes open*, for you know not the day or the hour" (Matt. 25:13). When our eyes are closed, it is darkness and we miss the rising of the sun. When we *leave home* and wander from the present moment, losing ourselves in a life of mindless worry, we miss the wonderful gift right in front of our eyes, the encounter with our beloved. Thây told a story during the 2004 winter retreat about a man named Daniel who was unable to see the beautiful gift of Angelina, his beloved, even though she was right there with him. His attachments and anger had blinded him to the gift of the moment.

The invitation of the Gospels is constant: remain awake in the light, who is Christ, for "in him was life, and the life was the light of all people. The light shines in the darkness, and the darkness did not overcome it" (John 1:4-5). To be a "child of the light" is to be mindful, awake, and attentive to the presence of God. This comes through clearly in another Gospel story, one that recounts an encounter between the risen Christ and two of his disciples on their way to the town of Emmaus (Luke 24:13-35). The "darkness" of the two disciples (who do not recognize the stranger on the road as Jesus) is the result of their being overwhelmed by Jesus' death. They are dispersed and blinded by their sadness. It is not sin that blinds them; it is worry and sorrow, the lack of mindfulness. Using Thây's words, they have not been able to touch the living Christ in the midst of their suffering. Jesus, however, does not abandon them in their sadness. He walks with them along the way. He is present to them even when they are not present to themselves. His walking meditation waters their seeds of mindfulness, inviting them to leave behind the pain of the past and to come home to the present moment.

Once they reach their village, they invite the "stranger" into their home. This single act of hospitality breaks into their dispersion, bringing them back home to the present moment. Gradually the situation begins to change. "Stay with us," they say to him. These words evoke the biblical references to God's faithful and eternal presence, a presence made possible in each moment through the Holy Spirit. So in a way, almost without knowing it, the disciples are brought back to their practice of mindfulness through their hospitality. Immediately their suffering is lessened. They wake up from the sluggishness of their sadness. "When you become mindful, understanding and loving, you suffer much less," says Thây.[58] By inviting a stranger to stay with them, to share a meal with them, they begin their own inner journey back home. Their blindness, brought on by the overwhelming sadness of the death of their dear friend and teacher, is beginning to give way to a new insight.

As the disciples' hearts begin to find inner calm and peace, their eyes begin to open. "Practice seeing with the eyes of compassion," says Thây, "and you suffer much less. . . . The 'eyes of compassion' means the eyes that look and understand."[59] St. Catherine of Siena said the same thing with these words: "Look into the depth . . . of divine charity. For unless you see you cannot love. The more you see, the more you can love."[60] The story from Luke's Gospel goes on to say that, as Jesus broke the bread and shared it with them at the table, "their eyes were opened and they recognized him" (24:30-31). The two disciples had moved from mindless suffering to mindful compassion. Their previous blindness and feeling of being overwhelmed by the darkness of their suffering blossomed into a moment of renewed *seeing*, a deep awakening in the Holy Spirit to the presence of the risen, living Christ. Their experience of Christ's *presence*, made tangible through the eucharistic breaking of the bread, gave the *present* moment a new sense of fullness.

3

The Breath of the Holy Spirit

Learning to Breathe Again

It sounds like a terrible understatement, but many of us can say with deep gratitude that Thây has dedicated his life to teaching people to breathe again.

> The first practice I learned as a novice monk was to breathe in and out consciously, to touch each breath with my mindfulness. . . . When you enter deeply into this moment, you see the nature of reality, and this insight liberates you from suffering and confusion. Peace is already there to some extent: the problem is whether we know how to touch it. Conscious breathing is the most basic Buddhist practice for touching peace.[1]

There is no doubt that the East is helping the West recover the simple art of breathing—that most basic of human actions, the one that will not let us escape from the present moment. We cannot breathe yesterday or tomorrow. We can only breathe in the here and now. "Every time you feel lost, alienated, cut off from life, or from the world, every time you feel despair, anger, or instability, you have to know how to practice going home. Mindful breathing is the vehicle that you can use to go back to your true home."[2] These simple, life-giving words remind many of us who live in the busy-ness of the modern world that we must make this breath-journey back home several times a day. The practice of mindful breathing is one concrete way of beginning the journey from the modern form of slavery and busy-ness we know as *workaholism*.

One of my Dominican brothers has a pad of scratch paper sitting on his desk, which, like many such notepads, has written on the top: "Things to Do Today." But this pad is different. It is not just one more tool to bolster our addiction to efficiency and work. The pad continues with these words: "Breathe in, Breathe out, Breathe in, Breathe out. . . . " As Zen teacher Ruben Habito says, "The spirituality of Zen can be characterized as the art of living in symphony with the breath."[3] What a hope-filled practice, and one that can guide us toward a deeper living of daily life: to live in symphony with one's breath and, in so doing, with the breath of the entire world. Thầy has spent many years teaching people his simple recipe for living and breathing with mindfulness:

> Breathing in, I calm my body.
> Breathing out, I smile.
> Dwelling in the present moment,
> I know this is a wonderful moment.[4]

One need not dig very deeply into any of the great religions of the world before finding some important reference to prayerful breathing as a symbol and disciplined practice of the spiritual life. The Judeo-Christian tradition is no exception, though unfortunately it is a gold mine that, in large part, has been covered over by centuries of growth and neglect. The Orthodox churches have done better at attending to the breath of the Spirit as part of their tradition of prayer, principally in connection with the practice of the Jesus Prayer. With the help of Thầy and other spiritual teachers from the East, we are finding the tools that we need in order to dig into our own backyard and rediscover our own lost treasures. In recent years, Christian meditation and centering prayer groups have begun this important task of spiritual excavation in the West, opening up a path back to the riches of a much-forgotten tradition. It is the beginning of a very hopeful renewal, and Christian teachers like John Main, Thomas Keating, Basil Pennington, and Lawrence Freeman must be lauded for doing much to rekindle this fire—especially through the teaching of the practices of contemplative meditation and centering prayer.

Within the Judeo-Christian tradition, the significance of breathing as a spiritual practice has its roots in the Book of Genesis, the first book in the Hebrew Bible. It is here that we find two narrative stories, both of which attempt to shed light on the beginnings of creation. The second of the two narratives, using the beautiful image of God as a potter whose hands mold the clay, describes the creation of humanity in this way: "The Lord God formed *adam* [literally "earthling," from the Hebrew word *adamah*, meaning "earth"] from the dust of the ground, and breathed into *adam*'s nostrils the breath of life, and *adam* became a living being" (Gen. 2:7). The author of this sacred text speaks of God's breath as a breath that gives life, sustains life, holds and enhances life. This same image appears in the Book of Psalms: "By the word of the Lord the heavens were made, and all their host by the breath of God's mouth" (Ps. 33:6). It is this very same divine breath that prompted Job to declare, "The spirit of God has made me, and the breath of the Almighty gives me life" (Job 33:4).

For Christians, the breath of God continues to be present among us as the Holy Spirit, connecting us not only with God but also with the world around us. Fr. Bede Griffiths notes, "The Spirit is the feminine principle in the God-head, the Mother of all creation. It is in her that the seeds of the Word are planted and she nurtures them and brings them forth in creation. The Spirit is the source of energy in the stars and atoms, of life in plants and animals. It is the source of evolution in the universe."[5] Thây has a deep appreciation for the role of the Holy Spirit in Christian belief, and reminds us, "If we touch the Holy Spirit, we touch God not as a concept but as a living reality."[6] The breath symbolizes the living, divine Reality present in each of us and in all creation.

The Gospel of John follows through with this image in a powerfully symbolic appearance of the risen Christ to his disciples. Having hidden themselves behind locked doors out of fear in the days following the crucifixion, Jesus comes into their midst to set them free. "Jesus came and stood among them and said, 'Peace be with you.' After he said this, he showed them his hands and his side. . . . Jesus said to them again, 'Peace be with you. As the Father has sent me, so I send you.' When he had said this, *he breathed on them* and said to them, 'Receive the Holy Spirit'" (John 20:19-23). John builds up to this scene throughout his whole Gospel, drawing a parallel between Jesus' death, resurrection, and breathing forth of the Holy Spirit and the creation story from the Book of Genesis. In other words, Jesus breathes new life into his disciples just as God had breathed into the nostrils of *adam* in the Book of Genesis, thus inaugurating a new creation. The Holy Spirit is, as Thây recognizes, not a concept, but a living reality.

In Hebrew the word for spirit, breath, and wind is the same word: *ruah*. It appears in the opening lines of the Book of Genesis: "Darkness covered the face of the deep, while a wind from God [*ruah*] swept over the face of the waters" (1:2). So when Jesus *breathes* the gift of the Holy Spirit onto his disciples, their Jewish faith and their Aramaic cultural background would have immediately connected them with the ancient story of creation, reminding them of oneness with God. Even in the wake of the cross, the risen Christ is still with them, faithfully breathing in them and through them by the gift of the Holy Spirit. Jesus reminds his followers, and he reminds us that the holy breath of God's Spirit that was present "in the beginning" is the same one that comes to our aid in this present moment, this eternal now, to renew and re-create us, as well.

The Spirit's presence, though, can be fully received only within a community of disciples who are willing to wait in hope and prayerful attentiveness in the face of adversity. Even though the disciples were devastated by the tragedy of the death of Jesus and plagued by fear, they did not disband, nor did they stop waiting for a new birth in hope (Acts 1:12-14). They persevered and supported one another, while remembering the teachings and promises of their beloved teacher. They looked deeply within themselves and discovered there, in their hearts of faith, the presence of the living Christ.

It is helpful to remember that as Jesus' breath flowed into the disciples, their fears were set aside, opening the way for them once again to connect with the living Christ. God's faithful love became real, tangible once again. How vital it is for us to recover this freedom from fear in our own day. Anger, depression, violence, and war have their roots in fear. Rather than seeing others as a threat to our own security, our mindful breathing opens us up to that which unites us. Through contemplative meditation and the practice of mindful breathing, we remain grounded in the present moment, in the presence of God, and are liberated from the shackles of fear.

This is precisely what happens to the disciples. Jesus' resurrection and gift of the Holy Spirit renew them in the gift of his faithful presence, and they are freed from the paralysis of fear. Says Thây, "The most precious gift we can offer others is our presence. When our mindfulness embraces those we love, they will bloom like flowers."[7] And blossom they do. The disciples are reborn into the full realization of Christ's risen life. In taking refuge in the gift of the Spirit, the disciples are re-created in a single moment of radical freedom, a single moment that fills every moment with the presence of God. Their fears are transcended as they find a way to trust again in the present moment. Hope is reborn among them. The mighty wind of creation, which God breathed into the nostrils of *adam,* is once again given to them as the holy breath of freedom and new life. Both breaths are manifestations of one and the same Spirit, the "Giver of Life."[8]

Jesus' gift of the Spirit to the disciples reminds us of the gratuitousness of God's love, the gratuitousness of life itself. Everything is grace; everything is a gift. This is one of the insights that the author of the Genesis narrative of God breathing into the nostrils of *adam* attempts to convey, and one that is vital for the Judeo-Christian understanding of God's Spirit. The Spirit always reawakens us to the gift of the first breath, the breath of Genesis. In the resurrection narrative mentioned above, Jesus breathes the Spirit and the Spirit's peace into his disciples as a *gift.* By awakening to this gratuitous gift we are freed from the idolatrous notion that we are the source of life and the moving force of the universe.

As St. Paul reminded his friends in ancient Corinth, we are simply vessels formed of clay, containing within us the treasure of the breath of God (2 Cor. 4:7). Jean-Pierre Lintanf, OP, a Dominican friar from France, reminds us of the gratuitousness of life that comes to us in the moment-to-moment act of breathing: "I pray to God who has given me, in my own mortal clay, a little of his own breath; so little, it is true, that at each instant I have to surrender my breath, so that it may be given to me anew."[9] The Spirit, like our breath, is a gift given anew in each and every moment.

Just as the Spirit is a gift freely given to us, so too is it a gift that we are called to give freely to others. Immediately before breathing his Spirit onto the disciples, Jesus said to them, "As the Father has sent me, so I send you" (John 20:21). Then he breathed on them and said, "Receive the Holy Spirit; whose sins you forgive are forgiven them" (20:23). It is very significant that Jesus links his breathing forth of the Spirit with the invitation to be a channel of freedom, reconciliation, and healing for others. In other words, the gift of the Spirit energizes the disciples to go out and radiate the healing love that they have received from the risen Christ toward all those who are paralyzed by fear or who find themselves downcast or brokenhearted.

They who have been transformed become a transforming presence for others. This is what genuine spiritual aliveness is all about. We need only think of people we have met who exude this radiant presence of life and holiness; it spreads out toward others, often without their even being aware of it. This is another part of the practice of mindful breathing that we must live daily. Just as we *receive* gratuitously the gift of the divine breath, so too must we be ready to *give* to others that same gift. We breathe in the gift, and we breathe it out again through loving-kindness and service.

I remember the very first meditation retreat that I made in 1994. It was a *Vipassana* retreat, and as an inexperienced meditator, it almost killed me! We sat for almost ten hours a day, for ten consecutive days. By the last day I was exhausted and empty. I just wanted it to hurry up and end. We were given a break for walking meditation and were told to return to the hall in a half hour for the final sitting meditation of the retreat. All we were told was that it would be a "special *metta* meditation" (I had no idea at the time what a *metta* meditation was). I went outside to take a walk and stretch my legs a bit when suddenly, caught completely by surprise, I began to weep and experience an overwhelming compassion for all who were suffering in the world. My heart felt like it had been torn open in a loving yet simultaneously painful embrace of the world. I was embarrassed by this sudden outpouring of emotion and could not stop crying.

We went back to the hall and sat down, as one of the teachers began to lead us in the *metta* meditation. We were instructed to send out to the world the compassion that we had cultivated during our ten days of silence. Of course, that was all I needed for the tears to start flowing again! What I found so powerful as I looked back and reflected on this experience was that something in my body and in my heart *already knew* that it was time to give to others the love that had been growing in my heart in silence throughout the retreat. Though I had no idea what a *metta* meditation was, my entire being knew intuitively that compassion was the only possible response in the face of the world's suffering. For ten days I had breathed in the gifts of healing and peace; now it was time to breathe out to the world those very same gifts.

The Latin motto of the Dominican order is *Contemplari et contemplata aliis tradere*, "to contemplate and to share with others that which is contemplated." Contemplation is authentic only if it flows out in loving-kindness to others. If all we do is breathe in all the spiritual energy of the universe, we literally implode—a spiritual ego intoxication. The prayer attributed to St. Francis of Assisi begins with this very intention: "Lord, make me an instrument of your peace." Francis did not pray primarily to have a profound experience of mystical union with God. He prayed for the grace to radiate peace and love. The breath of mindfulness, the breath of the Spirit, is like a seed that is meant to be planted, given away freely to others.[10] Authentic spiritual growth is measured more by what we breathe out than by how much we breathe in. As Jesus says, "You will know them by their fruits" (Matt. 7:16). Thây also points to a similar measure of an authentic practice of mindfulness: "When the energy of the Holy Spirit is in us, we are truly alive, capable of understanding the suffering of others and motivated by the desire to help transform the situation."[11]

I want to add one final detail in the story of Jesus' breathing forth of the Spirit upon his disciples after the resurrection (John 20)—one that we must not lose sight of: it happens within the context of community. In other words, Jesus does not leave the gift of his Spirit as the property of any one individual; he gives it to the whole community, what Buddhists call the *sangha*. Soon after this encounter with the disciples, Jesus "disappears" physically from the community and flows back into the fullness of Ultimate Reality, back into the heart of God. This is what Christians refer to as the "ascension" (Luke 24:50-51). Jesus takes leave of his disciples in the bodily, historical sense, but remains present as the risen Christ, alive in the community of disciples through the Holy Spirit. The Spirit is the divine breath which the community now breathes as the mystical, spiritual *body of Christ*. This is one of the most important and most profound insights in the writings of St. Paul: "We, who are many, are one body in Christ, and individually we are members one of another" (Rom. 12:5). The Jesus who lived among us, who walked and taught, who healed the sick and embraced lepers and sinners is no longer here, but *we who are his body are still here*. As Jesus himself says in the Gospel of John, "Now I am no longer in the world, but they are in the world" (John 17:11). The living Christ continues to breathe and live within the community of his disciples.

It is interesting that Thây speaks of a very similar belief regarding the Buddha's return. "The next Buddha who will come to us is described as the Buddha of Love, Maitreya. We practice in order to make his or her appearance a reality. We are preparing the ground for the Buddha-to-come. The next Buddha may be a Sangha, a community of practice . . . because love is practiced collectively."[12] This is precisely the focus of Jesus' breathing the Spirit into the community. It is now up to us to practice collectively the love of Christ. It is up to us to em-*body* the Holy Spirit. When Christians speak of the second coming of Christ, perhaps we too need to broaden our horizons and be open to an unexpected surprise. Maybe his second coming is already happening in us and through us. After all, we hold his holy breath in the temple of our hearts. We are his body now. The living Christ is very much alive in the *sangha*, the community gathered in his name (see Matt. 18:20 and 28:20).

Living Water Flowing from the Heart of God

Meister Eckhart very seldom speaks of the Holy Spirit in his sermons, but what he says is significant and refreshing. One thing that he does say, for example, is that the Spirit is the energy of love that links the Father with the Son. The Spirit holds it all together. Says Eckhart, "The first emanation [flowing forth] is that of the Son from the Father, which occurs in the way of birth. The second emanation is that of the Holy Spirit, by way of union: this emanation is by the love of the Father and the Son."[13] The energy from this divine flowing forth not only holds the Trinity together internally but also unites God with the universe, the eternal with the historical, the water with the wave. This unity between God's eternal being and the activity of the Spirit is made even clearer in another metaphor from the sermons of Eckhart:

> The Father is denoted by the heart and . . . is the source and mainspring of all divine activity. And the Son is represented by the arm, as it says in the Magnificat: "He has brought forth strength with his arm" (Luke 1:51). And thus the divine power proceeds from the body and from the arm *into the hand*, by which is signified the Holy Spirit.[14]

For Eckhart, then, the Holy Spirit is imaged as God's hand, which reaches out and touches the ordinariness of our living and our breathing, our working and our playing. In other words, it is through the unitive energy of the Holy Spirit that we are touched by God—not in spectacular, extraordinary ways, but precisely in the ordinary stuff of daily life. Says Thây, "The Holy Spirit is the energy of God. . . . That is why in our daily life, we should live mindfully, we should live with the Holy Spirit so we can live every moment of our daily life deeply."[15] Thây emphasizes the importance of practicing our spiritual life in the *ordinariness* of life in his presentation of the teachings of Lin Chi: "We do not have to prove that we are liberated or enlightened. We can live a very ordinary style of life. We only have to be an ordinary person."[16] The Holy Spirit is the divine energy that is moving and flowing through each and every breath, each and every ordinary moment of our existence. As we learn to live life mindfully, in conscious contact with this divine energy, we will discover that each moment offers us an opportunity to be in touch with the God whose hand first reaches out to touch us with the gentleness of a mother caressing the face of her newborn child.

To speak of divine power touching our daily life sounds very much like Thây's teachings on mindfulness. He, too, links mindfulness in the ordinary stuff of life with the Holy Spirit: "The Holy Spirit is the kind of energy that is capable of being there, of understanding, of accepting, of loving, and of healing ... the energy of mindfulness.[17] Thây, in fact, goes so far as to say that the Holy Spirit and mindfulness are the very same thing. Such an affirmation would not be common parlance for a Christian, given the fact that Christians understand the Spirit as the gift of divine life that flows gratuitously into us from God, through Christ. We certainly can, however, agree that the Spirit is the connection, the point of encounter, between the divine and the created world, between the ultimate and the historical dimensions of reality. To live mindfully of this divine, unitive energy is to live fully in the present, fully in the presence of God.

In Eckhart's view, seeing the Spirit as the divine presence reaching out to touch the universe is the key to living God's ongoing act of creation in the one eternal now, for as the Meister himself says, "God is creating the world *now* and in *this* day."[18] In other words, the divine breath that God breathed into the universe "in the beginning" is still flowing into each and every *now*, through the creative energy of the Holy Spirit. Thus, in each new moment we are being re-created in the image of God (cf. Gen. 1:27). In breathing the Holy Spirit into his disciples, Jesus gives birth to a new creation, a theme articulated more fully in the final pages of the Christian scriptures.

> Then I saw a new heaven and a new earth. . . . And I heard a loud voice from the throne saying, "See, the home of God is among mortals. God will dwell with them as their God; they will be his peoples and God will be with them. God will wipe every tear from their eyes. Death will be no more." And the one who was seated on the throne said, "See, I am making all things new." (Rev. 21:1-5)

We must not be led astray by what sound like future-tense verbs in this text from the Book of Revelation. The apostle writes these words for people living in a time of discouraging persecution and martyrdom. He speaks in this way so as to help the community see that the new heaven and new earth are already being manifest in their very midst. This very moment! Every moment, in fact, is the unfolding, the blossoming of this new creation. Every breath is a manifestation of the Spirit's re-creative action, by which the hand of God, the great cosmic Artist, paints the vibrant colors of the Word-made-flesh onto the canvas of the universe: "See, I am making all things new."

Let us for a moment call to mind the splendid creation mural of Michelangelo in the Sistine Chapel in Rome, in which God's hand reaches out to touch the hand of Adam, allowing for the overflow of divine life into humanity. If we can bring this image into our present consciousness we begin to realize that this divine overflow is happening in this very moment as powerfully and as creatively as it happened "in the beginning." By mindfully living this ongoing communion, this eternal touch of God in the Spirit, we are continually being re-created. We live enveloped in the divine energy of the Spirit, which flows from the life and heart of Christ, giving life to a new creation. With the Hebrew psalmist, we too sing the joyful song of praise: "O Lord, how manifold are your works! In wisdom you have made them all; the earth is full of your creatures. . . . When you hide your face, they are dismayed; when you take away their breath, they die and return to their dust. When you send forth your spirit [ruah, breath] they are created; and you renew the face of the earth" (Ps. 104:24-30).

St. Paul recognizes that this new creation, this new birth, does not come without its own labor pains, but when it comes it brings with it "the freedom of the glory of the children of God" (Rom. 8:21). Christ, "the firstborn of all creation" (Col. 1:15), who is also the "firstborn from the dead" (Col. 1:18), breathes the Spirit of God into us "so [that] we too might walk in newness of life" (Rom. 6:4). In fact, we are only able to walk in the newness of life because we have been "born of the Spirit" (John 3:6). So, although we are born only once in the flesh, we are being born anew in each moment, as we live in the resurrection consciousness that comes with being disciples of Jesus.[19] In this eternal now, which is enlivened by the Spirit of the risen Christ, death is overcome once and for all. We are re-created for eternity, "born from above," in the breath of the Spirit. Eckhart says emphatically that this is not some distant event that happened once upon a time. This birth of God is happening now, in us, in our universe, in this very moment. Asks the Meister, "What does it avail me that this birth is always happening, if it does not happen in me?"[20]

Born anew in God, through the Holy Spirit, in order to *walk in the newness of life*: this is one way to speak of the spiritual life in a Christian context. With keen insight, Thây understands this connection between the Holy Spirit and daily life, between living *in* God and living *in* the world: "When you pray with all your heart, the Holy Spirit is in you, and as you continue to pray, the Holy Spirit continues in you. You do not need to do anything else. As long as the

Holy Spirit is there, everything is fine. You are resting in God, and God will work in you. . . . The Holy Spirit is the energy of God that shines forth and shows you the way."[21]

David Steindl-Rast, OSB, a Benedictine monk and frequent participant in Buddhist–Christian dialogue, notes, "With a fine instinct, Thich Nhat Hanh traces genuine aliveness to its source . . . what the biblical tradition calls the Holy Spirit."[22] *Genuine aliveness*: this could be another name for the Holy Spirit. The very same Spirit-breath that flowed forth from the heart of God as a fountain of genuine aliveness for *adam*, the first human being, and which flowed forth from the heart of the risen Christ as new life for the community of disciples is available to us as well. This gift of genuine aliveness comes to us gratuitously each and every moment as God pours into us the Holy Spirit, teaching us to walk in the newness of life.

Peace: Many Voices, One Spirit

Eckhart's image of the Holy Spirit as the hand that communicates the power flowing from the heart of God is also helpful in understanding the unitive relationship between the particular and the universal, what in the East is called the experience of nonduality and what Thây calls *interbeing*.[23] To be in contact with the Holy Spirit in one part of the universe is to touch the same spiritual energy in all living beings. This is a foundational teaching in Buddhism.

> When we hold a piece of bread to eat, if mindfulness is there, if the Holy Spirit is there, we can eat the bread in a way that will allow us to touch the whole cosmos deeply. A piece of bread contains the sunshine. That is not something difficult to see. Without sunshine, the piece of bread cannot be. A piece of bread contains a cloud. Without a cloud, the wheat cannot grow. . . . One thing contains everything. With the energy of mindfulness, we can see deeply. With the Holy Spirit, we can see deeply.[24]

Eckhart, like many true mystics, struggles with the limitations of language in his attempt to speak of this unitive experience of nonduality. "There is nothing but one, and where one is, there is all, and where all is, there is one. . . . When the soul finds the One, where all is one, there she will remain in the One."[25] This is Eckhart's version of interbeing. In another sermon, using the image of bread in a way similar to Thây, Eckhart says, "In the Holy Spirit . . . there is one life, one being and one work. However many pieces of bread there were, there would still be only one body."[26] For Eckhart, the Holy Spirit is multiplicity and unity all rolled into one.

The nonduality of the Holy Spirit takes on more of a communal and universal expression in the context of the feast of Pentecost, as described in the Acts of the Apostles (2:1-13). In this story, the Holy Spirit is portrayed as a powerful energy of harmony, oneness, and peace, similar to the account of Jesus' breathing forth of the Spirit mentioned above (John 20). Multiplicity melts into unity as the Holy Spirit rushes through the gathered assembly like a strong driving wind that filled the entire house (Acts 2:2). The writer of the account certainly is inviting the reader to recall the *ruah-spirit* that hovered over the formless void and was breathed into the nostrils of *adam* in the Genesis story of creation. This Spirit-energy unites God with the entire universe. (In Hebrew, *ruah* can be translated as "wind," "breath," and "spirit.")

The disciples present for the feast of Pentecost were probably all Aramaic-speaking Jews, but in the anointing that came upon them by the Spirit, they surprised the large crowd and even themselves by suddenly speaking in different tongues to the people who gathered there "from every nation under heaven." So unexpected was this experience of universal communication and communion that one of those who was present among the crowd asked in amazed confusion, "Are not all these who are speaking Galileans? And how is it that we hear, each of us in our own native language?" (Acts 2:7-8). People from many countries, cultures, and languages experienced a common bond of unity in the Spirit. What might have been a chaotic free-for-all was, in fact, a deeply unifying experience. Through the power of the Spirit, the particular and the universal, the similar and the dissimilar were experienced as one. One voice, spoken in the power of the Spirit, became every voice, and every voice came together as one.

For Christians of all ages, the Pentecost event has a rich and profound significance. It is the moment in which the followers of Jesus awakened to the deeper meaning of what it means to "live according to the Spirit" (Rom. 8:5). It was a moment of new birth, but not just an interior birth of the divine within the human soul; it was the birth of community, the birth of universality and particularity all in one. The Holy Spirit which the disciples received at Pentecost broke through barriers of language, culture, and religion. They experienced unity within diversity.

So profound and unusual was the experience that some onlookers scoffed, exclaiming, "They are filled with new wine!" (Acts 2:13). The wine that they had drunk was the wine of harmony and peace. "To set the mind on the Spirit," says St. Paul, "is life and peace" (Rom. 8:6). They recognized in one another a common language, a common experience, a common spirit. They were mindful of something that, though not necessarily tangible, formed them into one people, with one heart.

Thomas Merton experienced this profound oneness, this nondual unity one day while walking through the streets of Louisville, Kentucky. He saw all of humanity in a single instant as one with himself. "It is because I am one with them that I owe it to them to be alone, and when I am alone, they are not 'they' but my own self. There are no strangers."[27] Like Merton, the disciples gathered for Pentecost touched a universal energy that flowed through them like an underground spring of water. They touched the possibility of a truly new world, healed of its fragmentation. Life seemed very real again. Thây knows this intimate experience from the very depths of his being, the fruit of a long life lived in the practice of mindfulness: "When we touch peace, everything becomes real. We become ourselves, fully alive in the present moment, and the tree, our child, and everything else reveal themselves to us in their full splendor."[28]

The Holy Spirit is the divine energy that makes everything fully alive, fully real, fully one. Once we learn to touch that genuine aliveness within us, we will be able to touch it in all persons and all things. The Holy Spirit cannot be bound by rules or cultural norms, nor is it the property of one religion or another. Jesus says very frankly, "What is born of Spirit is spirit. Do not be astonished . . . the wind blows where it chooses, and you hear the sound of it, but you do not know where it comes from, or where it goes. So it is with everyone who is born of the Spirit" (John 3:6-8). The Holy Spirit is a strong driving wind, blowing freely across all boundaries, uniting that which appears divided. It is the holy and universal Spirit of harmony and peace.

The final gift that Jesus gave to his friends was a renewing dose of the Holy Spirit. As he stated in his farewell discourse the night before his death, "The Advocate, the Holy Spirit whom the Father will send in my name, will teach you everything, and *remind* you of all that I have said to you. Peace I leave with you; peace I give to you" (John 14:26-27). It is the Holy Spirit who *reminds*, that is, *brings to mindfulness*, the teachings and the peace of Jesus. If we desire to live peace today, then we must allow the Spirit to *bring to mind* the gift Jesus left us. Says Thây, "We can realize peace right in the present moment with each look, smile, word, and action. Peace is not just an end. Each step we make should be peace."[29]

The Pentecost event is one example of how the early Christian community, filled with the Spirit, was able to put into practice the teachings and the peace of Jesus. "Our capacity to make peace with another person and with the world depends very much on our capacity to make peace with ourselves," says Thây, and "that is why the practice of meditation, looking deeply, is so important."[30] By awakening to the energy of the Holy Spirit within themselves, the early followers of Jesus were able to touch the peace and presence of God in others, as well. The boundaries that had once separated them were no longer a problem. The many different voices came together to form one harmonious voice of unity.

This new experience of oneness began to affect every aspect of the lives of the first Christians, so much so that "the whole group of those who believed were of one heart and soul, and no one claimed private ownership of any possessions, but everything they owned was held in common" (Acts 4:32). The Pentecost experience had given the disciples the opportunity to look deeply into the hearts of those people who were different from themselves and to see them as one with their own heart and soul. They experienced this as the fruit of the Holy Spirit. God was not divided between *us* and *them*, but was shared as the unifying presence of all. Says Eckhart, "The one to whom God is thus present in all things . . . alone knows peace."[31]

It is necessary for the very survival of our earth today that all who follow a spiritual path learn to touch in their practice the gifts of tolerance, understanding, and peace. Says Thây, "Where mindfulness is there is the capacity to understand . . . to accept, to become compassionate, to love."[32] It is this new world built on the foundation of understanding, unity, compassion, and peace that Jesus called the kingdom of God. This was the central focus of his entire teaching. "Strive first for the kingdom of God and God's righteousness," Jesus said, "and all these things will be given to you as well" (Matt. 6:33). For Jesus, the kingdom was both an inner and an outward reality—a nondual coming together of all multiplicity into one. The kingdom is both *within* us and *among* us (Luke 17:21), and we are invited to experience this fundamental unity with all reality on all levels: personal, communal, and cosmic.

Thây shares his version of this teaching with words that closely echo the teachings of both Jesus and Meister Eckhart, helping us all to see that we are truly one at the table of dialogue.

> The Kingdom of God is described as a mustard seed. . . . We hear repeatedly that God is within us. To me it means that God is within our consciousness. Buddha nature, the seed of mindfulness, is in the soil of our consciousness. It may be small, but if we know how to care for it, how to touch it, how to water it moment after moment, it becomes an important refuge for all the birds of the air. It has the power of transforming everything.[33]

To experience oneness with the God who dwells within us, the God who is the Ground of all being, is a gift that comes to us through the divine touch of the Holy Spirit. To consciously touch this divine presence is, as Thây states so well, precisely that which can transform everything, because to touch the Spirit in one part of the universe is to touch the Spirit in the entire universe. All the birds of the air, and in fact all living beings, find their true home in unity.

To be mindful of the gift present in one small piece of bread, filled with sunshine and clouds and earth, is to be mindful that all that exists is a gift filled with presence, a gift received so as to be shared. Jesus taught his disciples to pray, "Give us this day our daily bread." We ask for a piece of bread for today, *this* day, *this* moment. Because we know that when we eat *this* piece of bread with mindfulness and deep gratitude we are one in heart and soul with that transcendent energy which makes all things one.

The Mind of Love

Even though Meister Eckhart does not devote much space in his sermons to the topic of the Holy Spirit, he rarely does so without relating it in one way or another to *love*. Eckhart knows that a life lived mindfully, fully present to the divine breath of God's Spirit, is a life that will radiate love to those with whom it comes in contact. "The love with which we love is the Holy Spirit," he remarks.[34] Eckhart is saying something very important here. He is saying that the stuff of our love, its *suchness*, is of God; it is the Holy Spirit. In other words, in reaching out through a gesture, a smile, or a word of kindness to another person, we are acting from the deep well of divine love. We love the world around us with a love that finds its source in God, just as the gushing waters of the river are rooted in the deep, underground spring. The Christian scriptures, especially the Gospel and Letters of St. John, echo throughout with the simple phrase, "God is love" (1 John 4:8).[35] To love is to be in union with God, in and through the energy of the Holy Spirit.

In chapter 5 we will look at the Holy Trinity, the divine, nondual relationship between the Father, the Son, and the Holy Spirit, as a circle of love. We will consider Bede Griffiths' affirmation that within the Trinity there is an "energy of love [which] unites the Father and the Son."[36] This energy of love is the Holy Spirit. For Christians, then, the very capacity to love one another is made possible by the energy of the Spirit, the energy of divine love, which flows through us. We are literally taken up into the love of God and become channels through which that same love flows. But how does this happen in real life? It is here where Thây's teaching on mindfulness is of such great value. We cannot be a channel of God's love and peace if we do not learn to discover (literally *un-cover*) and touch with true mindfulness that gift which flows through us.

> The waves [of the ocean] are supposed to love each other. . . . But the wave may be so bound to the suffering and the difficulty she is having with the other waves that she is not able to realize that she is in an intimate relationship with water, and water is also the ground of all the

other waves. To love your God with all your might, what does that mean? It is this. . . . You have to devote twenty-four hours [a day] to touching the Kingdom of God, to touching the ultimate dimension that is deep in you. You can only love God with all your might when you are really a full-time student or practitioner. . . . It is not because you abandon all phenomena [matter] that you can touch the [ultimate] dimension of the noumena. If you throw away the historical dimension, there is no ultimate dimension for you to touch. You have to touch God through God's creatures. . . . Unless you know how to love your neighbor, you cannot love God.[37]

These profound words of Thây are helpful when it comes to the day-to-day task of loving God and one another. The First Letter of John, written to encourage the early Christian communities in their struggle to practice the command of love, says it this way, "We love because God first loved us. Those who say, 'I love God,' but hate their brothers or sisters, are liars; for those who do not love a brother or sister whom they have seen, cannot love God whom they have not seen" (1 John 4:19-20). We all know that in the daily attempts to put these teachings into practice, we are faced with obstacles and often feel confused as to how to overcome them. What Thây does is to show us that through the daily practice of mindfulness, we learn to touch that deepest part of ourselves, and in so doing, we touch the heart of our neighbor, which is also the heart of God. This is precisely what Thomas Merton meant when he attempted to describe his call to a life of solitude: "When I am alone, they are not 'they' but my own self." In touching love in the depths of his own heart, there was no separation from the rest of the world.

"There are those who are so discouraged that they no longer have the courage to love," notes Thây. "They have suffered a great deal just because they have made an attempt to love and have not succeeded. . . . We have to bring them the message that love is possible."[38] We live in difficult times in our world, and perhaps as much as any other time in human history, we so desperately need to remember that love is possible. We need to remember that love is worth the effort. Thây goes on to speak of what in Buddhism is called *bodhicitta*, the mind of love, and he encourages us to tap into the source of energy that *bodhicitta* provides. "If we have the energy of love, if we have *bodhicitta* in us, then we will be filled with life."[39] Is this not what all human beings really long for? Do we not all desire to live life fully, guided by the energy of love?

As a Christian I cannot help but hear in Thây's words an echo of St. Paul's invitation to "have the mind of Christ" (1 Cor. 2:16). Jesus lived each day, each moment, pouring his life out to others in love. To "have the mind of Christ" is to have the mind of love. This gift of Christ's mind of love comes to us through touching deeply within ourselves the gratuitous embrace of God. God reaches out to us—from deep within us—through the energy of the Holy Spirit. In other words, it is not so much we who *take on* the mind of Christ; it is more exact to say that we are *taken into* the mind of Christ. Love makes us its disciples. Eckhart says, "Divine love is not taken into us. . . . Divine love takes us into itself, and we are one with it."[40] One of the ancient prophets of Israel, Hosea, personifies this experience of being claimed by love: "I will now lure her, and bring her into the wilderness, and speak tenderly to her. . . . I will take you for my wife in righteousness and in justice, in steadfast love and mercy" (Hos. 2:14, 19). To have *bodhicitta* is to be one with the mind of love. When we allow ourselves to be *taken in* by love itself, and to live each moment mindful of this holy Ground upon which we stand, loving others will become as natural as breathing. This is, of course, a lifelong process of beginning and beginning anew.

To grow in the wisdom that comes from *bodhicitta* is the fruit of daily practice. It is this moment lived fully, immersed mindfully in the energy of love. If it is true, as Eckhart says, that "the love with which we love is the Holy Spirit,"[41] then learning to love in the ordinariness of daily life is the work of the Spirit; it is God touching our daily life. The Spirit is the hand of God reaching out to communicate the fullness of the energy of love and life to us in the present moment. Says St. Paul, "To set the mind on the Spirit is life and peace. . . . You are in the Spirit, since the Spirit of God dwells in you" (Rom. 8:6, 9). Each moment, each breath is an invitation to open ourselves to this indwelling Spirit, who is giving birth within us, in love, to a new creation.

For most of us this awakening to the mind of the Spirit, the mind of love, is a gradual process. We must not become discouraged as we walk this path. As the birth of this new creation unfolds within us, we will experience a deeper inner freedom and joy. St. Paul admits with candid realism that, "the whole creation has been groaning in labor pains until now; and not only the creation, but we ourselves, who have the first fruits of the Spirit, groan inwardly, while we wait . . . [to] obtain the freedom of the glory of the children of God" (Rom. 8:21-23). There are and will continue to be moments of mind-*less*-ness, what Thây referred to earlier as dispersion or forgetfulness, moments in which we fail to touch life deeply, and therefore fail in our attempt to love. This is the "groaning" process to which Paul alludes. No moment is lost, however. The Spirit touches us even when we forget to touch the Spirit.

Taking up again the earlier image of the underground spring of water, we know that the water pushes up from below the surface with every intention of gushing forth as a stream of loving-kindness—even when we have blocked the opening of the spring with our mindless dispersion, cutting off for a while the free flow of water. Eckhart employs this same image in an attempt to call us to hope and patience when faced with our own limitations.

> God's image, God's Son, is in the ground of the soul as a fount of living water (John 4:14). But if [we] throw earth, which is earthly desire, on it, [this] impedes and conceals it, so that we do not perceive or grow aware of it; *but the fount itself goes on living*, and when [we] take the earth away that was thrown over it, then it appears and we know that it is there.[42]

The moments of forgetfulness, the times that we allow our loving to be covered over with earthly desires and worries, are simply an invitation to breathe again and come back home to the present moment, to the energy of the Spirit. Thây adds his own words of encouragement: "If you manage to keep that source of energy alive in you, you can confront any kind of obstacles and you will be able to overcome them. That is why *bodhicitta* is so important. . . . In the process of love you learn a lot."[43] The fountain of love is eternal, and though the process of our reaching out in love can be blocked for a while, all we have to do is to come home to the breath of the Spirit, come home to the present moment, and allow the mind of love to re-create us anew. This is, it seems, the meaning of the practice of "beginning anew" which Thây teaches. Every moment is a chance to begin anew.

Learning to love, then, is a process. We must practice loving just as we practice mindfulness. Eckhart says in one of his sermons, building beautifully on the biblical image of the divine breath of God, "The greater the love is that is in the soul, and the more the Holy Spirit breathes on it, the more perfect the flame . . . not all at once . . . the Holy Spirit breathes gradually on the flame."[44] These words give us hope and encouragement, for they remind us that the process of learning to love ourselves and others is slowly fanned into a flame—one breath at a time.

This image of small flames being fanned into a great fire is part of the Pentecost story mentioned above (Acts 2:1-13). The disciples who were gathered in Jerusalem experienced what they later described as "tongues as of fire" descending and resting upon each of them. The large crowd from "every nation under heaven" looked on in astonishment and awe at the spectacle. As they looked deeply into each flame, resting upon such a great diversity of people, they began to see Fire itself. They glimpsed in the great multiplicity of flames a single burning Fire of Love.

The barriers separating them disappeared as the Holy Spirit opened their eyes to the mystery of the *one Fire* expressed in the many flames. This one Fire was symbolic of the love that united them. They truly experienced being of one mind and one heart—with God and with one another. Eckhart occasionally uses the image of fire to speak of the burning away of separateness, which then gives birth to oneness: "When fire is at work kindling and burning wood, the fire makes the wood quite small and unlike its former self, robbing it of solidity, cold, mass and moisture, and making the wood more like itself, the fire . . . the fire gives birth to itself in the wood."[45]

The Pentecost story from the Acts of the Apostles is fundamentally a story about awakening to the oneness of God and of all of creation from within the mind of love. When the Spirit of God moves us to touch the flame of loving-kindness in one human heart, we are then able to touch the eternal Fire which is Love. We touch God. We touch peace. The Fire gives birth to itself in us, and we remember, as Thây mentioned above, "that love is possible." Each new moment lived with the *mind of love* opens us up to the Holy Spirit, who breathes gradually on us, fanning the flickering flame of our hearts into the one great Fire of Love. The new creation is born in our very midst.

4

The Water and the Waves

Water-soaked Ground

Thây uses the metaphor of water and waves as a way of distinguishing between the eternal (*noumenal*) and the historical (*phenomenal*) dimensions of reality. "We are the waves, but we carry within us the water. We live our historical dimension, but we carry in us also the ultimate dimension."[1] Buddhists and Christians alike are called to touch this ultimate, eternal dimension of our being. In touching the wave, we touch the water, which is the true source of divine life bubbling up from within. Thây explains more fully how an awakened person understands this two-way relationship between the temporal and eternal dimensions of reality.

> In Buddhism, we speak of the ultimate dimension and the historical dimension. Take, for example, the historical dimension of a leaf. The leaf seems to be born in April and to die in November. . . . That is because of our way of looking, because we don't touch the historical dimension deeply enough. If we touch the historical dimension deeply enough, we will touch the nature of no birth and no death of the leaf. . . . If you do, then you will have another insight: The leaf is also eternal, deathless. The true nature of the leaf, your true nature, is the nature of no birth and no death.[2]

Thây's use of the expression "we carry within us" brings to mind a metaphor found in one of St. Paul's letters to the Corinthian community, one that also attempts to describe these same two dimensions of reality: "For it is the God who said, 'Let light shine out of darkness,' who has shone in our hearts to give the light of the knowledge of the glory of God in the face of Jesus Christ. But we have this treasure in clay jars, so that it may be made clear that this extraordinary power belongs to God and does not come from us" (2 Cor 4:6-7).

The treasure to which St. Paul refers is the very life and presence of God, which radiates upon the face of Christ, deep within the soul of every human being. And the great paradox is that this radiant presence of ultimate reality is somehow held within the fragile clay jar of our humanity. The eternal light shines within our limited, historical world. One of the great mystics of the Russian Orthodox Church, St. Seraphim of Sarov, uses imagery similar to that of St. Paul, saying that the Christian is a "vessel of grace," which holds divine light within. St. Seraphim goes on to say that this divine light is "the grace of the Holy Spirit, living in us, warming us, enlightening us, filling the air with his scent, delighting us with his fragrance, and rejoicing our hearts with an ineffable gladness."[3] The entire clay vessel of our humanity, then, is filled with the fragrant light of the Holy Spirit, just as the tiny wave is filled with the vast ocean.

Eckhart, too, plays with the image of the divine light, but he does so in a way typically Eckhartian, through the use of paradox, leaving us to deal with the unresolved tensions. At times he places the light within God and at other times within the human soul. In one sermon, for example, Eckhart links this luminous treasure with Christ, who shines "from all eternity in the Father's heart," and then later he goes on to say, "It is the light [in the soul] which lays straight hold of God . . . it wants to get into the silent desert [of the Godhead] into which no distinction ever peeped."[4] One of Eckhart's trademarks is his naming of the divine light a "spark" which, though hidden deep in the soul, "wants nothing but God, naked, just as He is."[5] He says elsewhere, "The spark of intellect, which is the head of the soul . . . is none other than a tiny spark of the divine nature, a divine light, a ray and an imprint of the divine nature."[6]

This treasure of divine light—whether it manifests itself in God or in the soul—is always the fruit of God's self-giving. God freely shares the very life of God with us, soaking the human soul with divine light. This is what Thây, St. Paul, St. Seraphim, and Eckhart all call, using different terms, the eternal, the Ultimate Reality, the divine essence that is our truest self, the Ground of our being. Human beings are stamped with the divine image in the very ground of the soul (grunt der sêle). In another place Eckhart says, "God is an essence that embraces all essence."[7] As Bernard McGinn points out, the unique contribution of Meister Eckhart was to use the term grunt to describe this "uncreated something" where God and the soul are one. "Eckhart does not qualify the gruntlôs grunt ("groundless ground") as either God's or the soul's. It is both."[8] Or, in the words of the Meister himself, "God's ground and the soul's ground is one ground."[9]

Aware that Christians and Buddhists come to this dialogue from different experiences, it is helpful to discover in Thây's writings a reference that—at least to Christian ears—sounds something like a Buddhist notion of the Ground of being. Of course, one cannot speak of "God's ground" per se in Buddhism, given that the Buddha does not give a name to God, but what

Thây says is important in helping to bridge the understanding of these concepts in our ongoing dialogue. He quotes from the Buddha:

> Verily, there is an unborn, unoriginated, uncreated, unformed. If there were not this unborn, unoriginated, uncreated, unformed, then an escape from the world of the born, the originated, the created and the formed would not be possible.[10]

The Buddha refers here to a movement (what he calls an "escape") from the created world into the ultimate, uncreated realm where true liberation is experienced. The wave, as Thây has shown over and over, is born in time and space and yet is simultaneously on a journey, flowing back into the eternal, uncreated ocean that is her true home. This movement corresponds very closely to what Eckhart and many of the mystics call by many different names (divine birth, breakthrough, emanation, return to the Godhead, etc.). Both Thây and Eckhart use the image of "going/coming home" to speak of this movement. This movement from the world of creation and form back into the uncreated world, back into God, is clearly articulated by Richard Woods: "Having become fully manifest in both image and likeness in humankind through the *birth of the Word* in time and place, the indwelling Triune God retracts the universe into itself through the birth of the soul back into God— Eckhart's great theme of *breakthrough*."[11]

For Eckhart, there are few aspects more important in the spiritual life than to awaken to this divine ground within, to flow into it and merge with it. The light of God dwells within us, which means that we, like Christ, are also the light of the world (Matt. 5:14). This realization, this awakening, is like stumbling upon a fresh, clear mountain spring of water—deep within our very being. Says the Meister, "God streams into the soul in such abundance of light, so flooding the essence and ground . . . of the soul [that it] wells over into the body, which is filled with radiance."[12] The discovery of this inner radiance that saturates our very being is the one important task in life, according to Eckhart, who, like a Zen master, calls out to us, "Awaken! Discover who you are! Close your eyes and see the radiant light within you."

A Drop in the Ocean

Eckhart, along with some of the monastic and lay mystics of his time, was rather daring to push the frontiers of mysticism at a time when the church was beginning to rein in those whose thought was a bit too creative for the guardians of orthodoxy. Though Eckhart remained committed to the church up to his death, he never allowed the environment of suspicion to keep him from speaking eloquently of the soul's divine union with God. Here he offers another fine image, one that appears in similar language in various Eastern traditions as well: "If you were to cast a drop into the ocean, the drop would become the ocean. . . . Thus it is with the soul: when she imbibes God she is turned into God, so that the soul becomes divine."[13] We can almost imagine Thây looking Eckhart in the eyes and responding, "Yes, Meister, how right you are," and then Thây adding his own affirmation of the relationship between the drop of water and the ocean: "We know that the wave is the water, and we know that the water is the ground of the wave."[14]

The wave is the water. The drop becomes the ocean. These phrases are not exactly common parlance in Western Christianity. In official theological jargon this is called the process of *divinization* or *deification*, but to some modern and Western ears this language can sound quite shocking. It is important, however, to note that this has been a common theme in both Western and Eastern Christianity since the earliest times. In the words of the *Catechism of the Catholic Church*, we are made "partakers by grace in the divine nature."[15] Thây comments in *Living Buddha, Living Christ* that "the idea of *deification*, that a person is a microcosm of God, is very inspiring. It is close to the Asian tradition that states that the body of a human being is a minicosmos. . . . A human being is a mini-God, a *micro-theos* who has been created to participate in the divinity of God."[16] In Christianity deification is often conceived of as a growing into one's essential oneness with the divine presence, the divine light, so much so that the soul is filled to overflowing with the warm, luminous energy of the Holy Spirit. Says Eckhart,

> It is just as true to say that humans became God as that God became human. Thus human nature was transformed by becoming the divine image, which is the image of the Father. . . . And just as the Son is one with the Father in essence and nature, so too you are one with God in essence and nature, and you have it all in you as the Father has it in Himself. You have not got it on loan from God, for God is your own.[17]

This process, of course, is God's work in the human soul. "It is not through his or her own activity or 'energy' that [the person] can be deified . . . but by divine 'energy,' to which his or her human activity is 'obedient.' . . . In 'deification' human beings achieve the supreme goal for which they were created."[18] So complete is the divine–human union that Eckhart can affirm with great simplicity and insight, "Where my soul is, there is God, and where God is, there too is my soul."[19]

Eckhart uses another metaphor, similar in many ways to that of the drop of water falling into the ocean, which also helps to illustrate this process called *deification*, or what Eckhart will refer to below as "passing into the naked being of God."

> God's seed is in us. If it were tended by a good, wise and industrious gardener, it would then flourish all the better, and would grow up to God, whose seed it is, and its fruits would be like God's own nature. The seed of a pear tree grows into a pear tree, the seed of a nut tree grows to be a nut tree, the seed of God grows to be God.[20]

Though this type of unitive, nondualistic language finally got the Meister into some hot water, one cannot deny the fact that Eckhart was firmly rooted in a rich Judeo-Christian mystical and biblical tradition. God's archetypal breathing of "the breath of life" into the nostrils of *adam* in the Book of Genesis (2:7) sets this tone very early. God literally pours the divine being into creation. Centuries later a New Testament text continues with the same theme, noting that Jesus has bestowed great promises on us "so that through them you may *come to share in the divine nature*" (2 Pet. 1:3-4). This "sharing in the divine nature" is the ultimate goal of the Christian spiritual journey. It is, in a kind of paradoxical way, the *natural* thing—what is supposed to happen. As one mystical author puts it, "The supernatural does not come to us as an exterior and violent imposition, but as an increase of life, freely accepted, liberating and ennobling us. It does not destroy our humanity; it makes us . . . children of God, gods by participation."[21]

We literally grow, like the seed, into the very being of God, who offers us "life in abundance." So, if what Eckhart and Thây say is true—namely, that the drop of water or the wave "become the ocean"—then what happens next? Do we just disappear? What happens when we merge into God? Eckhart smiles at the earnestness with which we ask the question, and then with the wit of a true master of wisdom, he replies: So, you want to know what happens with the drop of water? "It finds God; and the finding of herself and the finding of God is one and the same act."[22]

"Where does this happen?" we push on. Eckhart smiles again and says that the "place" into which we merge is *Nothing*—the vast emptiness of the Silent Desert. It is what the Buddha refers to above as the "unborn, unoriginated, uncreated, unformed" realm. "In the beginning" creation flows out of this empty ground of divine *nothingness*, and ultimately returns to and merges with the same *nothingness*. "Plunge into that with your essential being," says Eckhart, "and see that you are in *nothing else* but what you find there."[23] This mystical sense of the word *nothingness* refers, of course, to the Ground of being, which is free of all created *things* (i.e., no-*thing*-ness). Therefore, to say that God creates the universe out of nothingness (*creatio ex nihilo*) is to say that the primal source of creation is not any *thing*; it is beyond things. It is "unborn, unoriginated, uncreated, unformed." Eckhart calls it the Godhead.

As Thây explained in a *dharma* talk at Deer Park Monastery, "Creation is not being coming from non-being, but manifestation."[24] In other words, if creation flows from the uncreated *no-thing-ness* we call God, then what is created is a manifestation of *that* from which it flows, the divine Ground of being. If this is so, and if we agree with Eckhart's teaching about "God's ground and the soul's ground [being] *one* ground,"[25] then we must be able to affirm that this same uncreated *no-thing-ness* is as present in the ground of our soul as it is in God. Eckhart, in fact, says just that: "We have to come into the state of being *nothing* in order to enter into the same nature that God is. So when I am able to establish myself in Nothing and Nothing in myself . . . then I can pass into the naked being of God."[26] The author of the ancient Chinese *Tao Te Ching* has a similar insight:

> There was something formless and perfect
> before the universe was born.
> It is serene. Empty. Solitary.
> Unchanging. Infinite. Eternally present.
> It is the mother of the universe.
> For lack of a better name, I call it *Tao*.
> It flows through all things,
> inside and out, and returns
> to the origin of all things.[27]

Deification, then, is allowing the empty river of no-thing-ness to flow through us, inside and out, and to carry us back home where we merge with the Great Source. A film that appeared several years ago, *A River Runs Through It*, based on the novel of the same title, ends with these words: "Eventually all things merge into one, and a river runs through it." We flow back to oneness with the One, to no-thing-ness in the great Silent Abyss of the Godhead. This is what Eckhart's image of the seed of God growing into God is about. This seed is the divine spark of our being, and it is growing into divine fullness. The same is happening with Thây's wave. It is merging into oneness and fullness with the ocean.

Both of our teachers point to a subtle, though important, distinction when treating this topic of oneness and deification. The earlier quotation from Eckhart—the one about the drop of water cast into the ocean—has a second part to it that cannot be overlooked. "If you were to cast a drop into the ocean, the drop would become the ocean and *not the ocean the drop* . . . the soul becomes divine, *but God does not become the soul*."[28] The same could be said of the seed of God: it grows into God, but God does not become the seed. Thây adds his own well-thought-out clarification in this matter:

> We have to be careful. We cannot mix up the water with all the waves here. There is a causal relationship, but it is quite different. That is why the water should not be considered in the same way or on the same level with the waves. . . . You have to observe and contemplate the noumenal [ultimate] and phenomenal [historical] separately. . . . When you say that humankind was created by God, you are talking about the relationship between water and wave. . . . God is not a being in the phenomenal world. He or she is the ground of all being. It would not be difficult for Christians and Buddhists to agree on this.[29]

Thây's clarification that "God is not a being in the phenomenal world" is a necessary one for both Buddhists and Christians. The medieval Dominican theologian Thomas Aquinas, who greatly influenced Eckhart and all theologians of the era, made the distinction between God as a verb (*esse*: to be) and the created universe as a noun (*ens*: being). Commenting on Aquinas, Paul Philibert, OP, says, "God is not a static reality on a shelf. God is active everywhere in the sense that wherever anything exists, God's is the present, active force of its existence."[30] For Eckhart it is always important to point out that God is not *this or that*, God is not some-*thing*; God is *no-thing*. God is *is-ness*. There is no *why* in God.[31] The eternal, ultimate dimension, what Thây symbolizes with the metaphor of the water, is not a *thing* that can be grasped, put into a box. It is simply what Buddhists call *tathata*—*suchness*, "reality as it is."[32] It is the *Tao*, the Ground of all being. Says Eckhart, "If a [person] should seek to indicate something by saying 'it is,' that would be silly. . . . When everything is removed . . . so that *nothing* at all remains but a simple 'is'—*that* is the proper characteristic of God's name."[33] Again, in yet another sermon, the Meister says in his typically shocking manner, "God is nowhere . . . God is not here or there, not in time or place,"[34] because God is not a thing or a person. So, while we can affirm with Eckhart and Thây that "God's ground and the soul's ground is *one* ground," and "water is the ground of the wave," a believer in the Judeo-Christian tradition does not say that the soul is God. God is God, and the soul is the soul. The water is *not* the wave; the water is the *ground* of the wave. The water and the wave are one.

In all these words and images, all these references to drops of water and seeds of God, the spiritually attuned ear hears the lovely harmony at play in this mystical music between East and West. Though our paths vary, and the *what* or *Who* by which we name the ultimate dimension of reality is understood differently in the various traditions, we all gain from listening to one another's music and sharing the fruits of one another's table. We are more alike than different. "We spend all our time looking at each other as waves," continues Thây, "and we have not been able to realize that we are made of water and all of us contain each other."[35] This is what the mystics teach us. There is not one ground of being in the soul of a Buddhist and another in a Christian. The God called *Allah* by the Muslims is not a different God from the one called *Abba* by Jesus and his disciples. We are all waves, drops of water, in the one great Sea of Being. "What is the home of a wave?" asks Thây. "The home of the wave is all the other waves, and the home of the wave is water. If the wave is capable of touching [itself] and the other waves very deeply, [it] will realize that [it] is made of water."[36] The entire universe is made of water. The entire universe is made of the very *is-ness* of God.

Baptism and the Living Water

"There must be a relationship between water and waves," writes Thây. "Waves are water, waves are somehow born from water."[37] It is a curious coincidence (or is it?) that the metaphor of the waves and the water coincides so well with the sacrament of Christian baptism—the ritual initiation of those who set off on the path of following Jesus Christ. In a way, we could speak of baptism as akin to the Buddhist experience of enlightenment; it is a rite of passage, an initiation into the experience of Ultimate Reality known as God, the Great Mystery. It is the beginning of the Christian's journey to the groundless ground of the soul.

Continuing with the metaphor, Thây speaks of the wave's spiritual journey into the Great Mystery: "Enlightenment for a wave is the moment the wave realizes that it is water."[38] In this experience, the wave touches the ground of her being. In a similar way, we could say that enlightenment for those of us who follow Jesus is rooted in the sacrament of baptism, for it is in this moment that we realize (often gradually) that we are children of God—that we are made in the image of God. We begin to awaken to the truth that in the depths of our being, in that "place" which Eckhart calls the spark of the soul, we are divine.

It is precisely this relationship between the human and divine, between the historical and the ultimate dimensions of reality, that Thây wants to call our attention to through the metaphor of the waves and the water. The wave, which lives for a time in history, is born from water; its truest "self" is water. Its *wave-ness* is a temporary manifestation of the deeper reality called water. When the wave awakens and realizes that it is water, it experiences enlightenment. It is set free from all suffering.

Eckhart uses another metaphor—one of the most beautiful metaphors in all his writings—to speak of this same reality.

THE WATER AND THE WAVES 61

When master sculptors make figures out of wood or stone, they do not introduce the figure into the wood, but chisel away the fragments that had hidden and concealed the figure; they give nothing to the wood, rather they take away from it, letting fall beneath the chisel the outer layers, removing its rough covering, and then what had lain hidden beneath shines out.[39]

I would venture to say that this is one of the clearest, most insightful metaphors I am aware of in explaining the fundamental meaning of the sacrament of baptism. The trunk of wood holds deep within itself a pristine image of God, who is Ultimate Reality. To be plunged into the waters of baptism is our initiation on the journey toward awakening and growing into full consciousness of our true self—made in the image and likeness of God. In baptism the Holy Spirit gives us a glimpse of the divine spark of God's light within us. As Thây rightly points out, the Holy Spirit is in us as the very first cells of our body begin to form together, but this is "something [that needs] to be cultivated. . . . To be baptized is to recognize and to touch the Holy Spirit within you."[40] Unlike the Buddhist experience of enlightenment, which is sometimes the result of a very sudden and life-transforming awakening (sometimes called *kensho* or *satori*), most Christians would say that what baptism does is to set into motion this "cultivating of the Holy Spirit" of which Thây speaks; baptism is the first step in a very long journey. Gradually, as we glimpse more and more the divine core of our being, we learn to trust the divine Artist who carefully carves and chisels away all that covers over our eyes from seeing our true self. After all, a beautiful sculpture takes time to bring into fullness.

Jesus' own baptism prefigures the spiritual awakening that we, his disciples, are also called to embody. When Jesus came out of the waters of the Jordan River after his baptism, he experienced God's Spirit descending upon him, and he heard a voice speak from heaven, "You are my son, the Beloved; with you I am well pleased" (Mark 1:10-11). The voice very likely surprised him, wrapping him in a warm embrace of tenderness, intimacy, and love. Only with time would Jesus articulate this experience as an interior oneness with God, his *Abba*, or Father. He began to know that he was: "God's beloved child." He and the Father were one. Commenting on this pivotal experience in the life of Jesus, Swami Abhishiktananda, a French Benedictine monk who lived much of his life in India, had this to say:

It was at his baptism in the Jordan that Jesus experienced the disappearance of the separation, the dividing chasm, when the omnipresence of the Spirit annihilated the separation. In the Spirit he understood the Voice, which called him "Son," [and] when he replied "Abba," he realized in this "Abba" that "He and I are one."[41]

Jesus realizes in the Jordan River that he is more than a sack of flesh and bones. He, like the wave, is water; that is, he is divine at the very core of his being. There is no separation between him and the Father; he and God are one. This mystical oneness is available to us as well. The sacrament of baptism is the ritual awakening to the fact that, in and through Christ, we too are plunged into the depths of God's very being. The medieval Dominican mystic St. Catherine of Siena offers a marvelous image to help convey this mystical oneness. Said God to Catherine, "Just as the fish is in the sea and the sea in the fish, so am I in the soul and the soul in me, the Sea of Peace."[42] God is in us and we are in God. This was precisely the mystical enlightenment that led Jesus to exclaim toward the end of his life, "I am in the Father and the Father is in me" (John 14:11).

The aim of the sacrament of baptism, then, is to initiate us on this journey into God, "into the intimacy of the Trinitarian life . . . [a journey that] depends entirely on God's gratuitous initiative."[43] It is a pilgrimage toward inner freedom, the goal of which is to awaken us to the truth that we, like Jesus, are godly at our deepest core. We are one with God; we are beloved daughters and sons of God. Says Eckhart, "It would be little value for me that 'the Word was made flesh' for [us] in Christ . . . unless he was also made flesh for me personally so that I too might be God's child."[44] Or, to use Thây's metaphor, we Christians are invited to discover in the waters of baptism that we are one with the water, that our *wave-ness* is just one more unique and beautiful expression of God, the Sea of Peace.

This dis-covery (literally *un-covering*) of our true self, revealed in baptism, takes time. There is a blindness that hides our true self from us—like the layers of wood covering over the statue. In other words, we come into a world marked by sin and alienation; there is no escaping the woundedness that such a world inflicts on us. This is what in Western Christianity is referred to as *original sin*. We humans are born into a world that hides the beauty of our true self from us, a world that teaches us to strive to be something other than who we truly are. Like Saul of Tarsus, up until the time of his illuminating encounter with the risen Christ, we have scales over our eyes, blinding us from the truth of ourselves and alienating us from God (Acts 9:8, 18).

This struggle between our true self made in God's image and the false self that we are seduced into striving after is depicted symbolically in the story of Adam and Eve in the Garden of Eden (Gen. 3). Like all of us, Adam and Eve find themselves torn between two different voices that make a claim on their souls. First there is God's voice, which we hear again, and with perfect clarity, in the baptism of Jesus. God says to Adam and Eve and to all of us: "You are my child, the Beloved; with you I am well pleased" (Mark 1:11). There is another voice, though, a deceitful and seductive voice, which says, "God knows that when you eat of [the fruit of the tree in the middle of the garden] your eyes will be opened, and you will be like God, knowing good and evil" (Gen. 3:5). This voice invites us to strive to become someone *other* than who we are, to go in search of a self other than our true self. The promise that "your eyes will be opened" is a false one, for we are led to see and to search outside of ourselves for that which is already within. We actually become blinded to the truth.

The seducer speaks in a similar way to the wave, "So, you want to be like water? Come with me (i.e., outside of yourself, outside of this present moment), and I will take you to a pond where you can be like water." The wave, who already *is* water at the core of her being, takes off down a path that leads her to a false self, where she becomes stagnant and dries up. The promised source of water ends up being a prison leading to spiritual death. It is all an illusion, a journey filled with suffering, for the search leads her farther and farther away from the truth that lies deep within. We have all fallen into this familiar trap at some point in our lives—some of us more than others.

Baptism is an action of grace—a gift that sets in motion the healing of the blindness that hides our true self from us. Through baptism Christ heals our blindness. He shows us the path that leads from the darkness of not seeing who we truly are to an awakening in the light of truth. We begin this journey by entering into the water, which is symbolic of our entering into the paschal mystery of Christ's death and resurrection. We die to an old way of being and to the blindness of the false self, and we rise to a new life, washed clean and set free. As St. Paul says, "Just as in Adam all die, so too *in Christ* shall all be brought to life" (1 Cor. 15:22).

In baptism we touch the truth, the spark of our soul, and are reborn. "Nothing else resembles God so much as the human soul," says Eckhart.[45] This dimension of our being is our true nature, our ground; it is deathless and eternal. In a way not so unlike Thây's example of the leaf, Eckhart reminds us of our own eternal destiny, which takes us from the waters of baptism to a realm beyond birth and death. Passing beyond the limits of human life, "the soul flows with this richness and this sweetness into herself and beyond all things . . . back into her primal source. Then the outer person will be obedient to the inner person until death and will be at peace in the service of God forever."[46]

For Christians, this journey "beyond all things . . . back into [the] primal source" is paradoxical, for we enter into this fullness of life with Christ by being baptized into his death. In the Gospel of John's version of the crucifixion of Christ, water and blood flow from the pierced side of the crucified Lord. It is the blood of death and the water of life (19:34). In other words, we are plunged into the living water that flows from the emptiness of Christ's death. This gift of new life fulfills our deepest longings, as was announced by the prophet Isaiah many centuries ago: "Everyone who thirsts, come to the waters. . . . Listen carefully to me, and eat what is good, and delight yourselves in rich food. Incline your ear, and come to me; listen so that you may live" (Isa. 55:1-3).

Eckhart, in speaking of baptism, notes that "the soul is plunged into God and baptized in the divine nature, receiving divine life."[47] Eckhart then explains that this being "plunged into God" transforms us into Christ. We are *Christ-ened*, made one with Christ. Says the Meister, "You must not merely be *like* the Son (Christ), you must *be* the Son yourself."[48] In other words, baptism does more than make us imitators of Christ. We are *Christ-ed*, grafted into the very trunk of Christ. With Jesus we hear the voice of God speaking to us, and we too are given a glimpse into our essential divine nature. We *see* who we truly are.

For Eckhart, the whole of the Christian journey, from baptism onward, is simply the slow process of letting the chips of wood fall beneath the chisel of the master sculptor—laying bare the divine image that was always present. We always were and always will be the divine child of God. The anointing with the holy chrism oil, which forms part of the baptismal ritual, sacramentalizes our being *Christ-ened*, our oneness with Christ. There is no separation between Christ and disciple; both *inter-are*. In the words of St. Paul, we have "put on the Lord Jesus Christ" (Rom. 13:14), and in so doing, we find ourselves immersed in God—like the wave that awakens to the marvelous truth that she and the ocean are one. As Abhishiktananda says, baptism effects in us an annihilation of the experience of separation between God and ourselves. The only possible response to so great a mystery is to remove one's shoes, as did Moses, and say the holy name, "I am."

St. Paul speaks out of his own experience of being plunged into the mystery of union with Christ, when he exclaims, "It is no longer I who live, but Christ who lives in me" (Gal. 2:20). In another letter he writes, "All belongs to you, and you to Christ and Christ to God" (1 Cor. 3:22-23). Baptism is a journey into seeing our true self. This *seeing* very often unfolds gradually, not so unlike the blind man in the Gospel who was finally healed of his blindness only after being touched a second time by the healing love of Jesus (Mark 8:22-26). As disciples, we slowly grow into the baptismal consciousness of our divine groundedness. It takes time, but through grace and practice, we experience the slow opening of our eyes more and more. The illusory detours in search of a quick fix become less frequent. In fact, the wave begins to be suspicious of the false promises, as she gradually discovers within herself the vast ocean of peace. According to Thây, the wave realizes that water is her true home, water is her father, her mother. We learn to live so deeply immersed in God that, in the words of Eckhart, "all things simply become God."[49]

Called by Name

For Christians, baptism initiates us into a relationship with God. Through it I am invited to know God intimately. "Thus says the Lord . . . who created you, O Israel . . . I have called you by name, you are mine" (Isa. 43:1). God, the one who calls me by name (i.e., names my true self) from the depths of the baptismal water, is the very Ground of my being, "closer to me than I am to myself," says Eckhart.[50] This relationship with the ultimate dimension of reality is articulated—symbolized—in a personified manner. We say that baptism reveals to us the love of God as Father or Mother, and, like Jesus, we "hear" God speak to us as daughters and sons.

To speak of God using the language of *personal relationship* always brings one face to face with the limitations of human language. Is God a person? No, God is not a person like what we know. In attempting to speak of God, we say that God is three persons whose loving, nondual communion is the source of all personhood. "God is not a person, but not less than a person," notes Thây, quoting theologian Paul Tillich.[51] We could similarly ask, "Is nirvana water?" No, but the water's relationship with the wave tells us something about nirvana. We use the words, images, and metaphors that are available to us—limited as they are. We must constantly be reminded that this personal God is not a prisoner of our human concepts. All metaphors, all language will fall short of naming just *who* or *what* this Ultimate, Eternal Ground of Being is. Says Eckhart, "God, who has no name . . . is ineffable, and the soul in her ground is also ineffable."[52] So we do our best and try to speak the unspeakable.

Jews and Christians, of course, are not alone in employing the language of human relationship in speaking of God, or the Ultimate Dimension. In fact, many of the world's spiritual and mystical traditions, among them Hindus and Sufis, have found that only the language of personal relationship—including the language of sexual intimacy—comes somewhat close to describing the mystery of our communion with the divine. For many traditions, God is imaged as the supreme Lover who invites us into the depths of the divine abyss, the divine heart, as is so beautifully presented in the sacred Hebrew poetry, the Song of Songs:

> Arise, my love, my fair one,
>   and come away.
> O my dove, in the clefts of the rock,
>   in the covert of the cliff,
> let me see your face,
>   let me hear your voice,
> for your voice is sweet,

and your face is lovely. . . .
My beloved is mine and I am his;
    he pastures his flock among the lilies.
Until the day breathes
    and the shadows flee,
turn, my beloved, be like a gazelle
    or a young stag on the cleft mountains. (2:13-17)

In *Going Home* Thây expresses some difficulty with this type of personifi-
cation when speaking of God or the Ultimate Dimension. "Why spend your
time discussing whether God is a person or not, whether nirvana is personal
or impersonal?" he asks. "You are trying to compare the ground of being with
one expression at the phenomenal level. You are making a mistake."[53] I certainly understand Thây's discomfort. Not only is this language very foreign to
the Buddhist ear, but Thây is also painfully aware of the great risk in using this
type of language: we can end up making God in our own image and likeness.
We can easily manipulate God into acting according to our will. One need
only listen to some of the language being used to wage war and violence
around the world today to see how grave a danger this is. So Thây's words of
caution must be taken seriously. The language of person must not limit God,
for as the Buddha taught, the unborn, unoriginated, uncreated, and
unformed realm is not the same as the created realm. Having said this,
though, we are left with the challenging task of trying to say *something* about
mystical experience, aware that any attempt to speak of God, who is ultimately ineffable, is limited.

Throughout history, human beings have touched and tasted and have
come to know something about the ultimate dimension of life. This is what
is sometimes referred to as mystical experience. Mystics are left with a kind of
inner fire that burns within them in the wake of these experiences. Conscious
of the immense limitations, they feel impelled to say something about *that*
which burns in the human heart. Thây's use of the metaphor of the water and
the wave—which in itself is a marvelously simple and clear metaphor—
comes from the deep insights of his own mystical heart. But this metaphor,
like all metaphors, is limited. It too is drawn from the phenomenal world, the
world of poetry and symbol.

Thây alludes indirectly to the difficult yet necessary balancing act that
comes with entering into the realm of Ultimate Reality. He himself notes that
there is no mystical experience apart from the world of phenomena: "It is not
because you abandon all phenomena that you can touch the [ultimate]
dimension of the noumena. If you throw away the historical dimension, there
is no ultimate dimension to touch. You have to touch God through God's
creatures. You have to touch the ultimate dimension by touching the histori-

cal dimension deeply."[54] Might we not also add that the only way of *speaking* about God or the ultimate dimension is with insights and metaphors from the created world, the world of phenomena?

So one is left with no option apart from the limited, faltering language of human experience. And for the Judeo-Christian tradition, this limited, sometimes frustrating attempt to speak of God will often be done by employing the language of human love. Who knows? Perhaps, if we were to listen very attentively, we might hear the water whisper to the wave, "Come, my beloved, fall back into the cool abyss of my outstretched arms, into the dark, eternal cavern of my heart. Lose yourself in me for all eternity." Is this not a personified approximation of a truth that Thây and Eckhart and many other mystics are attempting to express? Did Jesus not hear something like this when the voice from heaven spoke to him as he stood dripping with water in the Jordan River? Once we touch fully the ultimate, eternal dimension completely we will no longer need language. We will be who we truly are, and this, finally, is freedom. In the meantime, we speak and listen and kindle the fire in our hearts.

Will or Grace?

Among the different expressions of Christianity there is debate around the question of when a person may be baptized. Though no one denies that the earliest practice of baptism was primarily a rite of Christian initiation for adults, within both the Catholic and Orthodox traditions infant baptism has been a commonly accepted practice almost since the time of Jesus. Many of the later branches of Christianity, however, opted for a different practice, emphasizing the importance of the ability on the part of the person to be baptized to willfully consent to faith in Christ as a prerequisite for baptism. Though this may seem of secondary importance in our present discussion, it actually is a key issue that needs to be considered, as it cuts to the heart of just what one understands baptism to be about. We bring it up here not to argue in favor of one side or the other, but instead for the purpose of looking at the topic of *grace* when considering the Christian mysticism of Eckhart in dialogue with the Buddhist mysticism of Thây.

I would like to approach this question by calling to mind from the Book of Exodus the ancient biblical story of the birth of Moses. Moses was born during a time in which Pharaoh, the king of Egypt, had decreed that all male children born to Hebrew women were to be killed. Moses' mother hid her son for three months, but "when she could hide him no longer she got a papyrus basket for him . . . [then] put the child in it and placed it among the reeds of the bank of the river" (Exod. 2:3). Not long after that, Pharaoh's daughter discovered the child, took him home to the royal household, and raised him as her own son. She called him Moses, because, she said, "I drew him out of the water" (2:10).

What does this story have to do with Christian baptism and Buddhist–Christian dialogue? In a direct way, the answer is, "probably very little." Symbolically, however, this story is quite illuminating when read as a kind of prefiguring of the sacrament of Christian baptism. The child Moses was "saved" from death by the intervention of several different actors. His mother put him into the basket and sent him down the river, while his sister—who was sent to see what would happen to the baby—was instrumental in suggesting to Pharaoh's daughter that the boy's mother be called to serve as a wet nurse for the "anonymous baby." The king's daughter herself also had a role to play in saving the child's life. Moses himself did *nothing* to save his life. It was saved as a result of the actions done by those who loved him. In other words—and this is what is important for our dialogue—it is the action of the community that introduced Moses into the plan of God's salvific love. The community did their part; God did the rest.

This story offers a fine narrative depiction of some of the different factors operative in the Christian understanding of baptism. First of all, it shows us that baptism is not only concerned with what *we do* or what *we believe*. It is a gift that we receive—a grace—that has everything to do with what God does through Christ, as it is lived out and passed on from generation to generation of believers. Our ancestors have been faithful in their response to Christ, and it is because of them that we have found our way to the banks of the river. In the words of St. Paul, "God chose us in [Christ] before the world began, to be holy and blameless in his sight, to be full of love" (Eph. 1:4). Baptism is not something we *do*; it is done to us. A sacrament initiates us into the saving grace of Christ. What *we do* is respond to the grace through the choices we make. So, while it is true that the baptized adult must exercise his or her will and choose each day to follow in the footsteps of Christ, it is vitally important for Christians to understand that long before we chose Christ, Christ chose us first (John 15:16).

To express this in the language of Thây's metaphor of the water and the wave, one might say: long before the wave realizes the great truth that she is *born of water*, the water has already made its own claim on the tiny wave: "You are my daughter, my beloved one." The water calls the wave by name long before the wave fully hears and understands that call. The wave awakens one day to discover who she *already is*. Likewise, Christians believe that we, like Jesus, glimpse the gift, the *grace*, of our true self as made in God's image at the moment of baptism, but the journey toward fully realizing in our lives this indwelling presence of God that is our deepest truth is a journey that unfolds over time. Says Bernard McGinn, "For Eckhart, grace saves primarily insofar as it activates the intellect to *become aware* of itself as *imago dei* [image of God]."[55] The Reality is always there—just as the statue is always hidden within the block of wood or stone. So, whether the sacrament of baptism is celebrated with a tiny infant or with a fully conscious adult, the challenge is still the same: to respond to the *grace* that is ours as a free gift. In the words of the evangelical hymn, "Amazing grace, how sweet the sound, that saved a wretch like me. I once was lost, but now I'm found, 'twas blind, but now I see."

Grace finds us; it is not the other way around. Thây articulates a kind of Buddhist notion of grace by reminding the wave that, "Water is your true home." The wave does not *make* the water her home; she simply discovers this wonderful truth. So it is with us, the followers of Jesus. Our entire life of faith is but a response to grace, the free and loving initiative of God. Says McGinn, "Eckhart . . . holds that grace is every gift we receive from God."[56] The rest is response, the choice to continue the journey, knowing that we, like Moses, have all been "drawn out of the water."

Both Christians and Jews believe that every human being carries within him or herself the imprint of the divine image. This is not something that we receive when we are baptized. As the psalmist says, "You [O God] knit me together in my mother's womb" (Ps. 139:13). We are the work of God's hands; God's very being is stamped into us. Without the breath of God within us, we, along with the entire universe, simply cease to exist. Picking up on Eckhart's image, the artist "does not introduce anything into the wood; instead he or she chisels away those fragments which hid and covered over the statue." The divine image is not any more present in the heart of an adult than in a child. It is not our conscious assent to the imprint of God's image in us that makes it present. It is our essential nature, our true ground, whether we know it or not. It is *the way it is*—suchness (*tathata*). The sacrament of baptism heals the blindness and awakens us to this *suchness*, our deepest and truest self.

The full-realization of that true self (i.e., the chiseling away of the fragments) is the work of an entire lifetime, the fruit of the many choices we make each and every day. It is for this reason that the Judeo-Christian tradition so deeply reverences time and history, for this is precisely the context in which we discover who we are and who God is, or better yet, *who we are in God*. The historical living out of our lives is the opportunity we have to become aware of this great mystery, and, for a Christian, the sacrament of baptism sets the whole process in motion.

Let us go back, then, to the question posed at the beginning of this particular section: Is it *will or grace*? Is baptism a grace we receive or a choice we make? The answer, of course, is yes. We receive a gift and we spend our lives opening it, giving expression to it. Baptism can never be reduced to a magic trick that works completely disconnected from human will. A sacramental baptism that is never acted upon, never integrated, never lived out is hardly any baptism at all. At the same time, though, we must also refrain from reducing baptism simply to "my choice to accept Jesus Christ." God chooses us first. The water gives birth to the wave, not vice versa. Grace is always a free gift; its blossoming takes the gentle and constant work of a good gardener. It is the journey of a whole lifetime.

Sacrament: Touching the Water

Having commented on the Christian understanding of grace, we must also be honest and admit that the work of gardening and giving expression to the grace of baptism—what Thây calls "cultivating the Holy Spirit"—is not always easy. In fact, in many parts of the world, the task of "cultivating the garden" is in a state of crisis. We are often baptized Christians by name, though many of us have not awakened to the riches that such a grace entails. We are swimming in the ocean of God's presence and yet still spend much of our lives frantically searching for water. I would characterize the situation as a crisis of mindfulness. To a great extent, we have lost the capacity to practice the unfolding of the grace of baptism. We have the ancient rituals in place and our theological libraries are filled with writings on the sacraments, but we have forgotten how to make it all real, how to live out our full baptismal enlightenment. It is here, it seems to me, where Thây's practice of mindfulness sheds such needed light onto the path for so many Christians today.

Because we are in a crisis of *practice*, we need spiritual guides who can show us the path again. We need people steeped in the practice who can help us discover within ourselves the all-encompassing presence of God. We need to experience *being* who we are—sons and daughters of God—filled with the luminous presence of the living Christ. This was the role of the desert fathers and mothers in the early centuries of Christianity. Christians sought them out in their desert huts and caves in order to learn how to practice their faith. These hermits and wandering ascetics were teachers who simply taught by their example. It was not a question of long treatises and theological discussions. They taught through practice.

Thây addresses this lack of real spiritual guides in our day. Though it is painful reality, it is only through honestly recognizing the truth that we can embark on a path of healing.

> Spiritual leaders . . . simply do not know what to do. They have not been able to transmit the deepest values of their traditions, perhaps because they themselves have not fully understood or experienced them. When a priest does not embody the living values of a tradition, he or she cannot transmit them to the next generation. He can only wear the outer

garments and pass on the superficial forms. . . . Buddhism, like Christianity and other traditions, has to renew itself in order to respond to the needs of the people of our time.[57]

I believe that Thây's practice and his teachings on mindfulness offer a valuable treasure in our present times for all of us who are seeking paths toward spiritual renewal. Thây is a spiritual teacher who *has* been able to respond to the challenge. Though my experience is much more limited than that of others, I can attest to the fact that Thây is a masterful teacher—and he teaches principally by example. I've witnessed this with my own eyes. I've watched Thây doing walking meditation with perfect recollection and simple joy, dwelling fully in the present moment. I remember him pausing one day, in the middle of one of his *dharma* talks, to contemplate a lovely flower arrangement done by one of the nuns. It was as if time had stopped. There was no hurry, just sheer delight in the beauty of the moment. As far as I was concerned, he did not need to say another word. His contemplative presence said it all. The way Thây looks at people, his smile, his gentle voice, his simple stories, his openness to listening to others—all of this speaks volumes to people hungering for spiritual guidance.

Thây does not need to talk *about* the Buddha. He *is* a Buddha, and so what he does witnesses to the teachings of the Buddha. His teachings are uncomplicated, down-to-earth, freeing. He sits in meditation with his monks and nuns, he eats with them, travels and gives retreats with them. During my stay at Deer Park Monastery, he welcomed a group of eight of us into his living area one day for tea and some time for informal conversation. Even *that* time was a teaching. He taught us by just being with us, including the pauses in which we just sat in silence. Thây's unhurried presence is very much a part of the spiritual nourishment our world hungers for today. I wonder if, perhaps one of the greatest gifts I, as a Catholic priest, can give to others is simply to sit with them in contemplative silence? This, unfortunately, was not part of our seminary curriculum.

How do we Christians recapture this largely forgotten dimension of our life? How can we recover those pieces of our own tradition that were once less complicated? How do we teach people in our modern world the value of just *being together*, just *wasting time together*—unproductively—because we believe that being with one another is to be with God? We do believe, after all, that when we are together we are the body of Christ. What might Christian catechesis look like if it were based on a model of sharing our faith not in a classroom but by being together, sharing our lives together, mindfully, with no hurry, no business agenda, nothing that needed to be accomplished? How can we pass on the Good News of Jesus through example and within the context of daily life—rather than as one more extracurricular activity to tack onto our busy week? I guess the main theme running through these questions is: Have we reduced Christianity to a series of things we *do*, while forgetting *simply to be?*

I actually think that Christianity has done a pretty good job passing on the legacy of doing our faith—practicing Jesus' call to love and serve one's neighbor. This does not mean that all Christians are doing it, but at least most of us are aware of that part of the tradition. Around the world there are many exemplary Christians doing exemplary things: working with the poor, teaching in schools for the underprivileged, caring for the sick, feeding the hungry, building a more just world. In fact, it is precisely in this field of service and love that many Christians have found a fulfilling way to engage and en-flesh their baptismal vocation. This is a great legacy, and one that I am very grateful to be a part of. Serving others—especially the poor—is a very valid way of living the teachings of Jesus with mindfulness. To serve soup in a soup kitchen or to sit and hold the hand of someone dying of AIDS in a hospital is practice, and it does lead us to a tangible experience of being in the presence of God. This is so because loving service leads us beyond just thinking about God, into simply being with God in the person of our neighbor.

It is rather humorous to note that for many years there were almost as many Western Christians flocking to India to work with Mother Teresa of Calcutta as there were those who went to ashrams and zendos to learn the practice of meditation. I know, because I am one of them! The spiritual hunger is not much different in both cases: people want to live their faith in a direct and experiential way. We are all searching for a deeper meaning to life—not just intellectually, but practically, experientially. There is an insight here that we need to pay attention to. Just as direct and selfless contact with the poor and destitute can awaken one to an encounter with the living Christ, the same is true for many who experience the ego-stripping practice of meditation and contemplative prayer. Christians, especially the young, want to discover a God who is real and tangible. All of us who define ourselves as spiritual seekers are looking for a *real presence* that is more than a theological teaching. We want something that will invigorate and liberate us really and experientially. We are looking for a living faith and a living God beneath and beyond the memorized words of catechetical formulas and theological dogmas.

I must admit that these are *not* the kinds of questions that Meister Eckhart was asking in his day. Eckhart was not concerned much at all with practical ways and methods. In fact, he was a bit skeptical of all that sounded to him like *methods*—afraid that people would get so caught up in the methods that they would lose the God whom they were seeking. This is good advice for our own times as well. But as much as I have great respect for the wisdom and teaching of Eckhart, I think that Thây has something to offer that was simply not part of Eckhart's immediate concern.

Thây's teachings on the practice of mindfulness have a way of bringing the teachings of Buddhism home through real and tangible experience. "Even children can understand the teaching on impermanence," he remarked the day we shared tea with him, "through the practice of mindfulness." The more I understand and practice mindfulness, the more I begin to realize that it shares much common ground with the rich and ancient sacramental tradition in Christianity. In fact, I would be so bold as to say that Thây's teaching on mindfulness is a kind of *sacramental Buddhism*. For Christians, a sacrament is a sign of something holy that makes real that which it symbolizes. Through sacramental gestures, we touch sacred reality here and now. The eucharistic action of taking, blessing, breaking, and sharing bread in the context of remembering the words and gestures of Jesus at the Last Supper is a *sacramental action*. Through this eucharistic gesture, we come into tangible, spiritual union with the living Christ.

When Thây teaches his disciples walking meditation, inviting them to walk slowly and gently, dwelling fully in the present moment, touching and healing the earth with each mindful step, he is doing what in Christian parlance we would call a sacramental gesture. Each mindful and meditative step connects me in a spiritual way to ultimate reality. Mindful breathing is another example. For Thây it is about more than just inhaling oxygen. Mindful breathing connects us with the energy of life, what Christians call the Holy Spirit and through the Holy Spirit, we touch God, the Giver of life. Mindful breathing brings us into communion with plants and trees, as well as with the endangered Brazilian rain forests. Mindful breathing shows us how we are to be part of the world community committed to healing our polluted and contaminated world. The same is true when Thây invites the sound of the bell. This sacramental gesture is more than a device for telling us that it is time to meditate; it calls us home to the present moment—here and now in the kingdom of God.

What Thây has done with the practice of mindfulness is to show us how every moment of life is a sacramental moment—a moment in time that unites us with eternity, with the ultimate dimension of life. Thây comes very close to making this connection between mindfulness and sacramentality in a section of *Living Buddha, Living Christ* in which he comments on different expressions of Jewish piety.

"Piety" is an important word in Judaism, because all of life is a reflection of God . . . so when you enjoy something you think of God and enjoy His presence. It is very close to the Buddhist appreciation of interbeing and interpenetration. . . . Piety is the recognition that everything is linked to the presence of God in every moment. The Passover Seder, for example, is a ritual meal to celebrate the freedom of the Israelites from bondage in Egypt and their journey home. During the meal, certain vegetables and herbs, salt, and other condiments help us touch what happened in the past—what our suffering was and what was our hope. This is the practice of mindfulness.[58]

From a Christian point of view, what Thây is speaking about here is the sacramental life. In fact, what he says about the Jewish Seder sounds very similar to his own teaching on the mindful consumption of food. It is something so simple, yet it encompasses such profound consequences. For Thây, eating is much more than providing for the material needs of our bodies; it is a sacramental act that connects us with the sun and the clouds, with the earth and the farmers who farm it. "When we hold a piece of bread to eat," says Thây, "if mindfulness is there, if the Holy Spirit is there, we can eat the bread in a way that will allow us to touch the whole cosmos deeply."[59] This is sacrament at its best. In the recitation ceremony for the Five Mindfulness Trainings, the fifth training shows us how eating becomes a sacramental act of healing, transformation, and peace:

> Aware of the suffering caused by unmindful consumption, I am committed to cultivating good health, both physical and mental, for myself, my family, and my society by practicing mindful eating, drinking and consuming. I will ingest only items that preserve peace, well-being, and joy in my body, in my consciousness, and in the collective body and consciousness of my family and society. . . . I will work to transform violence, fear, anger, and confusion in myself and in society by practicing a diet for myself and for my society.[60]

Christianity does not have to reinvent the wheel here. What we need to do is to recover the connection between the sacramental life of the church and daily practice. Much of Christianity has a rich liturgical and sacramental life, but unfortunately it has been largely limited to something that is done on Sunday mornings within the walls of a church building. The bridge linking liturgy and life has broken down. This is indeed one of the great tragedies of modernity. Luckily there are still places in our world today where life is lived according to the rhythms of mystery and spirit. Large parts of India and Africa, as well as substantial pockets in Asia and among the indigenous peoples of the Americas continue to touch the ultimate reality within the small details of daily life. These peoples have a treasure to share with the rest of us. To the extent that we are able to heal this rupture within our own soul, we will be part of the healing of our wounded world.

Touching the Water, Touching God

How, then, do we go about this great healing? First of all, at least speaking from a Christian perspective, it seems to me that we must liberate sacramentality from the limits of the sanctuary and bring it back into the realm of daily life. This is the great insight of Thây's practice of mindfulness. For centuries Christians lived without this divorce between spirituality and daily life. Faith was made tangible through the sacramental use of bread and wine, candles and prayer beads, holy water and sacred icons, kneeling and prostrations, oil and incense. People did sacramental "walking meditation" by going on pilgrimages and visiting holy shrines; they celebrated with prayer and ritual the seasons of planting and harvesting, and in this experienced the entire earth as one great sacrament of God's abundant love. The liturgical feasts were celebrated both at the local church and at home. In all of these sacramental actions people touched the presence of God in the events of everyday life.

How can we bring the water and the oil, the bread and the fire, the incense and the ashes—the raw materials of Christian sacramental life—back into the realm of daily life? How do we renew and encourage the practice of sacramental mindfulness among ordinary people today? How do we provide nourishment and guidance for a world hungering for meaning?

I would like to begin to answer these questions by sharing a personal experience, an experience of spiritual renewal and insight that I received from the people of Latin America. I think it offers a glimpse of how we might cultivate sacramental mindfulness today through the recovery and rejuvenation of traditional spiritual practices. By the time I went to Latin America to study theology and to minister as a young Dominican friar, my spirituality had already been thoroughly influenced by modern Euro-American secularism. In my limited understanding, the gospel message had come to represent a blueprint for social change, and I was sent out as one of its "enlightened" architects. Let me state clearly that I recognize and agree wholeheartedly with the social implications of the gospel and of the following of Jesus. However, I also recognize now—certainly more clearly than before—that this is just one piece of the whole of the Christian message.

Thanks to the simple, uncomplicated faith of the people of Latin America, many of whom are still rooted in the indigenous traditions of their ancestors (both pre-Christian and Christian), the blindness caused by my limited vision slowly began to heal. In the mountain villages of Honduras I ran into a tradition that deeply moved me. Since I often stayed in the small, one-room huts of the families that I visited, I experienced their daily life up close. In many places, the parents and grandparents bless their children each morning before they leave the house for school or to work in the fields. Sometimes this blessing is done with holy water that has been blessed previously by a priest. This daily routine is done without much fanfare. The children (and adults, if there are still grandparents in the house) simply walk up to their elders in the household and, with a slight bow of the head, receive a blessing. The parent or grandparent simply places his or her hand on the child's head, sometimes accompanied with a sprinkle of holy water, and says something like, "God bless and protect you today, son." That is all. It is very simple, yet for me, as an outsider, it is quite moving. I often would ask for a blessing as well. This very simple sacramental gesture is a concrete way for the family to touch the presence of God in the goings and comings of the day.

Blessings and the use of holy water are still common practice in the Catholic Church today. Unfortunately, though, they have become more and more confined to the official duties of the ordained priest. What deeply impressed me in Honduras was that this particular sacramental gesture was a daily spiritual practice done within the small circle of the family, and its ministers were the parents and grandparents. The shift of the past several centuries toward limiting almost all sacramental expressions of faith to ordained ministers is truly a tragedy, for in so doing, we are removing sacramentality from the very realm where it should be flourishing—the daily life of ordinary people. For too long now, spirituality has become the property of experts, and that always runs into the danger of turning access to God into a commodity that can be sold. If there is anything that Jesus was passionate about during his life, it was the need to "give God back to the people." Jesus forcefully denounced the concentration of religious power in the hands of a few self-appointed experts.

What the families in the mountains of Honduras have helped me to rediscover is the beauty and simplicity of a spiritual practice lived harmoniously within the ordinariness of daily life. Not only do they bless their children; they bless their animals and houses too. In many parts of Latin America the people bless the seeds and the fields before planting. They sprinkle holy water on the sick and on those who have died. They bless newborn babies and the midwives who deliver them. They use holy water to bless prayer beads and holy pictures, even new bicycles and taxis! It is somewhat comical to see people arriving at the church for the celebration of mass with plastic Coke bottles filled with water to be blessed, which they then take home to be used in their myriad of daily sacramental celebrations.

I was a bit skeptical of all this at first (filled, as I was, with all my "enlightened" theology). Is this not superstition, I wondered? Little by little, though, with the patient example of the people and with some insights shared by others along the way, I began to see that this is the way the people touch God in their daily life. They do not have access to God and spiritual things in the official, sophisticated religious world, so they and their ancestors before them have developed ways of celebrating God's presence through simple pious practices that are "unofficial." Everything about their world offers them an opportunity to be mindful of God's presence. As Thây says, " If you throw away the historical dimension, there is no ultimate dimension to touch. You have to touch God through his creatures. You have to touch the ultimate dimension by touching the historical dimension deeply."[61] Through gestures as simple as blessing their children and their homes with holy water, these people have been able to keep the presence of God alive and real in the midst of daily life. This sacramental mindfulness is, I believe, one way that Thây's teachings on mindfulness can be translated into Christian practice.

The use of holy water as a way of sacramentally touching the divine in daily life has the potential of bringing Christians into a deep experience of what Thây calls *interbeing*. For Christians, to touch water mindfully is to touch our entire story of salvation. We touch, for example, the gratuitousness of creation, as well as the ancient story of Israel's journey through the Red Sea into freedom. Through touching water deeply, we reconnect with the water that God made to spring from the rock in the desert (Ps. 105:41), as well as the water of the Jordan River, where Jesus was baptized and experienced his profound oneness with God. Water brings to mind the crucifixion of Jesus and the water and blood that flowed from his pierced side. We remember Jesus' promise to the Samaritan woman he met at the well one day: "The water that I will give will become in [you] a spring of water gushing up to eternal life" (John 4:14). Water puts us in touch with our own baptism and the presence of Ultimate Reality in the depths of our own being. When an elderly grandmother in a small village in Honduras blesses her tiny, sick granddaughter with holy water, she is not only touching God, but through her sacramental use of water and through the gesture of human touch, she knows that God is touching her granddaughter too. She knows without knowing. She knows that the water and the wave are one.

What we have considered here holds true for many other possible expressions of sacramental mindfulness. We Christians could look similarly at the practice of mindfulness through the sacramental use of bread or oil or silence or listening to scripture. The possibilities of learning to practice in this way are infinite. The ultimate dimension of reality is so close to us, "closer to us than we are to ourselves," says Eckhart. It is all right here and right now. It is the present moment, and it is also the moment of presence, God's presence. It is the wave dancing upon the water, and it is the water dancing within the heart of the wave.

5

Jesus and God

"Coming Home"

The Trinity as Pilgrimage of Love

The Christian doctrine of the Trinity is a mystery that lies beyond words (even though a lot of words have been written on the topic!). Some might ask, and many do: why try to speak about something of which one cannot speak? Perhaps the only way to answer that question is to say that we do not really know how to speak very well about love either, though we attempt to do that, mostly through poetry and music. We *must* attempt to say something about love; to be silent would seem almost blasphemous. So, too, is the case with the Trinity, for the Trinity is the Christian story of love. Anything and everything that we say falls short. As long as we are clear about this, we can continue.

The Trinity offers a platform for fruitful interreligious dialogue with Buddhism and Hinduism, since it is only through the lens of nonduality, what Thây calls *interbeing*, that one can even begin to intuit the energy of love that is at the heart of the Trinity. The Christian scriptures point to different levels of this nondual intercommunion, both within God and between God and the universe. Within the Trinity there is a commingling between the Father, the Son, and the Holy Spirit that is simultaneously *oneness* and *otherness*. We human beings participate in this mutual communion. The Gospel of John, for example, quotes several statements by Jesus that point to this paradoxical intercommunion:

Believe me that I am in the Father and the Father is in me. (14:11)

Whoever has seen me has seen the Father. (14:9)

As you, Father, are in me and I am in you, may they also be in us . . . so that they may be one as we are one, I in them and you in me, that they may become completely one. (17:21-23)

On that day you will know that I am in the Father, and you in me, and I in you. (14:19-20)

Jesus said to them again, "Peace be with you. As the Father sent me, so I send you." When he had said this, he breathed on them and said to them, "Receive the Holy Spirit." (20:21-22)

The starting place and the ending place within the Trinity is always the Father, the Source. The Father is "beginning without any beginning,"[1] as well as the final "place" where this intimate communion finds its completion. The Son and the Spirit, and with them all being, come forth from the Father and return to the Father—in one great, eternal flowing. In referring to the *going forth* and the *returning home* within the Trinity, Eckhart was fond of quoting from the Book of Ecclesiastes (1:7): "All streams run to the sea, but the sea is not full; to the place where the streams flow, there they continue to flow."[2] Not only does this happen within the Trinity, but, as we shall see, the entire universe is on one great pilgrimage—a journey that begins in God, flows out from God, and leads us *home to God*.

This cosmic pilgrimage begins with an act of pure love: the begetting of the Son by the Father. From the undivided state of oneness and silence, dwelling wholly within the Godself, the Father flows outward in self-expression, "giving birth to the Son," and thus is born love. This is what Eckhart refers to frequently in his sermons as *bullitio*, an inner "boiling" within God, "an emanation from the depths of silence . . . inwardly boiling without any boiling over."[3] Fr. Bede Griffiths, the English Benedictine monk who spent the second half of his life living as a Christian *sannyasi* (Hindu monk) in India, notes, "In the Christian Trinity we have the Father. He is the Ground, the Source, the Origin, the One beyond. And the One is always expressing itself in the Logos (the Word). That is the principle of *differentiation* in the Godhead."[4] Griffiths continues, adding the second piece of the equation: "In the Logos the whole world comes into being."[5] In other words, there are two emanations, two divine outpourings going on simultaneously: one within God (Eckhart's *bullitio*) and the other an outward "boiling over" (what Eckhart calls *ebullitio*). This second one is God's self-expression—via the Logos—in creation.[6]

Eckhart's inner and outward *boiling*—part of his language of *flowing*—is one way of describing God's self-expression through the Logos. Just as God *flows out* through the Word, so too is there an eternal *flowing back*—all part of the one great trinitarian pilgrimage. Everything finally comes home in God. This energy of flowing is music to Eckhart's ears. The entire universe, according to the Meister, is soaked with divine presence as a result of the gratuitous outpouring of the Son, the Logos, into creation. This "universe soaked with God's presence" has its origin within the inner dynamism of oneness and otherness (differentiation) within the Trinity. The swirling of energy within the Trinity—which is none other than the Holy Spirit—*overflows* into the created realm. Says the Meister, "In the same source where the Son takes rise, where the Father speaks His eternal Word, and from the same heart, the Holy Spirit also takes rise and flows forth."[7] Again, relating the divine over-flowing to grace, Eckhart says, "I sometimes mention two springs. . . . One spring, from which grace gushes forth, is where the Father bears forth His only-begotten Son. From that source grace arises, and there grace flows forth from the same spring."[8]

Christianity, using Jesus' own mystical experience and prayer as its inspiration, names this eternal Source, the spring from which grace gushes forth, "the Father." Eckhart uses the term "Father" in two ways. Sometimes he uses the name to speak of the Trinity's differentiation (as in, "Father, Son, and Spirit"). At other times, though, he uses the name "Father" to speak of *that reality* which is nameless: the undifferentiated Source, the great "Silent Desert into which no distinction ever peeped."[9] He also calls this undifferentiated Source "the One," and he notes that the "One is beginning without beginning."[10] He likes to imagine what the "One" was like "prior" to the trinitarian differentiation, that is to say, "prior" to the Father's outflowing in the Logos.[11] It is, of course, rather pointless to speak of something as "prior to eternity," but for Eckhart it is an important question, for it is *there*, in the undifferentiated Source, that we experience nonduality. Eckhart wants to lure us into the spring "that has not yet gushed forth" where we are invited to taste the trinitarian intermingling with nondual abandon. It is *there*, says the Meister, that we experience true oneness.

The river that flows out of the great underground Source is, of course, the Word, the Logos, the Son who flows forth from the Father "in the beginning" (John 1:1). It is the "spring of water gushing up to eternal life" (John 4:14), which breaks through into history (i.e., "becomes flesh") and flows out in the four directions, irrigating the earth and producing trees with healing leaves and abundant fruit (Rev. 22:2). The Book of Genesis uses this metaphor of God in one of the versions of the creation story: "In the day that the Lord God made the earth and the heavens, when no plant of the field was yet in the earth and no herb of the field had yet sprung up . . . a stream would rise from the earth, and water the whole face of the ground" (Gen. 2:4-6). The dynamic movement of *flowing* is the work of the Holy Spirit. Through the energy of the Spirit the entire universe is *soaked* with God.

Says Eckhart, using another of his metaphors, and speaking on behalf of the great river of life, "When I subsisted in the ground, in the bottom, in the river and font of the Godhead (i.e., the undifferentiated Source) no one asked me where I was going or what I was doing: there was no one to ask me. When I flowed forth, all creatures said 'God.'"[12] For Eckhart, this is the essence of the Christian Trinity, in as few words as possible. The Trinity is the Godhead (the Ground, the Font, the Source) differentiated. The Father, Son, and Holy Spirit are not three gods but three different movements within God, three unique manifestations of the Water.

Fr. Bede relates this differentiated unity of the Trinity to the Mahayana Buddhist doctrine of *sunyata*, or emptiness (the absence of inherent existence). Building on the teachings of D. T. Suzuki, who is credited with having introduced Zen to the West, Bede notes that "*Sunyata* is not static, but dynamic. . . . In the void there is a constant urge to differentiate itself. The whole creation is the differentiation of the void. . . . At the very moment of the differentiation it returns to itself. It is always coming out and returning. That is why the Buddhists say that *Nirvana* and *Samsara* are the same. Ultimately they are one."[13]

In *Living Buddha, Living Christ*, Thây comments on this differentiated movement of going out and returning in a discussion of the ten names of the Buddha. The first name, he says, is *Tathagata*, which describes the Buddha as "he who has arrived from suchness, remains in suchness, and will return to suchness." Thây continues, "Suchness is a Buddhist term pointing to the true nature of things, or ultimate reality. It is the substance or ground of being, just like water is the substance of waves. Like the Buddha, we too have come from suchness, remain in suchness, and will return to suchness. We have come from nowhere and have nowhere to go."[14] This kind of language, of course, would send Meister Eckhart into ecstasy! Thây's reference to the fact that we come *from*, remain *in*, and return *to* suchness is a good description of both the dynamic movement of pilgrimage within the Trinity, and the trinitarian outpouring into humanity and the universe as a whole.[15] We Christians would say that we come from the essential ground (*suchness*) of the Father, we live in and remain in that ground now, and we are on a journey of return to that original source through the power of the Holy Spirit.

Just as Thây calls the suchness "nowhere," so too does Eckhart: "God is nowhere . . . God is not here or there."[16] This divine *nowhere*, so common to mystical language, is an invitation to go beyond concepts, beyond the this and that of time and space, in order "to pass into the naked being of God."[17] It is in letting go of the *some-where* and *some-thing* of heaven that we are able to live mindfully in the eternal present here and now. Eckhart calls the nowhere of the final return an *unbecoming* as well: "When I return to God . . . my breakthrough [back into God] will be far nobler than my outflowing. . . . When I enter the ground, the bottom, the river and fount of the Godhead, none will ask me whence I came or where I have been. No one missed me, for there God *unbecomes*."[18]

This language of emptiness and *no-where* (what the Buddhists call *sunyata*) is not common in everyday Christian circles. We are more accustomed to saying that God is *Someone*, and that God is *everywhere*. How, then, are we to understand that God is *not here* and *not there*, that God *unbecomes*? For me personally, it was a short parable from the ancient *Chandogya Upanishad* that gave me the light I needed to begin to grasp this mystical insight.

> [A] guru tells the disciple to take a fruit from a tree, break it open and then take a seed and break it open, and he asks the disciple what he can see. The disciple says, "I see nothing," to which the guru replies, "In that nothing, that hidden essence which you cannot see, the power of the growth of the whole tree consists." So also there is a secret essence in all creation, in everything which exists, which is the source of all being; and "Thou, Svetaketu, art that."[19]

As the outer covering of all created reality is stripped away, layer by layer, we eventually end up with nothing. It is like peeling an onion layer by layer. But we could do the same with a book or a tree. All outward matter is simply a manifestation of an invisible essence hidden at the core of all that *is*. So, when the last layer of the onion is peeled away, and the last page of the book, including the cover, is torn out and thrown away, and all the bark and wood of the pine tree are removed—what is left that is common to them all? Where is that which made all these material things exist? *That* is nowhere; it cannot be seen. It is neither the layers of onion, nor the pages of the book, nor the wood of the tree. *That* is *is-ness*, and it is nowhere, and it is everywhere. We are *that*, too.

The language of God must necessarily make use of the language of paradox, for without it, we lose the mystery of this *One* who is far beyond all our human imaginings. The Trinity is not any-*thing*. It is beyond things. It is *is-ness* flowing out of *is-ness*, only to flow back into *is-ness*. Because the Trinity *is*, all things *are*.

Bede Griffiths, using this circular image of the Trinity's going out and returning (*exitus* and *reditus* in the theology of Thomas Aquinas[20]), speaks of it as a dynamic flow of love, moving from unity, into diversity, and back into unity: "The Logos is the principle of differentiation in the Godhead, which differentiates itself in the world. And at the very same moment of differentiation, there is a movement of return in the Holy Spirit. The circle is completed. The *energy of love* unites the Father and the Son."[21] This is a unique insight of Christian mysticism in general, namely, that the entire trinitarian pilgrimage is fueled by love. Says Fr. Bede:

> The Father conceives us in the Word and wills us in the Spirit, and he expresses his love in bringing us forth. . . . The very love which sends us forth from him draws us back to him all the time. If we respond, then we grow in this world and gradually we are transformed, as Jesus was in the resurrection, and we return to the Father. . . . In the final state creation and humanity return to God . . . redemption in Christ has

overcome the disintegrating forces of sin and has restored humankind to unity. In him we are able to return to the source. We are able to return to God and exist eternally in God, each participating in the one divine reality, yet remaining distinct. . . . The basis of this is the Christian understanding of the Trinity. The Father is in the Son in a total self-giving to the Son, and the "I" of the Son is one with the Father. . . . That is also what we experience in our lives in the experience of love, when we can share and participate in the identity of the other. The ultimate state is when we all reach that state of pure identity in difference.[22]

As one Catholic theologian, Robert Barron, says, "God is a community, a play of contrast, an energy of love or, to use Balthasar's favorite image, a drama. The Father goes out from himself in the Son and then returns in the Spirit . . . allowing for the playfulness and 'theatricality' of love."[23]

John Tauler, another Dominican mystic and a disciple of Eckhart, captures well this interflowing energy of love within the Trinity, emphasizing that this "divine circulation" is as much about us as about God. In a Christmas sermon he noted:

God rests within himself in the unity of essence, and he flows out in the distinction of persons. And so He turns inward, comprehending himself, and he flows outward in the generation of his image (that of his Son). . . . This delight streams forth as ineffable love, and that ineffable love is the Holy Spirit. Thus God turns inward, goes outward, and returns to Himself again. . . . This divine circulation should also be adopted by us if we are to attain spiritual motherhood in our soul.[24]

What is of vital importance in the insights of each of these Christian theologians is that this trinitarian *flowing out* and *flowing back in* is all about love, the dynamism of love. As the song goes, "Love is what makes the world go 'round." At the heart of the Trinity is the transforming power of love. How important it is for us Christians to discover this priceless gift. It is for this reason that we must try to speak of this unspeakable mystery.

It is time to free the Trinity from the dusty pages of theology books and return it to the loving hearts of believing men and women. I think this is what is behind Thây's words, "If the church practices well the teachings of Jesus, the Trinity will always be present and the church will have a healing power to transform all that it touches."[25] Yes! That is it exactly.

We are all pilgrims, then, making our way through history as part of this great pilgrimage of love. We are on a journey back home, back to our original source in the loving heart of God. Says Eckhart, "All have a call to return whence they flowed forth. All their life and being is a calling and a hurrying back to what they came out of."[26] It is important that we hear this mystical teaching with Thây's earlier quote as background music: "Like the Buddha, we too have come from suchness, remain in suchness, and will return to suchness. We have come from nowhere and have nowhere to go."[27] The great mystics have all heard the same music of loving silence.

The Trinity and Interbeing

For Christians, the question inevitably arises: Then how do we get back home to God? For Thây the answer is quite simple: through the practice of mindfulness. We Christians can find much to imitate in this teaching, for only through mindful spiritual practice does the Trinity move from the theology books to becoming a reality in our lives. Yet there is more to the answer for us. We recognize that our way home to God is through and with Jesus Christ. In John's Gospel, Jesus speaks of our going home with him to the Father in this way: "In my Father's house there are many dwelling places. . . . If I go and prepare a place for you, I will come again and will take you to myself, so that where I am, there you may be also" (14:2-3). The very Logos, the Son, who flowed forth from the Father "in the beginning," leads us and all of creation back home. Our fidelity to "following Christ" leads to the fulfillment of our pilgrimage of faith.

The medieval mystic St. Catherine of Siena clearly understood that for Christians the journey home to God was possible only *in* Christ and *through* Christ. In one of her divine conversations, God said to Catherine, "Look at the bridge of my only-begotten Son, and notice its greatness. Look! It stretches from heaven to earth . . . bridging the chasm between us and rebuilding the road."[28] Catherine knew well the fragility of her own spiritual life. She was aware that in every human heart there is a broken-down road in need of divine healing in order for us to *come home to God*. For Catherine, it is through our entering into the heart of Christ that we find the pathway back to the heart of God.[29]

This pilgrimage home to God is captured in narrative in Jesus' parable of the prodigal son (Luke 15:11-32). After leaving his father's house with his portion of the inheritance, the younger son in this story embarks on a wild journey out into the world—the sinful, broken, limited world. We are not accustomed to hearing this parable told in reference to *God's* Son, Jesus Christ, but it really is a trinitarian parable. St. Paul says, "For our sake God made him to be sin who knew no sin, so that in him we might become the righteousness of God" (2 Cor. 5:21). The prodigal son "becomes sin" so as to open up a pathway home to those who are "lost and cannot find the way."[30] Upon returning to his father's house, the son is met with great rejoicing, and the father, after embracing him, exclaims, "Let us eat and celebrate; for this son of mine was dead and is alive again; he was lost and is found" (Luke 15:23-24).

The reference to the "dead son" who is now alive and back home with the Father reveals the trinitarian subscript of the story. It also points to our own redemptive story. Our "becoming lost and found again" happens *within* the heart of Christ. Says Fr. Bede, "Redemption in Christ has overcome the disintegrating forces of sin and has restored [us] to unity. In [Christ] we are able to return to the source. We are able to return to God and to exist eternally in God, each participating in the one divine reality, yet remaining distinct."[31]

The Trinity, then, is more than an abstract doctrine about the inner workings of God. What is perhaps of most importance for us is to see how *we* participate in the trinitarian journey, flowing out from the spacious heart of God and returning—*in* Christ and *through* the loving energy of the Spirit—back home to God. We are all *going home*, to use the metaphor from Thây's book, to the extent that we live each and every moment mindful of this deep, inner pilgrimage of faith. The steps we take today on this journey are both a returning to our original home in God and a living out of the fullness of God's kingdom here and now. One cannot help hearing in this pilgrim movement an echo from T. S. Eliot's *The Four Quartets*:

> What we call the beginning is often the end, and to make an end is to make a beginning. The end is where we start from. . . . With the drawing of this Love and the voice of this Calling, we shall not cease from exploration, and the end of all our exploring will be to arrive where we started, and know the place for the first time.[32]

Fr. Bede reminds us that this participation in the trinitarian pilgrimage is universal, all-encompassing, leaving no one excluded. We are all "drawn by love" back home to the Source: "Just as the universe is one, humanity is one, and every individual human being is part of this one humanity . . . evolving through time and space and throughout all the races and religions of the world, moving toward the point when it finally converges on the One."[33]

Swami Abhishiktananda, who spent the last years of his life living in a hut along the Ganges River in India, struggled to integrate the mystery of the Trinity with his lived experience of the Hindu teaching on *advaita*, or nonduality. He says this of his own encounter with the transforming power of trinitarian love, "The Trinity is the face-to-face of the Father and of the Son in the nonduality (*advaita*) of the Spirit. The Spirit is divine love which opens being up in a face-to-face relationship so that love can be expressed, and which closes it in *advaita* so that love can be consummated."[34]

The Father—silent, empty, and alone in the eternal abyss of the Godhead—expresses himself as *other* in order to manifest love. This outward expression of love flowing forth from the Father is a mystery, for though Father and Son are seemingly *two*, they remain essentially *one*. As Eckhart masterfully shows, "It is the nature of love to arise and flow out of two as a one. One as one is not love; two as two is not love; but *two as one* must needs produce natural, willing, ardent love."[35] The Father and the Son are not *one* and they are not *two*. They are *love*, and love is *two as one*. Lest we forget, we are also brought into this great mystery of love to the extent that we surrender our separateness and flow into the *One* who is "closer to me than I am to myself."[36]

This language of mystical oneness within the Trinity is very similar to Thây's teaching on interbeing. For this reason it is surprising to read the following comment from Thây in *Going Home*: "If we can bring into Christianity the insight of interbeing and of nonduality, we will radically transform the way people look on the Christian tradition, and the valuable jewels in the Christian tradition will be rediscovered."[37] I say "surprising" because in several places in the earlier *Living Buddha, Living Christ* Thây makes very strong comments linking the Trinity with nonduality. For example, Thây says, "The fact that Jesus is both the Son of Man and the Son of God is not difficult for a Buddhist to accept. We can see the nature of nonduality in God the Son and God the Father, because without God the Father within Him, the Son could never be."[38] The Trinity is the expression of nonduality par excellence within Christianity, for it holds oneness and otherness together as a dynamic communion of love.

Perhaps we need more opportunities for Buddhist–Christian dialogue on the insight and experience of nonduality and interbeing. In the Christian scriptures the language of nonduality is most notable in the Gospel of John, as we have seen in the quotations at the beginning of this chapter. It is in this Gospel more than any other that Jesus' own experience of unity with the Father and with his disciples is most clearly articulated: "As you, Father, are in me and I am in you, may they also be in us" (John 17:22). This deep insight on the part of Jesus seems very much in line with Thây's teaching on interbeing. St. Paul also regularly alludes, through his rich metaphor of the body, to the intercommunion that exists among the members of the Christian community: "The body does not consist of one member but of many. . . . If one member suffers, all suffer together with it; if one member is honored, all rejoice together with it" (1 Cor. 12:14, 26). The church, according to Paul, and in the language of Thây, "inter-is."

This mystery of two as one, which is the mystery of love, is always connected with the action of the Holy Spirit in Christianity. The Spirit, the divine breath, is the key that holds the mystery of the Trinity together. Says Benedictine monk Cyprian Smith, "In some ways this 'Spirit' is the deepest mystery of all, for it shows how that which comes out is still enclosed within; that which is spoken is still silent; that which is distinct is still one."[39] In the Trinity, through the energy of the Spirit, the three "persons" of God *lose themselves* in one another in a nondual intermingling of love. Eckhart reminds us of our own intimate participation in this great mystery of love:

> In the love that one gives there is no duality, but one and unity, and in love *I am God* more than I am in myself. The prophet says, "I have said you are gods and children of the Most High" (Ps. 82:6). That sounds strange that *a person can become God in love*, but so it is true in the eternal truth.[40]

We become God in love. Eckhart holds nothing back in this statement. For him there is no duality, no separation. "If I am to know God," he says, "then I must really become He and He I. I say further: God must really become I and I must really become God, so fully one that this 'he' and 'I' become and are one 'is.'"[41] For Eckhart, this is who God is, and this is who we are in God. If God is love, as the First Letter of John holds (1 John 4:8), then *love is God*, and our loving is *God loving*. Through love we are brought into the loving that is God. Says Eckhart, "Likeness and love raise, lead and convey the soul into the prime source of the one, that is, the Father of all things in heaven and earth."[42]

The First Letter of John takes this reflection to another level—outwardly—like rings of water radiating out from the place where the pebble falls into the pond. It shows us how the experience of nonduality and interbeing includes our neighbor as well: "God is love, and those who abide in love abide in God, and God abides in them. . . . Those who say, 'I love God,' and hate their brothers or sisters are liars; for those who do not love a brother or sister whom they have seen cannot love God whom they have not seen" (1 John 4:16-20).

As Thây teaches, "We can touch the noumenal (ultimate) world by touching the phenomenal (historical) world deeply. . . . If you think that you can touch God by abandoning everything in this world, I doubt that you will touch God. . . . If you throw away all the waves, there will be no water for you to touch."[43] Thây's insightful words help to shed light on *interbeing* as experienced through the Christian lens of love of neighbor. If we were to replace Thây's word "touch" with the word "love," we would have a statement almost identical with the First Letter of John: "If you think that you can love God by abandoning everything in this world, I doubt that you will love God. . . . If we throw away loving our neighbor, there will be no God to love." This is certainly the kind of love that has the power to transform the world and give birth to true peace.

The Great Birth

Our participation in the trinitarian circle of love means that God the Father's pouring forth of the divine Son does not just happen in some celestial realm beyond time; it happens within us as well. Though it may seem somewhat strange to our ears at first, the mystics frequently say that *God gives birth to the divine presence within us*. In fact, Meister Eckhart says emphatically, "What does it avail me that this birth [of God] is always happening, if it does not happen in me?"[44]

This kind of mystical language, strange though it may seem, is not foreign to Buddhism either. Says Thây, "Waves are . . . born from water. That is why we adopt the language that waves are sons and daughters of water. Water is the father of waves. Water is the mother of waves."[45] Through this image, Thây wants to help us touch the ultimate dimension of reality within the concrete living out of our daily lives. *This* is the miracle of mindfulness. Eckhart's great passion is not much different. He, too, wants to help his listeners experience deep within their souls the *water–wave* relationship, that is, the intimate relationship between God and the human soul. Eckhart, like Thây, wants us to be aware of the divine presence that grounds our very being, the source of all life deep within us. It is not about learning a lot of abstract ideas but about experiencing God in our daily lives as the ocean of loving presence that grounds us.

So how does God give birth? How does God "the Father" give birth? Christianity, as we have seen, adopts the language of Jesus, who, living in a particular culture and time, referred to the Ultimate Dimension of Reality as *Father*. It is unfortunate that the metaphor of father, one that is deeply rooted in the biblical tradition, is a stumbling block for some Christians today— especially for many women who have suffered for too long as second-class citizens at the hands of patriarchal religion. But the title *Father* simply cannot be ignored. It was used by Jesus in his own teachings and prayer to God, and so we do ourselves a disservice if we try to sidestep it. It is important, I believe, to hold onto the metaphor, while expanding its boundaries. As we will see, Eckhart does just that. He helps us to discover the gentle Mother-Father God to whom Jesus tenderly directed his own prayer, and in whose hands confidently placed his entire life (Luke 23:46).

The Aramaic word for *father* used by Jesus was *Abba*. Given the patriarchal culture of the day, it is significant to note that the *Abba* to and about whom Jesus spoke was gentle and loving—anything *but* a domineering, patriarchal tyrant. Jesus' *Abba* was one who provided bread for hungry children (Luke 11:3) and stayed up day and night waiting for a runaway son to return home (Luke 15:20). Jesus even asked his *Abba* to forgive his assassins, as he hung dying on the cross (Luke 23:34).

The title *Abba* is only one of many different metaphors for God found in the Judeo-Christian scriptures. God is imaged as a potter who fashions human beings out of clay (Gen. 2; Jer. 18:6), as well as the rock of our salvation (Ps. 62:2; Matt. 7:24). God is a shepherd who carries the sheep in gentle, loving arms (Isa. 40:11), and God is a lover who roams through the night searching for the beloved (Song of Songs). God is even imaged as the one who "knit me together in my mother's womb" (Ps. 139:13). The important thing is not to get lost in the metaphors but instead to use them collectively as a way of discovering the deeper truth that lies deep within us.

So for Jesus, sharing his *Abba* with his disciples was akin to inviting them into the intimacy of his love. As he himself said, "Those who love me will keep my word, and my Father will love them, and we will come to them and make our dwelling with them" (John 14:23). Jesus showed his disciples that his *Abba-God* is a treasure of divine life that lives deep within us—a source of compassion and loving kindness. As Thây says, "God the Father is not out there in space, but is in our hearts. The question is how to touch him."[46]

So how *do* we touch this God-presence within us? How does God *give birth* to the divine life within us? The key that unlocks this mystery for Christians is the incarnation—the coming together of eternity and history, of God and humanity, in the person of Jesus. By following Jesus we discover that God is woven into the very fabric of our human lives. Through our life in Christ, we who are waves learn to recognize that water is the deepest truth of our existence. "Thy will be done on Earth as it is in Heaven," says Thây, quoting from the Lord's Prayer. "This means you have to be alive and touching both dimensions, the ultimate as well as the historical. Heaven is here on earth, and earth is there in Heaven. Wave is in the water and water is in the wave."[47]

Thây's words are a wonderful expression of Christian theology. Through Jesus, we discover what it means to live in both dimensions simultaneously. We see in Jesus both heaven *and* earth, both God and humanity, and we awaken to this marvelous reality in ourselves. Again Thây says, "The wave is always water. The wave does not have to die in order to become water; it is water right now, right here. The kingdom of God is the same; it is not situated in space and time. You do not have to die in order to enter the Kingdom of God; in fact you are already in it now and here."[48]

As the sign hanging on the tree at Deer Park Monastery proclaims so boldly, "The Kingdom is either now or never!" To use a parable that Jesus himself used, God and God's kingdom are like yeast, which a woman kneads into three measures of flour until the whole mass of dough begins to rise (Matt. 13:33). In other words, as we reflected upon in the last chapter, the world of history and matter is saturated with the divine; both dimensions mix together and become one. Not only do we see this in Jesus, but through him we see this in ourselves as well. Through Jesus, God, the master bread baker, mixes divine life into the dough of our humanity. We, like Jesus, experience the mystery of being "bread of life" (John 6:35).

God's becoming flesh in the dough of humanity, what is commonly called the *incarnation*, reveals to us this marriage between heaven and earth, between God and creation. Cyprian Smith, in his book on Meister Eckhart, speaks of the importance of understanding the incarnation on the historical as well as the mystical level.

> The Christian religion is a religion of the flesh. . . . The paradox of Jesus is our own paradox. Like the Jews of Jesus' own day, we find it "mind-blowing" to be faced with someone who is both God and [human]. . . . Eckhart is concerned above all with union, how God and [humans] can come together and become one. Now this happens in two ways. First, God and [humans] are united in the historical event which took place in Bethlehem 2000 years ago. Secondly, they are united here and now in the mysterious event which Eckhart calls the Birth of God in the Soul, or the Speaking of the Word in the Ground of the Soul. The historical Incarnation in the past, and the "mystical" Incarnation in us, here and now, are two aspects, distinct but inseparable, of one single mystery.[49]

Our present interest is not so much the historical birth of Jesus as the mystical coming together of heaven and earth in us—the birth of God's Word within us. Just as God's divine Son was born in history through the Virgin Mary, the mother of Jesus, so too does God give birth within each human soul on a spiritual level—two dimensions of "one single mystery." Eckhart goes so far as to say that we are all "mothers of God!"

The title *Mother of God* (*theotokos* in Greek) was officially approved as a title given to Mary, the mother of Jesus, at the Council of Ephesus in 431.[50] It is a paradoxical title that not all Christians understand or accept. "How can God have a mother?" many ask. It is a good question, for unless the title is rightly understood it seems to place Mary, a mere human being, in a situation of being preexistent to God. This is definitely *not* what the title means. It is, instead, a title that points to a deeper mystical reality. It points to all of us, reminding us of our own call to live this nondual reality of being human *and* divine, wave *and* water—all at the same time. What Mary lived in a unique way, by giving birth physically to the eternal Word of God, we live spiritually.

We will reflect on this paradox by navigating our way into Eckhart's teaching on the birth of God's Word in the soul. In a series of Christmas sermons on the topic, Eckhart leads us into some pretty tricky waters. He stretches the metaphorical boundaries so much that, at times, it almost sounds comical. He begins very simply by saying, "God the Father gives birth to the Son . . . in the soul's ground."[51] Then, realizing the limitations (both metaphorical *and* physiological) of a Father giving birth, he tries to untangle himself from his own knot by tacking on a few more words: "Fatherhood has a maternal name . . . for it is properly a mother's work to conceive."[52] For those keeping tabs, Eckhart's birthing Father has now safely been transformed into a Mother. And if that is not enough, he adds one last touch, "God [the Father] lies in childbed like a woman who has given birth, in every good, out-drawn and indwelling soul . . . eternally welling forth from his paternal heart."[53] So, in case anyone has gotten lost in the labyrinth, the end result is a father who is lying in childbed like a mother, giving birth to a divine child from a paternal heart. Needless to say, it is not Eckhart's finest piece of poetry.

Poetry aside, though, Eckhart is saying something very profound. In the divine Ground of the Godhead, what Eckhart called in the Middle German of his day the *grunt*, God's very life is being poured out—born—in the world.[54] This *grunt*, which exists within the human soul as much as it does in God, is given other names by Eckhart, as well: the silent, empty desert, the spark, the castle, the void, nothingness, etc.[55] It is the place from which all being flows forth, what Eckhart calls in one sermon "bare beingness."[56] It is *there*, he says, "in the noblest part, the ground . . . in the very essence of the soul . . . in the silent middle . . . [that] God bears the Word in the soul . . . in the true unity of divine nature."[57] For Eckhart, there is simply no better way to speak about this overwhelming mystery than to call it a *birth*. God is eternally pregnant, says the Meister, and gives birth to the divine Son (Christ, the eternal Word) in us.[58]

This birth of the Word, this birth of God within us, is what Thây refers to when he speaks of "heaven on earth." It is God giving birth to the divine self in the everyday-ness of our earthly existence. Thây employs very similar language in speaking of the Buddha and the manifestation of the Buddha's awakening in us.

> The Buddha described the seed of mindfulness that is in each of us as the "womb of the Buddha" (tathagatagarbha). We are all mothers of the Buddha because we are all pregnant with the potential for awakening. If we know how to take care of our baby Buddha by practicing mindfulness in our daily lives, one day the Enlightened One will reveal himself or herself to us.[59]

Though Eckhart's birth of the Word and Thây's birth of the Buddha are not pointing to exactly the same reality,[60] it is interesting to note how both use the *birthing* metaphor to articulate the relationship between the ultimate and historical dimensions of reality. In other words, the awakening to one's essential

Buddha nature and the Christian living out fully of the divine-human mystery of the incarnation are both experiences of an eternal reality that is being born within us in the midst of daily life. Giving birth, then, for both teachers, has to do with incarnating, literally *bringing into the flesh* of everyday existence, that which is eternal.

Mary, the mother of Jesus, is the icon par excellence that best points to this dual mystery. In the Christian story she is both a mirror image of what happens in God and a paradigm of what is to happen in us, as well. We glimpse God as eternal Mother by contemplating the historical birth of her son, Jesus. Or to say it the other way around, the eternal birth of the Word within God echoes out into history through the birth of the enfleshed Word in the womb of the Virgin Mary. Mary is, in the most profound sense of the word, a symbol or sacrament of God. The birth of the divine Word in her virgin womb reveals to us something about God, and something about ourselves as well. Mary's virgin womb is a symbol of the divine womb, the empty, Silent Desert of God.

The Book of Genesis begins by saying, "In the beginning when God created the heavens and earth, the earth was a formless void and darkness covered the face of the deep" (Gen. 1:1-2). This *formless void* reappears symbolically in the scriptures, announcing the new creation that will come forth from the virgin womb of Mary. Mary is the new *formless void*, the Silent Desert of God's Nothingness. From her virgin void, God gives birth to the new heavens and the new earth (Rev. 12:1-6).

Eckhart rarely spoke about his own spiritual or mystical experiences, even though one cannot help but sense that they somehow permeate all his writings. There is one passage, though, that is believed to be precisely that—a personal sharing of his own experience of the mystical birth of the Word in the depths of his own heart and soul. The fact that he shares this experience, even though in the third person, is in itself a commentary on how important this experience was in his own spiritual journey. This is how he describes what seems to have been a rather indescribable experience: "It appeared to a man as in a dream—it was a waking dream—that he became pregnant with Nothing, like a woman with child, and in that Nothing God was born. [God] was the fruit of the Nothing. God was born in the Nothing."[61] Eckhart's paradoxical language defies any logical explanation. He knew deeply, though, that what we call God is not any-*thing* tangible or objectively describable. God cannot be grasped or forced into any measurable human category. At the same time, though, this Nothing out of which God is born is everything. It is fullness and eternity within us.

As mentioned in chapter 4, this is one way of understanding the ancient formula *creatio ex nihilo*—creation coming from nothingness. All that exists flows not from any-*thing* but from a Source beyond thing-ness, what the mystics have called with a faltering tongue, *No-thing-ness*. "Put aside *this* and *that*," says Eckhart, "and what remains is nothing but God."[62] This is precisely what Mary did. Her *fiat*, her "let it be with me according to your word" (Luke 1:38) was the offering of her virgin emptiness to God. Mary is a mirror image of the divine *Nothingness*; her entire being is the great void, the Ground where the new Genesis, the new creation, the new birth of God takes place. As St. Paul wrote, "If anyone is in Christ, there is a new creation" (2 Cor. 5:17).

In Mary, the eternal, creative Word that was spoken by God "in the beginning," becomes flesh in history. This is the unique role that she plays in the Christian story of salvation. Unfortunately, however, this is also the very place where we have often failed to bring the story to its just completion. We sometimes end the story here, falling into the temptation of idolizing Mary and forgetting that she is a symbol of our own deepest spiritual reality as well. Like her, we are also a new Genesis, where God is giving birth to the divine Word. Like her—at least on the spiritual and mystical levels—we too are called to cultivate the inner desert of virgin spaciousness if we are to live fruitful lives as followers of Christ. In our own divine *nothingness*, God is being born today.

From a scriptural point of view, Mary's virginity proclaims a profound spiritual truth: only when we are empty and detached from the illusion that we are some-*thing* separate from God, can we give birth to God. Mary's heart is empty enough, poor enough to be graced with the gratuitous surprise of the birth of God. "Blessed are the poor in spirit," said Jesus, "for theirs is the kingdom of heaven" (Matt. 5:3). Mary shows us that we are *all* called to give birth to God within the fragile framework of our human limitations, our poverty of spirit. It is not our being *something* that prepares us for God's mystical birth in our soul, but our emptiness, our spaciousness, our nothingness that prepares us for the divine birth. That is why Luke's Gospel goes into detail to record that Mary gave birth to her firstborn child in a poor stable, "because there was no room for them in the inn" (Luke 2:7). Only when there is *no* room, *no* place, *no-thing* can God be born in us. Then, and only then, do we lose ourselves long enough to find ourselves immersed in the kingdom of heaven. When the divine *Nothingness* gives birth within us, it also annihilates us; it *nothings* us. We lose ourselves and are swallowed up into *Nothingness*, merging into "the fullness of the one who fills all in all" (Eph. 1:23).

This theme of the divine Nothingness is found in different ways in most of the world religions. In the words of Meister Eckhart: "If I should have gone out of myself and were entirely empty, then indeed the Father would bear His only begotten Son in my spirit."[63] Mary did just that. Bernard McGinn picks up on Eckhart's teaching, relating it to our own spiritual lives: "Only in the silence and stillness of the ground is God free to touch the soul with his own essence and without images. The motif of pure interiority and utter stillness

provides the key. . . . Eckhart is uncompromising in insisting on the importance of utter passivity as the only possible preparation [for the birth of the
Word]."[64]

Mary, the Virgin, is a symbol of the emptiness of God, the vast, undifferentiated spaciousness of the eternal Godhead. This is a theme that Buddhists
find very compatible with their own experience and insights. D. T. Suzuki,
commenting on the writings of Eckhart, fully concurs with the Meister's
insistence on the empty void at the heart of the Godhead. "It is the unmoved,
a nothing where there is no path (*apada*) to reach. It is absolute nothingness;
therefore it is the ground of being from whence all being comes."[65] He goes
on to ask how Christians understand this emptiness of God, as presented by
Eckhart, and then makes an important link with the Buddhist notion of
emptiness called *sunyata*: "What would Christians think of 'the divine core of
pure (or absolute) stillness,' or of the 'simple core which is the still desert onto
which no distinctions ever creep'? Eckhart is in perfect accord with the Buddhist doctrine of *sunyata*, when he advances the notion of the Godhead as
'pure nothingness' (*ein bloss niht*)."[66]

Mary's virgin nothingness is an invitation to cultivate within our own
heart and soul a spaciousness that is free for God alone. As Eckhart reminds
us, in order for this birth to happen, "God needs and must have a vacant, free
and unencumbered soul, containing nothing but Himself alone."[67] Mary's
soul, her entire being, was pure, uncluttered, receptive to the unexpected gift
of love. She waited in perfect mindfulness and absolute inner stillness for the
visit of the long-awaited divine Guest, the Messiah, her Beloved, the Christ.
Mary's *yes* to God, her groundedness in the eternal Now, opens the door for
every Christian's *yes* to the mystical birth. Just as Thây says that "we are all
mothers of the Buddha," so too, following the example of Mary, we are all
called to be *mothers of God*.

This is what interests Eckhart: that we say yes to the mystical birth in the
soul. Eckhart is like a midwife whose great desire is to help us give birth to
God in our lives. "This eternal birth occurs in the soul precisely as it does in
eternity . . . for it is *one* birth," he reminded his friends six centuries ago.[68] To
help this birth happen in us, Eckhart asks, "Where is the place where the Word
is spoken?" He then gives his own answer, "As I said just now, it is in the purest
thing that the soul is capable of, in the noblest part, the ground—indeed, in
the very essence of the soul which is the soul's most secret part."[69] And in
another sermon, he goes on to say, "In this birth, God streams into the soul in
such abundance of light, so flooding the essence and ground that it runs over
and floods into the powers and into the outward person."[70]

What, then, do we do to make this birth happen? We wait in silence. Eckhart insists on the practice of silence—the need to make room in our noisy

and busy lives for God to do something surprising, something new. "The very best and noblest attainment in life is to be silent and let God work and speak within."[71] The practices of silence and contemplative meditation nourish in us the mindfulness necessary for remaining rooted in the present moment, the moment of God's eternal birth. A great challenge for contemporary monasticism and religious life—both lay and vowed, East and West—is to help sow the seeds of silence into the dry terrain of our modern world. It is a question of spiritual survival. In the words of Timothy Radcliffe, OP, former spiritual master of the Dominican order, "We have to learn the art of silence. In study and in prayer, we learn to be still, attentive, so that we may receive from the Lord what he gives to share. . . . Finally we come to love this silence as the deepest center of our lives."[72]

I personally cannot express the gratitude and hope that filled me during my days with Thây's monastic and lay disciples during the 2004 winter retreat at Deer Park Monastery. Their practice of mindful silence was like a soft rain falling onto a dry, thirsty desert. The intentional, respectful silence permeates the entire monastery, but in a way that is not caught up with the attachment of legalism. No one is afraid to speak when necessary, and yet there is the marvelous freedom to refrain from small talk. How desperately needed is this practice in every corner of our globe today. I dream of the day when Israelis and Palestinians, Hindus and Muslims, Catholics and Protestants—our whole world—will be able to sit down together in mindful silence, look deeply into each other's eyes, and smile, as the walls that we have built to separate ourselves from one another crumble to the ground. The practice of silence, so necessary in our world today, is akin to the farmer who, after preparing the ground and planting the seed, must wait in silent expectation for new life to be born. This requires great patience and steadfast hope. Says Jesus in a short parable, "This is how it is with the kingdom of God; it is as if a farmer were to scatter seed on the land and would sleep and rise night and day, and the seed would sprout and grow, he knows not how. Of its own accord the land yields fruit, first the blade, then the ear, then the full grain in the ear" (Mark 4:26-28).

So we learn to wait patiently during the silent process of germination and growth, the days and months and years of silent, mystical pregnancy. Nothing is gained by rushing the process, as Thây teaches so gently through the practice of walking meditation. "Just await this birth in you," says Eckhart, "and you shall experience all good and all comfort, all happiness, all being and all truth."[73] Thây, in a talk *also* given on Christmas, invites us to practice the birth of new life in the *now* of the present moment:

> The child in us is always alive; maybe we have not had enough time to take care of the child within us. . . . A child is always able to live in the

present moment. A child can also be free of worries and fears about the future. Therefore, it is very important for us to practice in such a way that the child in us can be reborn. Let the child be born to us. Tonight we celebrate the birth of a person who is very dear to humanity, a person who has brought light to the world, Jesus Christ. We hope that children like him will be born to us in every moment of our daily lives.[74]

6

Christ

The Amazing Grace of God

Grace: Healing the Blindness

As we have seen above, the reality of our true nature is that we are historical and eternal beings, human and divine, wave and water, heaven and earth. Or, in the image that St. Paul uses: "We hold the treasure of divine life within the earthen vessel of our humanity" (2 Cor. 4:7). The "place" where these two dimensions meet is what is commonly called in the Christian tradition the *soul*. Says Eckhart, "The soul is created as if at the junction of time and eternity. . . . [It] bears God's image and is like God."[1] For Christians, it is Jesus' incarnation that makes this "junction" between time and eternity accessible to us. He who was "the firstborn of many brothers and sisters" (Rom. 8:29) reveals to us the wonderful truth that we too are God's daughters and sons. As St. Catherine of Siena said, Christ is the bridge that links us with God.

To use a Hindu term, Jesus is for Christians the *Sat-Guru* (the "True Teacher"), the one who lifts the veil from our eyes to reveal (literally *un-veil*) for us our true self—made in the image and likeness of God. Through this revelation, we are able to exclaim with St. Paul, "All of us, gazing *with unveiled face* on the glory of the Lord, are being *transformed into the same image . . .* as from the Lord who is the Spirit" (2 Cor. 4:18). The revelation of Christ effects in us the divine transformation. We see at last who we truly are, who we *always were*, and this seeing helps us to claim our deepest truth. We learn to say, with Moses and Jesus, and all the enlightened beings of all eternity, "I am."

This is beautifully portrayed in the story of Jesus' healing of a blind man in the Gospel of John (ch. 9). After the healing, the blind man says with great confidence, when questioned by the authorities, "One thing I do know is that I was blind and now I see" (9:25). The story is about much more than a physical healing; it is about the blind man's encounter with Jesus and his subsequent discovery (*un-covering*) of the divine life within himself. He is given the gift to see who he truly is and always was. This is symbolically alluded to in the text when some of the neighbors of the man ask, "Is this not the man who used to sit and beg?" The answer placed on the lips of the now-healed blind man is an echo of the Holy Name of God that Moses was given at the burning bush. He simply answers. "*I am*" (9:8-9). He claims his deepest truth and affirms his divine oneness with God. He, like Jesus (who just a few verses earlier said, "*I am* the light of the world"), is both human *and* divine. Without this gift, this grace, we all remain blinded. We fail to experience the great breakthrough of seeing with the eyes of God.

As we hear in the First Letter of John: "Beloved, we are children of God now; what we shall be has not yet been revealed. We do know that when it is revealed *we shall be like God*, for we shall see God as he is" (1 John 3:2). Through our spiritual practice, we are learning to see our true self in each and every moment. Through Jesus, we dis-cover and reconnect to our own inner divine life. Our eyes are opened and we see that we are like God. This is why the early church called the sacrament of baptism "illumination." Baptism awakens us to see not what makes Jesus different from us, but instead what makes us like him. *This* is the mystery, the great gift we receive.

It is important to remember that Jesus was as totally human as any other human being. He was born of a woman, lived a normal human life, and died. It is when Christians speak of Jesus' divinity and our own that we note a distinction. It is summed up this way: We believe that Christ, the Word of God, is divine by nature, whereas we humans are divine by grace. In the words of Donald Goergen, OP, "Jesus cannot *not* be united to God, for God is his very *ousia* (substance, being). . . . Jesus' very own act of being is the Word of God, he *is* the Word of God. I am not God. My act of existence is a created act, but I *become* one with God through grace."[2] Using St. Paul's image of the earthen vessel, we could say that Jesus' vessel is divine; mine, on the other hand, is earthen and is filled with a divine treasure (2 Cor. 4:7). This is the meaning of grace in Christian life. It has to do with the experience of gratuitousness. Our Godliness is given to us as a free gift.[3]

"Grace," says Eckhart, "is the indwelling and co-habitating of the soul in God."[4] Though we often speak of God dwelling *within us*, what Eckhart is saying, and what might be more helpful in our understanding of grace, is to say that we dwell *in God*. In another place, Eckhart uses an interesting analogy to speak of grace: "God, the heavenly Father, gives the Son and the Holy Spirit all that is good; but to creatures He *gives* nothing good, but only lends it. The sun gives heat to the air, but the light is loaned, and so, as soon as the sun sets, the air loses the light, but retains the heat."[5] God gives the divine self fully and eternally to Christ (as the heat that "stays" in the air), but to us human beings God gives the divine life moment to moment, day to day (as the sunlight that "comes and goes"). In other words, the Sun gives itself equally to all. The difference is that we human beings do not hold claim to what is given; we always receive it as a gift. It is not the stuff of God's giving that changes but the manner in which it is received. For us, God's creatures, the gift is never ours "to keep," but it is always ours to receive.

Eckhart tackled this difficult point in another place by employing an idea from the letters of St. Paul, namely, that of being "adopted children," children through grace: "You did not receive a spirit of slavery . . . but you have received a spirit of adoption. When we cry 'Abba! Father!' it is that very Spirit bearing witness with our spirit that *we are children of God*" (Rom. 8:15; see also Gal. 4:5). We are not just *like* God's children. We *are* God's children. This, for Eckhart, was the whole reason for the incarnation, to reveal to us that we are "by the grace of adoption what the Son is by nature."[6] He later said in defense of his teachings on the divine spark and the ground of the soul, "Don't think that there is one Son by which Christ is God's Son and another by which we are named and are sons; but it is the same . . . by being joined to him as heir, we are coheirs."[7]

Eckhart, of course, was much more interested in highlighting and celebrating the divine ground of the human soul and our oneness with God than in pointing out the differences between Christ's divinity and our own. The environment of suspicion in which he preached, however, forced him to express the delight of our inner divine spark with a bit of caution. Like all the great mystics, his experience of oneness with God went far beyond any words capable of describing it.

From a Judeo-Christian point of view, to be human is to be created in God's image, which is to say that the seal of God is stamped into our very nature. As Eckhart described earlier, the seed of God is planted within us. That seed, though, lies dormant until it is awakened to life. For a Christian, it is Jesus' paschal mystery of death and resurrection that awakens the seed within each person to grow into its fullest expression of divine life. Through baptism, the person "is watered by grace,"[8] says Eckhart, and "the seed of God grows to be God."[9] It is the risen Christ who pours the water of the Holy Spirit into us. The seed sprouts, the experience of sin and separation is healed, and we discover anew the oneness that is our truest self.

The reason why the understanding of grace is so essential in the Judeo-Christian tradition is because of the mystical experience of love. In other words, love is experienced throughout history as God's initiative; God loves us first, and *then* we discover that *we are love* (1 John 4:19). As Jesus said to the woman from Samaria who came to draw water from the village well one day, "Whoever drinks the water *I shall give* will never thirst; the water I shall give will become in that person a spring of living water welling up to eternal life" (John 4:14). Our collective experience teaches us that we first *receive* the living water of love from God, a love made tangible in the life of Jesus, and only then do we *become* that same living water. This is the working of grace.

Thây frequently uses the metaphor of the wave *touching* the water, and in so doing, the wave realizes who she truly is. As he says, "The practice of touching things deeply on the horizontal level gives us the capacity to touch God."[10] This one sentence offers us a wonderful definition of spirituality. We touch God to the extent that we touch everyday life with loving kindness. At the same time, though, and in order to highlight the gratuitous work of grace, a Christian might preface Thây's words by first saying that through Jesus Christ, the water *embraces* the wave, revealing to her that which is the deepest truth of who she is. Only after being touched by God can we in turn touch God; we respond to grace. Thomas Merton points to this distinction with great clarity:

Contemplation . . . knows God by seeming to touch God. Or rather it knows God as if it had been invisibly touched by God . . . touched by God who has no hands, but who is pure Reality and the source of all that is real! Hence contemplation is a sudden gift of awareness, an awakening to the Real within all that is real. A vivid awareness of infinite Being at the roots of our own limited being . . . received as a present from God, as a free gift of love. This is the existential contact of which we speak when we use the metaphor of being "touched by God."[11]

I write these words knowing that this uniqueness of Jesus is one of the difficult bridges to cross in Buddhist–Christian dialogue. Thây speaks on this very topic:

Jesus is a wave, like you and me, like the Buddha, because you can touch him as one wave in the historical dimension. . . . The relationship we have with Jesus is the relationship between one person and another person. . . . This person is an extraordinary person; he is a teacher and he carries within himself the Way: "I am the Way." And the Way is the Tao. The Way is the Dharma. . . . Jesus is our Lord because he embodies the way, he embodies the Dharma. There is a kind of love between both of us. "Jesus loves me, this I know." We know this because first of all Jesus is the Son of Man—he is a living being. . . . But when you say, "I love God," then God here is the Father, our ultimate dimension. We know that the kind of love we address to our Father, our heavenly Father, would not be of the same nature.[12]

Everything Thây says here is quite compatible with Christian theology. But there are subtle differences, nuances that must be looked at honestly if we are to be true to the spirit of openness and transparency required for this kind of dialogue. I remind the reader that I do not speak here as an expert in this field, but, like many others, I am trying to grapple with these questions, to listen attentively to the many different voices. I recognize that at times there is harmony and at other times we must step back and simply listen with respect to the unique melody each of us sings.

Christ, the Word of God

We can perhaps get a better glimpse of this unique role of Jesus in Christian theology by considering what it means to call Christ the eternal *Word of God*—one of many titles used in the New Testament (John 1:1-14; Rev. 19:13). At the same time that we recognize Christ as God's Word, it is important to remember that we, too, are the Word of God. We could not exist if we were not spoken into existence by God (Gen. 1:26). So how is Christ as *Word of God* different from the rest of creation as *Word of God*? This is one of the subtle differences referred to above.

Eckhart tackles this question with a simple comparison. Christ *is* God's Word, while we are an *echo* of God's Word. Commenting on Psalm 61[62]:12 ("God spoke once, but I heard God twice"), Eckhart says, "That is true. God spoke but once . . . but the prophet says, 'I heard two,' that is, 'I heard God and the creatures.'"[13] Eckhart emphasizes the oneness first: God spoke only one Word—the Word who "became flesh and lived among us" (John 1:14). This Word is the divine Son, the Christ. But no sooner has Eckhart affirmed the oneness than he nuanced it, holding onto the tension of nonduality. The entire creation, says Eckhart, including ourselves, flows from this one divine speaking—not a *different* Word altogether, but reverberations of that very same divine Word which is spoken eternally from the mouth of God.

Commenting on Eckhart's insight, Cyprian Smith says, "Within the Trinity God utters himself totally and expresses himself totally, so that the utterance is not different from himself; it, too, is God. The created universe, however, is not a total expression of the reality of God. . . . It is not the Word; it is only an echo of the Word. Yet it is the same Word which is being uttered in both cases. The speaking forth of the Son, within the Trinity, echoes and resounds in the creation of the universe."[14] Thomas Merton again adds a note of exquisite clarity, hinting at the oneness, the loss of separateness, between God's voice and our own:

> It is a deep resonance in the inmost center of our spirit in which our very life loses its separate voice and re-sounds with the majesty and the mercy of the Hidden and Living One. God answers Himself in us and this answer is divine life, divine creativity, making all things new. We ourselves become God's echo and God's answer.[15]

Eckhart, using a bit of humor to emphasize his point, says, "All things speak God. What the mouth does in speaking and declaring God, is likewise done by the essence of a stone. . . . All creatures would like to echo God in all their works."[16]

For Eckhart, then, there is only *one* Word of God ("God spoke once") that resounds in every atom of the universe ("I heard two"). This is why the shaman from the Lenca tribe in Honduras (mentioned previously) was able to say that a person who sits at the foot of a pine tree in the predawn hours of the morning, listening attentively, will hear the pine tree singing to God. The pine tree's song is an echo of the song of God. The tree's song and God's song are *one* song. There *is* only one song.

In the Apostles' Creed—a statement of basic Christian beliefs, not so unlike the Four Noble Truths of Buddhism—there is a phrase that reads: "I believe in Jesus Christ, his [God's] *only* son, our Lord." Thây comments on the creed's use of the phrase "*only* son," saying that Buddhists do not see Buddha as unique in this way. "There are so many Buddhas, countless Buddhas of the past, of the present, and of the future. . . . All Buddhas embody the supreme enlightenment, the supreme compassion."[17] The creed's use of the phrase God's "*only* Son, our Lord" can be confusing to Christians, too. A very legitimate question would be: Are we not *all* children of God? Thây's words offer us a chance to seek some clarity.

If the creed's use of the phrase "only son" is not to be understood as referring to Christ as the exclusive heir to the fullness of God's life, then what does it mean? It can only be understood in light of Eckhart's teaching in the above paragraphs concerning the *one* (and *only*) Word which emanates from God's eternal speaking. Just as in the *one* Word the entire universe is spoken into being, so too in the *one* and *only* Son is all of humanity born. This parallels closely Thây's teaching on the relationship between the ultimate and historical dimensions of reality. Just as the water and the wave are intimately related through cause and effect, such is the relationship between the Word and the echo, between the Son of God and humanity.

The Hindu version of interbeing, or nonduality, is called *advaita* and is often described or defined as *not two, not one.* So, for example, the Word and the echo of the Word are not two separate entities, nor are they one and the same entity. This paradox is captured quite beautifully in the third verse of the well-known song "Morning Has Broken":

> Mine is the sunlight! Mine is the morning.
> Born of the *one* light Eden saw play!
> Praise with elation, praise every morning,
> God's re-creation of the new day.[18]

There is *one* light, according to the lyrics of the song, and yet there are many manifestations of this *one* light. Every morning is a new expression of the *one and only* light. So it is with all of creation and with us human beings as well. We are not God, nor are we separate from God. In a mystical sense, we are all the *one and only* Son who flows forth from the heart of God, for God gives birth to only *one* Son, *one* Word, in the *one* ground of all being. As Jesus himself said, "Father, that they may all be one, as you are in me and I in you" (John 17:21).

Eckhart puts it in his own words: "You must not merely be *like* the Son, you must *be* the Son yourself."[19] Just as we are called to *be* the Son, so are we called to *be* the Christ. This was part of the mystical insight of St. Paul: "It is no longer I who live, but Christ who lives in me" (Gal. 2:20). Again, "There is no longer Greek and Jew, circumcised and uncircumcised . . . slave and free; but Christ is all and in all" (Col. 3:11). It is in this sense that one must hear the words of the creed that refer to Christ as God's "*only* Son, our Lord." I venture to say that Thây would be very comfortable with the statement that there are *many* Buddhas, and there is *only one* Buddha. Not two, not one.

So where does Jesus stand in this relationship between the ultimate and historical dimensions of reality, between God who speaks and the Word that is spoken? Is he a wave or is he water? In one of his sermons Eckhart says,

> God is a Word, an unspoken Word. . . . Who can utter this Word? None can do so but he who is this Word. God is a Word that utters itself. . . . God is spoken and unspoken. The Father is a speaking work, and the Son is the speech at work. . . . When God speaks into the soul, he and she are one. . . . The Father always speaks the Son in unity and *pours forth all creatures in him.*[20]

The divine Son is God's speaking. He is "God uttering himself as he is in himself . . . not speaking *about* himself, but speaking himself."[21] This speaking, which happens eternally in God, happens in us as well. As Merton stated above, "God answers Himself in us, and the answer is divine life." Because of this, we *hear* God's very being enfleshed in our own human history through the Son, who is the Word.

God is both spoken *and* unspoken, says Eckhart. God remains within while flowing out. God is silence and God is Word. God's speaking is made manifest in the silent ground of the universe and in the silent abyss of our soul. The Hebrew psalmist attempts to capture the paradox of this unspoken speaking in this way, "Day unto day pours forth speech, and night to night declares knowledge. There is no speech, nor are there words; their voice is not heard; yet their voice goes out through all the earth, and their words to the end of the world" (Ps. 19:2-4). In this eternal time and place—where voices not heard go out to all the earth—silence and Word are one. The Silent Desert of the Godhead and the Word spoken from the silence are one. Here, too, the water and the wave are one. And in this very place of paradox and mystery, we hear the words of Jesus: "Father, that they may be one, as we are one, I in them and you in me, that they may become completely one" (John 17:22-23). In God's *one* Word and in God's *one* and *only* Son is *every* word, and *every* child of God.

The Body of Buddha, the Body of Christ

There is a teaching in the Buddhist tradition that considers the different bodies or manifestations of the Buddha. In both *Living Buddha, Living Christ* and *Going Home* Thây turns to this teaching in an attempt to draw some parallels with Christian doctrine—especially regarding the relationship between what Thây calls the historical Jesus and the living Jesus. This teaching does, in fact, offer some very keen insights into Christ, for just as the Buddha has different bodies, so does Jesus Christ have different bodies.

Thây notes that the historical Buddha "was born in Kapilavastu, near the border between India and Nepal, got married, had one child, left home, practiced many kinds of meditation, became enlightened, and shared the teaching until he died at the age of eighty."[22] But this is not the Buddha who most interests Thây. He is much more interested in the *living* Buddha: "The living Buddha [is] the Buddha of ultimate reality, the one who transcends all ideas and notions and is available to us at any time. The living Buddha was not born at Kapilavastu, nor did he pass away at Kushinagar."[23] Thây then reaches out across the religious borders to invite those of us who are Christians to be equally bold in discovering the *living* Christ. "The living Jesus is the Son of God who was resurrected and who continues to live. . . . We can appreciate Jesus Christ as both an historical door and an ultimate door."[24]

How can we—both Buddhists and Christians—help each other discover the living presence of both Buddha and Jesus in our own times? How do we continue to breathe new life into these ancient and venerable spiritual traditions? This seems to be one of the greatest challenges in our day and age. Thây sheds light on these challenges through his teaching on the three bodies of the Buddha, one of which is called *Nirmanakaya*, which is

> the body of transformation—and it is this body that we are dealing with in daily life. We bow to this manifested or transformed body. It is said that sometimes he manifests himself as a child, sometimes as a woman, and sometimes as a politician. We need to have a little bit of intelligence and vigilance in order to recognize his or her presence when he manifests himself. It is not so difficult. Wherever and whenever there is mindfulness, true presence, compassion, and understanding, Buddha is there.[25]

This teaching is insightful for Christians, and in fact for any religious or spiritual tradition that is trying to practice a living faith that is more than a set of ancient rules. It is helpful to remember that the word *Buddha* means the enlightened one, and so what Thây is trying to help us discover is this body of the enlightened one that is hidden within every person—similar to Eckhart's statue hidden in the block of wood. It takes mindfulness and a contemplative vision to see the enlightened one, the one who is made in the image and likeness of God in each and every person we come in contact with in daily life. We can all profit by trying to see each and every person as a Buddha in the process of awakening, a human being made in the image of God.

Jesus challenged his disciples in this same respect. He invited them to open their eyes and *see* the action of God in our daily lives: "Look at the fig tree and all the trees; as soon as they sprout leaves you can see for yourselves and know that summer is already near. So also, when you see these things taking place, you know that the kingdom of God is near" (Luke 21:29-31). After Jesus' death and resurrection from the dead, one of the disciples, Thomas, refused to believe that Christ was still alive in their midst. "Unless I see the mark of the nails in his hands . . . I will not believe" (John 20:25). Jesus came into their presence and said to Thomas, "Put your finger here and *see* my hands. . . . Do not doubt but believe" (20:27). Jesus wanted them to go beyond his historical life and to see him as the *living* Christ, the presence of the *living God* in all persons and things.

It is for this reason that the risen Christ "disappears" from the midst of his disciples after the postresurrection appearances. The disciples are forced to know Jesus on another level, as an inner reality. Jesus, the man, leaves his beloved community behind, only to be with them as a presence living within and among them. "Were not our hearts burning within us?" asked the two disciples who encountered the risen, living Christ on the road to Emmaus (Luke 24:32). This must be our question, too—the question that burns daily in our hearts. It is this mystical encounter with the living Christ that must continue to nourish Christians today. Thây has a deep understanding of the need for Christians to live in touch with the Christ who lives now, in this present moment. The title of his book *Living Buddha, Living Christ* was chosen very intentionally. We, Buddhists and Christians alike, must fan the flame of our respective traditions into a living reality.

Not only are we Christians challenged to open our eyes to the Christ who lives within us, but equally important is the call to see Christ outside of ourselves, in our neighbor. In other words, we are called to both an inner mysticism and an outer mysticism—what might be called the nonduality of compassion. The Christian scriptures invite us to see the body of the living Christ, God's living presence, in those around us, those who are shunned and made to be invisible in a world that discards what is not profitable. It is not that God is more present in them than in others or in ourselves. That is impossible, for God is equally the Ground of *all* being. It is that God wants to open our eyes to *see* the body of Christ in those whom we can easily overlook, those who are pushed out of sight in a world blinded by greed and power.

Several years ago Mother Teresa told a story of a young nun who returned one afternoon to the convent after caring for the poor in the streets of Calcutta. "Her face was radiant, full of light," said Mother Teresa, "I asked her where she had been." The young sister answered, "I have been touching the body of Christ." When Mother Teresa asked her to explain, the sister told of bathing and cleaning the wounds of a man who had been found in the streets, his body covered with maggots. "For three hours," she repeated, "I have been touching the body of Christ."[26] The young sister had understood that Christ is living today, and one of the places that we see and touch his body is in the poor.

The manifestation of Christ's living body in the poor and outcast is poignantly presented in a pivotal text at the end of the Gospel of Matthew. The story is told as a final reckoning of the nations before God. Those who have fed the hungry, clothed the naked, and visited the sick and imprisoned are invited to take part in the everlasting kingdom. Somewhat confused, they ask:

> "Lord, when was it that we *saw* you hungry and gave you food, or thirsty and gave you something to drink? And when was it that we saw you a stranger and welcomed you, or naked and gave you clothing? And when was it that we *saw* you sick or in prison and visited you?" And the king will answer them, "Truly I tell you, just as you did it to one of the least of these brothers or sisters, you did it to me." (Matt. 25:37-40)

This is a truly remarkable teaching, not only because of the compassion that lies at the heart of it, but because Jesus is giving over his body to the world, to all of humanity, to the entire universe, and in a special way, to the poor. Jesus relinquishes the particularity of his body, allowing it to merge with the universal body of all humanity, the body of the cosmos. It seems that this is the insight to which Thây is inviting us to awaken when he says that whenever there is mindfulness, true presence, compassion, and understanding, then the enlightened one is present. As Christians we would say that the body of the one to whom I reach out in compassion is the body of Christ.

It is St. Paul who makes the metaphor of the body one of the centerpieces of his teaching on Christ. For Paul, all of us who make up the group of followers of Jesus Christ are, in fact, his body: "For just as the body is one and has many members, and all the members of the body, though many, are one body, so it is with Christ. . . . Now you are the body of Christ and individually members of it" (1 Cor. 12:12, 27; also Eph. 5:30). Paul understood this teaching through a mystical experience that set in motion his whole journey to becoming a follower of Christ. He (called Saul at the time) was on his way one day to the city of Damascus, zealously persecuting Jesus' disciples every chance he got, when the risen Christ, the *living Christ*, appeared to him in a vision and spoke, "Saul, Saul, why do you persecute me?" What is important to note in this exchange is that Christ did not ask him: Why are you persecuting my disciples, but why are you persecuting *me*? Saul asked aloud, "Who are you, Lord?" And the answer came to him, "I am Jesus, whom you are persecuting" (Acts 9:4-5).

"I am Jesus, whom you are persecuting." Paul was not persecuting Jesus per se, so why did Jesus refer to himself as the one being persecuted? This mystical encounter with Christ was the impetus behind Paul's transformation from being a zealous murderer to being a great man of God. It was the presence of the living body of Christ—hidden in the collective body of his disciples—that transformed Paul's life. It was an experience of nonduality, of interbeing. Paul realized that Jesus is not just Jesus. For Paul, *we* are Jesus, too. *We* are the body of Christ. To persecute the disciples of Jesus is to persecute the body of the living Christ. To cut down a rain forest in Brazil out of greed is to cut down the body of Christ. To execute a criminal, no matter how guilty he or she may be, is to execute Christ. That is why Mother Teresa of Calcutta, this time responding to a reporter's question after visiting the men on death row at California's San Quentin Prison, remarked, "What you do to these men, you do to God." She knew that the men condemned to death were as filled with God as anyone else. They too are the body of Christ.

For St. Paul and the early Christians, what at first was a limited and somewhat exclusive experience—namely, that *they*, the disciples of Jesus, formed the living body of Christ—later grew to include both universal and cosmic dimensions. Paul himself (or at least one of his close disciples) wrote several years later, "Through Christ, God was pleased to reconcile *all things* to himself, whether on earth or in heaven" (Col. 1:20). Again, the Letter to the Ephesians says that in the fullness of time God will "gather up *all things* in [Christ], things in heaven and things on earth" (1:10). *All* things, *all* persons—in fact the entire universe—pulsates like one great cosmic body with the spiritual energy of the risen Christ.[27] Nothing, no one, is excluded from this cosmic embrace, for as St. Paul proclaims, in the end "Christ is all in all" (Col. 3:11).

For Christians, this teaching takes us back to the gift of the Holy Spirit. It is through the Spirit that the body of the risen Christ permeates the entire universe. The Spirit is a *presence* that contains an *absence*. The body and historical life of Jesus of Nazareth are gone, but his risen body is still here. This paradox is captured in the encounter between the angel and the women who visit the empty tomb after Jesus' death and resurrection. The angel says, "I know that you are looking for Jesus who was crucified. He is not here, for he has been raised" (Matt. 28:5-6). He is not here; he is *everywhere*. Bede Griffiths, in his book *The Marriage of East and West*, notes, "At the resurrection Jesus becomes the head of the cosmic whole, and the whole creation becomes his body, and this body of creation, redeemed from the forces of sin and division, is what constitutes the Church."[28]

Eckhart picks up on the same scripture text, also opening it up to its universal, cosmic dimensions. The risen Christ, he notes, is not *here*, because "God is nowhere . . . God is not here or there, not in time or place." If that is true, asks Eckhart, "Where are we to look? . . . Where is Christ sitting?" As always, he provides his own answer: "He is sitting nowhere. Whoever seeks him anywhere will not find him."[29] What Eckhart is saying is that if we try to look for Christ here or there, in this place or that place, in this church or that church, we will not find him. He is nowhere, because he is everywhere. When Jesus breathed forth the Holy Spirit from the cross (John 19:30), there was nothing left. He died. But as soon as there was nothing left, suddenly there was a fullness. "To have nothing," says Eckhart, paraphrasing St. Paul, "is to have all things."[30] The Holy Spirit is the cosmic energy that flows from the empty body of the cross out into the entire cosmos. This life-giving breath of the risen Christ is no longer confined to the limitations of history. "It is the fullness of the one who fills all things in every way" (Eph. 1:23).

Thây calls to mind a similar doctrine in the Buddhist tradition. While there is no resurrection account in the life of the Buddha, there is a spiritual body that remains in the absence of the historical Buddha. Says Thây,

> When the Buddha was about to die, he recommended to his students to touch the other body . . . which is the teaching body of a Buddha, the *Dharmakaya*. . . . The Buddha recommended to his disciples that after his passing away physically, they should take refuge in his Dharma body. . . . The Buddha said, "My physical body is not so important; I have used it, but I have also offered you my Dharma body which is more important, and you should try to keep that Dharma body alive for your happiness." You need the Dharma, you have faith in the Dharma, you love the Dharma.[31]

The Buddha still teaches through the living Dharma which he left to his disciples. His teaching, like that of Jesus, is a living word. Just as the Buddha encouraged his disciples to take refuge in the living teaching body of the Dharma, so too did Jesus invite his disciples to take refuge in him: "Abide in me as I abide in you. Just as the branch cannot bear fruit by itself unless it abides in the vine, neither can you unless you abide in me" (John 15:4). Jesus went on to say that he would leave the breath of the Holy Spirit with his disciples to teach them once he had gone: "The Spirit of truth [will] come and will guide you into all the truth" (John 16:13). Again, "The Holy Spirit, whom the Father will send in my name, will teach you everything and remind you of all that I have said to you" (John 14:26). It is heartening for both Buddhists and Christians to know that, in the absence of our respective teachers, the body of their teachings lives on, guiding us toward truth and life.

Bede Griffiths, using categories taken from Hinduism, points out in a teaching he gave at his ashram in India in 1989 that the historical body of Jesus, what Hindus call the *gross body*, is not the same body as his resurrected body. After death, says Fr. Bede, the gross body passes first into an intermediate stage, that of the *subtle body*, before coming into the final stage as a *spiritual body*.[32] Following this ancient Hindu teaching, we could say that it is Jesus in his subtle body who appears to the disciples in the days after his resurrection, prior to his final return (ascension) to the Father. But the body of the risen and ascended Christ is a spiritual body, the Spirit's body. It is ever-present through the Holy Spirit, which "blows where it chooses. You hear the sound of it, but you do not know where it comes from or where it goes" (John 3:8). Through the Holy Spirit, Christ lives on as teacher and Lord within the body of his disciples and within the body of the cosmos.

During a Buddhist–Christian seminar in 1994, Fr. Laurence Freeman, OSB, brought up the theme of the risen and ascended body of Christ. Says Freeman,

> I think the Christian's understanding of the Resurrection also involves a cosmic dimension. Jesus is the embodiment of God in human form. . . . When the human form of Jesus dies, a process takes place that anticipates what is going to happen to the whole cosmos. The human bodily form of Jesus is reabsorbed in its total physical energy and form into the source of the universe, into God. . . . Everything in the cosmos came from God, is an emanation of God, and will return to God. So I think what we see in the Resurrection is a transformation of matter back into its original source. That happens to the body of Jesus in his human form—body, mind, and spirit—but it is also an anticipation of what will happen to the whole cosmos in time, at the end of time.[33]

At the same seminar, the Dalai Lama also commented on the different *kayas*, or bodies, of the Buddha, noting differences among the various schools of Buddhism:

The ancient Indian *Vaibhasika* school maintains that Buddha's nirvana constitutes the end of Buddha's existence. . . . Even the continuation of the Buddha's consciousness ceases. . . . This is not, however, the standpoint of many other Buddhist traditions, including Tibetan Buddhism. . . . [We believe that] Buddha's consciousness and mindstream has continued and is ever-present. Buddha, in the emanation form of a human being, may have ceased; but he is still present in the form known as his *sambhogakaya*, the state of perfect resourcefulness.[34]

Both Freeman and the Dalai Lama make reference to the emanation in human form of Jesus and the Buddha, understood in unique ways by our different traditions. What is of value here is that both Buddhists and Christians recognize a living presence of these two great teachers who continue to inspire us and guide us today—through their teachings, through their spiritual energy, through their embodied communities, through the universe, through the poor. We continue to touch and to be touched by both Jesus and the Buddha today.

The Eucharistic Body

Bede Griffiths continues in his 1989 talk to name yet another manifestation of the living *body of Christ* present today, what we might call the *eucharistic body of Christ*. In the Christian community's eucharistic sharing of bread as the *body of Christ*, notes Bede, we are not communing with the gross body of the Jesus of history. "Jesus in the eucharist is the Jesus of the resurrection, in the glorified state where he is totally one with God."[35] In the Eucharist we commune with the spiritual body of the risen Christ. He goes on to say that when a Christian receives "the body of Christ" in the eucharistic celebration, there is simultaneously an intercommunion with the entire cosmos. The Holy Spirit, present in the eucharistic body of Christ, says Bede, is the divine presence that is *one-ing* humanity and the entire cosmos into wholeness, healing it of all divisions. We receive the spiritual body of Christ, who, in turn, becomes the soul of our gross body.

What happens in the Last Supper is a *re-membering*, that is, a "bringing of all the scattered members back together" into communion. The fragmented body of Christ present in our world—with its separated families, its divided nations, its decimated rain forests, and its broken human hearts—is reunited. Eckhart refers to this cosmic oneness: "Just as all angels are one in their original pure nature, so all blades of grass are one in their original pure nature, and there all things are one."[36] The eucharistic re-membering *reminds us*, takes our minds back to the original oneness. Thây, of course, speaks in the same vein, in his typically simple and easy-to-understand fashion, "When we look at one flower, we know that this flower is made of all these non-flower elements. . . . We see all in the one and also the one in the many."[37]

Thây's words, "We see all in the one and the one in the many," are another way of saying "communion." In many of the Christian churches, the phrase "receiving communion" is one of the ways to refer to receiving the Eucharist in the Lord's Supper. "Receiving communion" takes on a whole new meaning when we consider the cosmic healing dimension of the Eucharist. To think that, by our participation in this sacramental ritual of breaking and sharing one piece of bread among many, we are taking part in a universal healing of brokenness, is an awesome reality. Perhaps an even better phrase, one that Thây would probably use, might be to say that we are "tasting communion." In other words, our eucharistic sharing helps us to *taste* the reality of communion for which our hearts long, and which we once knew, "in the beginning," when all was one. In the Letter to the Ephesians we hear that God's plan is "to gather up all things in [Christ], things in heaven and earth" (Eph. 1:9-10). In the eucharistic sacrament of thanksgiving, we have the opportunity to touch this healing and unifying body of Christ, to participate in the re-membering of our universe.

Thây has a profound appreciation for this cosmic communion and once again links it with the practice of mindfulness:

> If Christ is the body of God, which he is, then the bread he offers is also the body of the cosmos. Look deeply and you notice the sunshine in the bread, the blue sky in the bread, the cloud and the great earth in the bread . . . the whole cosmos has come together in order to bring you this piece of bread. . . . Eat it mindfully. Eat it in the presence of God. Eat it in such a way that the Holy Spirit becomes an energy within you.[38]

Thây's words help us to see how the eucharistic *re-membering*, when celebrated with a true spirit of mindfulness, connects us with the world around us. The whole cosmos is present in the eucharistic bread. Every small action, every breaking and sharing of bread in loving communion, touches and heals the whole.

We must not underestimate the importance of touching the eucharistic body of Christ with true mindfulness. For through this sacramental action, we participate in the mission of Christ to reconcile and unite *all things* on earth and in heaven, helping to give expression to a world where there are no more divisions. "Christ is our peace," says St. Paul, "In his flesh [i.e., in his body] he has made both groups into one and has broken down the dividing wall, that is, the hostility between us" (Eph. 2:14).

How important it is for us who are Christians to remember that Jesus longed for a world healed of all divisions. That is why he reached out to touch the many untouchable sectors of the society of his day. He wanted to welcome them into the oneness of God's trinitarian heart. Jesus wanted to seat them at the table of love, wash their feet, and feed them with the bread of life. He wants to do the same today through us. Unfortunately, the Eucharist is sometimes manipulated into an instrument of division. Rather than beating our swords into plowshares (Isa. 2:4), we sometimes do just the opposite. The bread of *communion* has at times been made into a weapon of war. Communities and families have been divided rather than united. Sinners have been left hungering for God, rather than welcomed home and fed with the bread of mercy. This must not be so; this is *not* the mind of Christ.

The eucharistic body of Christ is to be a healing body, one that serves to re-member the body's many disparate members, to re-unite all those who are separated. As Paul Philibert, OP, says, "Our eucharist is our *sangha*, our oneness celebrated. Christ gives himself to us in the Spirit as a body re-membered."[39] In the very sacramental act of receiving the eucharistic body of Christ, we re-member the oneness of our true home in God. Nourished by this gift, we go forth with new eyes, to see the many parts of the body coming together as one, healed of all division. We taste the kingdom that we have already received.

After the death of Jesus, a group of women went to the tomb in search of the body of Jesus. An angel appeared to them and said, "I know that you are looking for Jesus who was crucified. He is not here, for he has been raised" (Matt. 28:5-6). Indeed, Jesus has been raised above the divisions and pettiness of our world. From his place of oneness with the Source of all life, he breathes on us the Spirit of unity. His risen body now belongs to the entire cosmos, and all creation forms part of this body. Christ cannot be confined to any this or that, to any here or there. In the words of Meister Eckhart, "Cease to be this or that, and to have this and that, then you are all things and have all things, and so, being neither here nor there, you are everywhere . . . you are everything . . . what remains is nothing but God."[40] In the end, says St. Paul, we become one with the risen, cosmic body of Christ, "the fullness of the one who fills all in all" (Eph. 1:23).

7

Suffering

For those involved in dialogue among the world's religions, the fact cannot be denied that both Christianity and Buddhism treat the theme of suffering with great intensity.

> Siddhartha [the Buddha] and Jesus both realized that life is filled with suffering. The Buddha became aware at an early age that suffering is pervasive. Jesus must have had the same kind of insight, because they both made every effort to offer a way out. We, too, must learn to live in ways that reduce the world's suffering.[1]

There are thousands of books written on the theme of suffering, and this is certainly not the place to offer a survey of this literature. I will attempt in this chapter to reflect on some of the writings of Eckhart and Thây regarding this theme, adding along the way insights from others, as well as reflections from my own experience and meditation on the reality of suffering, especially as reflected in the icon of the cross of Christ. Much of my own insight into the transforming power of the cross comes from my years of sharing in the life and sufferings of the poor of Latin America. Dialogue on this theme, I believe, is of great importance in a world where suffering and violence confront us daily. I write these reflections aware that our traditions approach this topic from different perspectives, yet confident that the common ground we share can provide us all with the insight and courage needed to help "reduce the world's suffering."

Noble Truths

The Buddha's fundamental teachings on suffering, as outlined in the Four Noble Truths,[2] place the theme of suffering at the very center of Buddhist teaching and practice. One author says that the Four Truths "lie at the heart of Buddha's spiritual message."[3] Says Thây:

> The First Truth is the truth about suffering [*dukkha*], and no one can see the path unless he or she sees suffering. . . . Everyone knows that if

you run away from suffering, you have no chance to find out what path you should take in order to get out of the suffering. So our practice is to embrace suffering and look deeply into its nature. . . . [By doing this] we find out what has created our suffering. If we have seen this, we know how to stop, to cut the source of nutrition for suffering, and then healing will take place.[4]

One of the first things that catches the attention of a Christian in these words is the Buddhist emphasis on establishing a practice that will allow one to overcome suffering. In Buddhist teaching, a person is encouraged to acknowledge and name his or her suffering, and then through spiritual practice and discipline—what Thây calls embracing and looking deeply into the suffering—one gradually moves toward overcoming it. This teaching, which deals with suffering and its roots in a very direct way, is experienced by many people in our day as refreshing and hopeful, as it actually offers a practical path to liberation. It turns the experience of being at a dead end into an open door for those who are caught in suffering's endless cycle.

The Buddhist journey *out of* suffering and *into* freedom is at the heart of the Christian Gospels as well, though in a different way. Jesus certainly spent much of his public life reaching out to those who suffered, in an attempt to bring them into a new life, free from suffering. Perhaps one of the differences between the Christian and Buddhist approach to suffering is that, more than talking about overcoming personal suffering, Christians are likely to talk about helping someone else overcome suffering: the poor or the sick, for example. It may be a question of where we begin, our starting point. Buddhists emphasize beginning with the individual spiritual journey, leading the practitioner to a liberation that is then able to express itself through selfless service and loving-kindness to others. Christians, it seems, emphasize almost from the outset the practice of love of neighbor, trusting that, in the end, selfless love of others will lead one to a deep and lasting inner liberation.

The Judeo-Christian focus on the practice of love as the starting point for overcoming suffering begins with the story of creation. Creation flows, as we have seen previously, from a God who is love, a God whose love acts to free the world from suffering. At the same time, though, the belief of these two traditions is that human beings come forth from God endowed with free will, which is a reflection of the very freedom of God. This freedom to choose, to act, to decide can be employed either as a path that enhances life or destroys it, one that works to free the world from suffering or add to it. Sometimes we choose healthy, life-ennobling actions, and other times we make choices that lead to suffering and death. The Book of Deuteronomy, one of the original five books of the Law of Moses, records this admonition from God: "I have set before you life and death, blessings and curses. Choose life that you and your descendants may live" (Deut. 30:19). The choice for life is the choice for love, and this choice must always go hand in hand with the overcoming of suffering.

In the West, the emphasis on working to overcome one's own personal suffering is more common in the world of psychotherapy than in the religious milieu. There are, however, some examples in the West where therapy and spirituality have teamed up to help people face and overcome their personal suffering. Perhaps the best known of these marriages of psychology and spirituality can be seen in the different Twelve Step programs that have grown out of Alcoholics Anonymous. With their focus on daily practice, combined with psychological and spiritual wisdom, these programs have helped countless numbers of people look deeply into their suffering and find a path leading out of it. The Twelve Step programs have very much in common with the Four Noble Truths of Buddhism, in that both focus on naming the suffering, trusting that there is a way out of it, choosing a path of detachment based on honesty and discipline, and beginning the journey toward freedom. The millions of success stories attest to the sound principles underlying these programs. One of the striking similarities between the Twelve Step traditions and the Four Noble Truths is the understanding that suffering is fundamentally the result of craving, attachment, and desire. The alcoholic or drug addict suffers from a craving that has reached addictive proportions. Only through the brutal honesty of living "one day at a time" can the addict begin to "look deeply" enough to embark on the journey to liberation.

Thây's program for living "one day at a time" is centered on the practice of mindfulness, especially as spelled out in the Five Mindfulness Trainings. Thây proposes these trainings as a kind of "rule of life" that can help people overcome personal and societal suffering. The trainings, or precepts, give hope to those working to overcome suffering by way of very concrete practices. In other words, for Thây it is important to get beyond the *idea* that suffering can be overcome and actually live in such a way that this becomes possible and practical. As he himself points out,

> All the Five Mindfulness Trainings begin with "Aware of . . ." "Aware of the suffering caused by. . . ." This is the practice of mindfulness, of looking deeply into the nature of ill being. There is suffering in yourself and in the people around you. You practice looking deeply into the suffering in order to see the causes, the roots of the suffering. The Five Mindfulness Trainings are not a declaration of faith only. They are the real path of transformation and healing.[5]

This is, as we have mentioned previously, the great gift of Thây's teaching; he helps us to see how practicing an ethically honest and loving life actually relieves our own and others' suffering. Spirituality is not primarily about following rules, but about living a life that generates happiness and well-being for oneself and for others.

His Holiness the Dalai Lama, the spiritual leader of the people of Tibet and one who frequently remarks, "My religion is kindness," treats the theme of overcoming suffering in a way very similar to what Thây and the Twelve Step programs teach. As he and Thây both note, these teachings date back to the Buddha himself and basically proclaim that suffering exists, that it is caused principally by attachment, and that there is a way to bring an end to it. The Dalai Lama, however, commenting on Jesus' Sermon on the Mount in an interfaith seminar held in London in 1994, takes the discussion a step further by making a very insightful and helpful distinction between different kinds of suffering.

> There are certain types of suffering that are amenable to solutions and can thus be overcome. Once we realize this, we should seek their solution and the means to overcome the suffering. But there are other types of suffering that are inevitable and insurmountable. In such cases, it is important to develop a state of mind that will allow you to deal with this suffering in a realistic way. . . . Such an attitude will protect you, not necessarily from the physical reality of suffering, but from the unnecessary, added psychological burden of struggling against that suffering.[6]

The Dalai Lama's frank recognition that there are types of suffering that are inevitable, and that these particular kinds of suffering call us to a spiritual practice that is not focused primarily on overcoming them as they are manifest outwardly (i.e., a particular physical or social ill), but instead call us to the inner task of developing a healthy "state of mind," is an extremely enlightening teaching. For many people, the ability to discern the question, Just *what kind* of suffering am I up against? is, as we say, "half the battle." Spiritual guides must not underestimate the tremendously important service that they can offer to people, often caught in the terrible dilemma of making difficult life decisions, by helping them discern the kind of suffering that they are facing in any given moment and the options available to them.

This is often the case, for example, with people struggling with terminal illnesses such as cancer. In those cases in which doctors see a very viable possibility of stopping or, at least substantially slowing down the spread of the cancer, the choice to undergo the grinding chemo and radiation treatments is often the result of a healthy spiritual discernment. In other cases, though, when there does *not* seem to be any real hope for recovery or for an improved quality of life, the tendency (quite understandable from an emotional point of view, and often complicated by the medical industry's smorgasbord of options) can be to begin grasping for any and all possible life-saving miracles. This can actually work against the spiritual life. It is at these points where the teaching of the Dalai Lama is so very helpful: "In such cases, it is important to develop *a state of mind* that will help you to deal with the suffering in a realistic way." It is the development of a healthy and holy "state of mind" that is the fruit of spiritual practice.

People from all walks of life are faced with these kinds of heart-wrenching discernments every day. I know a man who has spent almost twenty-five years in prison, the first several years of which were filled with anger and despair. As he peered into the future through the steel bars of his prison cell, all he saw was a dark, unending tunnel. There was no light to be seen anywhere. Slowly, though, a light did begin to appear—not on the outside but deep within himself. His outward situation, his external suffering, was inevitable. To continue fighting it was akin to opening a festering wound over and over again. What he really longed for was for the wound to heal. For this to happen, he needed to undergo the dying process of letting go, letting go of the anger and of the lost dreams, letting go of his ego and the control of his destiny. For at least the past fifteen years, he has lived a life of deep peace and tranquility, a contagious kind of calm that has helped many other inmates make the spiritual journey through the dark tunnel and into the inner light as well. This is one of the dimensions of "overcoming suffering" that our spiritual masters are inviting us to embrace.

Eckhart, interestingly enough, approaches the topic of suffering from a perspective very similar to what is taught by the Buddha's Four Noble Truths and Twelve Step traditions. His most thorough treatment of the topic is in a treatise entitled *The Book of Divine Comfort*, which was written in or around 1308 for Agnes, the queen of Hungary, who was overcome with grief after the death of her husband and the assassination of her father, both of which occurred in 1301. Several years after the dual tragedy, Agnes entered a monastery, where she lived for the next fifty years until her death in 1364. Eckhart begins his entire program for "overcoming suffering" with a succinct theological statement, which forms the basis for everything that follows: "In God there is no sorrow or suffering or distress. If you would be free from all adversity and pain, turn and cleave entirely to God."[7] For Eckhart, the steps that lead to liberation are possible only if one is faithful to the practice of the presence of God, that is, living mindfully of the fact that, in *this* moment and in *this* place, I am *in God*. For Eckhart, suffering, when taken *in God* "is perfect suffering, for it arises from pure love of God's sheer goodness and joy."[8] Once I root myself firmly in this practice, teaches Eckhart, no suffering can touch that part of my being where God and I are one.

Detachment: Let Go and Let God

Though Eckhart does not repeat exactly the Dalai Lama's teaching that spiritual freedom in the face of suffering depends on the development of a particular "state of mind," he does in many ways point us down a very similar path. Eckhart approaches the topic, as he always does, by inviting us to set off on the path to freedom by journeying deep within ourselves, into the very ground of our being, where we are one with the Ground of God. Though it may sound at first somewhat dualistic—as if Eckhart were calling us to run away from the outward life by "hiding out" somewhere within—this is not what Eckhart is proposing. In no way does he advocate a life built on seeking some false interior refuge that will distance us from suffering. For Eckhart, the call to "cleave entirely to God" in the inner ground of the soul is his particular way of inviting his disciples to meet life's tragedies head-on, grounded in God, with a God-awakened state of mind.

It is important to note that in Eckhart, as in the Dominican tradition as a whole, there is a profound theological appreciation for creation and the things of the world, the so-called outward life. In fact, the order was founded partly in response to the world-rejecting theology that formed the basis of the Albigensian spiritualist movement in thirteenth-century southern France. In response to the dualism of the Albigensians, the Dominicans promoted a very positive view of the created world and the unfolding of human history. After all, the first story of creation in the Book of Genesis resounds with the phrase "And God saw that it [creation] was good" (Gen. 1:12ff.). There is no doubt that certain sectors of both the church and the state were abusing their worldly power and hoarding the gifts of creation at this time in history. In fact, it was precisely these abuses that gave rise, in great part, to both the Albigensian movement and the mendicant reform of monasticism, carried out principally by St. Francis and St. Dominic.

The tensions between these different views of the material world were still "blowing in the wind" by the time Eckhart appeared on the scene, which is one of the reasons why he is careful to distinguish between the goodness of creation and the suffering caused by the attachment to created things. For both Eckhart and the Buddhist tradition, suffering comes not from the material world per se but from a spiritually unhealthy attachment to that world.

Eckhart reminds his disciples that the world of creation, what Thây calls in earlier chapters the "phenomenal world" is to be understood as a kind of pathway leading us beyond itself into that which is its ground. The wise disciple, notes Eckhart, does not get stuck on the path but learns that the real secret is to "love God alone *in* creatures and creatures *in* God alone. . . . [Only then will the person] find true, real and equal comfort everywhere."[9] Creation, for Eckhart, is filled both *with* God and exists *in* God. Its "mission" is to point beyond itself to God. Few have described the divine presence underlying creation so beautifully as the poet Elizabeth Barrett Browning:

> Earth's crammed with heaven,
> And every common bush afire with God;
> But only he who sees, takes off his shoes
> The rest sit round it and pluck blackberries
> And daub their natural faces unaware . . .
> If a man could feel,
>
> Not one day, in the artist's ecstasy,
> But everyday, feast, fast, or working-day,
> The spiritual significance burns through
> The hieroglyphic of material shows,
> Henceforth he would paint the globe with wings,
> And reverence fish and fowl, the bull, the tree,
> And even his very body as a man . . .[10]

To help his disciples to learn the wisdom of living life amidst the beauty of creation, free from attachment, and grounded "in God alone," the Meister's simple advice goes something like this: taste God in all that surrounds you, and then let it all go, remaining only with that which you tasted.[11] What we have here is a summary of one of Eckhart's most important teachings: the practice of *detachment*. "When I preach," he says in one sermon, "it is my wont to speak about detachment."[12] Bernard McGinn remarks, "There are few motifs to which the Dominican appealed more often in his vernacular preaching [than] the need for separation from all earthly attachments in order to attain the freedom to find God."[13] Eckhart defines detachment as "nothing else but a mind that stands unmoved by all accidents of joy or sorrow, honor, shame, or disgrace, as a mountain of lead stands unmoved by a breath of wind."[14] Detachment is the path that leads to freedom. "Let go of yourself and let God act with you and in you," says Eckhart emphatically.[15]

"Let go of yourself and let God!" Sounds like solid advice. Let go of the tendency to cling to false gods—those seductive security blankets that are transitory and offer only a false sense of security—and learn to "cleave entirely to God." Only then can you experience inner liberation. Eckhart goes on to say, "The truly perfected [person] should be wont to be so dead to self, so truly lost in God in his own form and so transformed in God's will, that his entire blessedness consists in unknowing of himself and all things, and knowing only God."[16] Eckhart's "unknowing of self" is an echo of the teaching of Jesus in the Gospels: "If any want to become my followers, let them deny themselves and take up their cross and follow me" (Matt. 16:24). It is an invitation to die to the tyrannical control of the ego-mind and awaken immersed in "the mind of Christ" (1 Cor. 2:16).

There are perhaps few areas where our attachments can be so subtle and so deceptive as in the area of religion and spirituality. It is so easy to be very "spiritual" just as long as it is on my own terms! We can write lovely treatises about detachment and about God, and then become attached to what we have written! Eckhart mentions "people who like the taste of God in one way but not in another."[17] Without realizing it, they have become attached to an image or feeling about God, leaving the true, living God behind in the process. Thây also warns against trying to grab onto the Buddha: "You believe that going to the temple you will see the Buddha, but by doing so you are turning your back on the real Buddha. You are running after something that is not really the Buddha, or maybe a Buddha in bronze or copper, not the real living Buddha."[18]

Along with the danger of clinging to God, Eckhart also calls attention to a similar trap: becoming attached to a particular way of seeing or understanding truth. When this happens, we blind ourselves to the Ultimate Reality. Says the Meister, "Cease to be this or that, and to have this and that, then you are all things and have all things, and so, being neither here nor there, you are everywhere . . . you are everything."[19] Again he says, "Put aside *this* and *that*, and what remains is nothing but God,"[20] the ultimate Truth, the one who transcends all of our limited categories and self-serving egos. Though we must attempt to say something about God, we must be careful not to put God in a box. To underline the importance of being detached even from our notions of God, Eckhart, in one of his most masterful sermons, cries out, "Let us pray to God that we may be free of God that we may gain the truth and enjoy it eternally."[21] As soon as we think we have finally *got* God and *got* the truth, we can be sure that we have missed both. No one possesses the truth. On the contrary, we are possessed by the truth. Truth is the Ground upon which every *this* and *that* stands.

Eckhart ultimately wants to lead us beyond being attached to any kind of religious sign or symbol, so that we might have a direct experience of the living God who is beyond all our categories, all our wildest imaginings. We would do well to heed his words of wisdom, which sound very much like Thây's caution about running around in search of the Buddha:

If a [person] thinks that he or she will get more of God by meditation, by devotion, by ecstasies or by special infusion of grace than by the fireside or in the stable—that is nothing but taking God, wrapping a cloak around his head and shoving him under a bench. For whoever seeks God in a special way gets the way and misses God, who lies hidden in it.

> But whoever seeks God without any special way gets God as he is in
> himself. . . . If [you] asked life, "*Why* do you live?" if it could answer it
> would only say, "I live because I live." That is because life lives from its
> own ground, and gushes forth from its own. Therefore it lives without
> *Why*, because it lives for itself.[22]

"I live because I live." This is living from the experience of detachment. This
is what it means to awaken to an enlightened life: to "live because I live."
When we live because we live, we discover ourselves to be *in God*.

The practice of detachment, as our teachers point out here, is no piece of
cake. We would all like to be allowed to hold onto at least a couple of our
security blankets, but it is only by dying to the self-centered ego that we discover the path that can lead us to authentic love. Says Eckhart, "Love must be
so pure, so bare, so detached, that it is not inclined towards myself nor
towards my friends nor anywhere apart from itself."[23] In other words,
detached love means to love for love's sake—because loving is a good and
noble thing to do—*not* because there is some kind of a payback.

Addressing Jesus' commandment to love our neighbor as ourselves, Eckhart asks, "Why am I more glad that something good happens to my brother
or to myself rather than to another? [It is] because I love my own more than
another's. But if I love [the other] as myself . . . then it will seem all the same
to me. . . . Love will begin with God and straightway be with my neighbor. If
I detach myself fully from my own and have one equal love, then I shall love
all things equally."[24] Eckhart's invitation to let go of self-serving pseudo love
demands a lifetime of practice. Like the water of a cool mountain stream that
flows steadily over the rocks and boulders in its pathway, slowly softening
them over many years, so too is the process of detachment. We are softened
from our grasping and clinging one day at a time.

Eckhart continues his discussion of the connection between detachment
and love. Sometimes what we call love is only a detachment in disguise. When
this is so, suffering increases. But even the suffering can become our teacher,
and by looking into it deeply, we begin to see the path that leads beyond it.

> All suffering comes from love and attachment. So if I suffer on account
> of transitory things, then I and my heart have love and attachment for
> temporal things, I do not love God with all my heart and do not yet love
> that which God wishes me to love with Him. Is it any wonder then that
> God permits me to be rightly afflicted with loss and sorrow?[25]

At first it may sound like Eckhart is opting for a simplistic formula: love God
and hate the things of the world. His argument is much more nuanced than
that, however. Sounding like a Buddhist master, Eckhart pushes on: "All sor-

row comes from love of [those things] which loss has deprived me of. If I mind the loss of outward things, it is a sure sign that I am fond of outward things, and *really* love sorrow and discomfort. . . . [So] I turn to creatures . . . and turn away from God, from whom all comfort flows. Is it to be wondered at that I am sad and grieved?"[26] So, as Thây says, we look into the sadness and the grief and learn from it. What I previously thought to be so lovely has actually brought only sorrow and discomfort. The path becomes clearer, thanks to the suffering.

It is important to pay attention here to the way Eckhart carefully distinguishes between the *craving* for things (which is the cause of suffering) and the things *craved* (which in and of themselves are neutral). As he says in the previous paragraph, suffering does not come from enjoying "outward things," but instead because "I mind the loss of [those] outward things." It is the longing for "what I wish I had" that is the cause of the suffering. So for Eckhart, we should not be too terribly surprised that we suffer; we cling to passing shadows that appear one day and then we are plunged into depression when they disappear the next day. The key is to know this, to become aware of it. With the insight that comes from the experience, we learn to rejoice in the gift of the present moment without holding onto it.

The line that separates the thing itself from the craving can seem rather fine at times, but the distinction is tremendously important. Another way to say it is that our inner tranquility and peace are jeopardized not by worldly things per se, but by clinging to them. The Buddha's Second Noble Truth, let us recall, is that attachment gives rise to all suffering. This truth is central to Eckhart's teaching as well. The good news, though, as we just noted above, is that the suffering *teaches* us and helps us to see the path to freedom. Thây illustrates with a simple example what happens when we do *not* discern wisely the consequences of our craving: "The Buddha teaches us to remember that it is not the object of craving that makes us suffer, it is the craving that makes us suffer. It is like a hook hidden in the bait. The bait looks like an insect, and the fish sees something it thinks is tasty, not knowing that there is a hook inside. It bites and the hook catches it."[27]

We have all fallen for the baited hook a few times (or a few hundred times) in our lives! We learn from our mistakes. Like a child, we learn that the round coil on the top of the stove is sometimes not very friendly, so we just stay away. The real tragedy, though, and one that unfortunately is not so uncommon, is when one gets caught in an unending whirlwind of suffering and cannot seem to get out. This is the experience of many addicts, as in the case of a man who gambled his entire family into poverty. This is what the Buddhists refer to as the cycle of *samsara*—lifetime after lifetime of birth, suffering and death. There are some people, says Eckhart, who lose themselves completely in outward attachments. "Finally they go out so far that they never get back home or find their way in again. Thus they have not found the truth, for truth is within, in the ground, and not without."[28] There are few things more heartbreaking in this world than to meet someone lost in this kind of suffocating suffering, especially if the person still insists that there is no problem.

Eckhart comments on the tragedy of unending suffering with an example that might offer us some insight into what signs or red flags we should watch for to avoid falling unknowingly into the terrible pit. He imagines a person losing a great sum of money or a friend, or an eye, or a hand. In other words, this is the kind of "inevitable suffering" of which the Dalai Lama spoke—something that has happened and which cannot be reversed. How does this person keep from becoming consumed by the pain? In his example, Eckhart points us to one of the red flags. Eckhart asks, "[How are people going to] take comfort and be free from care, if they [constantly] turn toward the loss and the tribulation, impressing it upon themselves and themselves upon it, so that they look at it and it looks back at them, and they talk and converse with the loss, and the loss converses with them, and they gaze each other in the face?"[29]

This is Eckhart's version of *samsara*—becoming mentally obsessed with our losses and our sufferings, gazing at the empty void day and night, allowing them to consume us with even greater emotional suffering. For Eckhart, this kind of spiraling obsession must be addressed immediately if one is going to get out of the destructive pit.

One way to recognize that a person has been caught in this unending whirlwind of pain is the complete inability to dwell in the present moment. Everything becomes an obsession with the past or a panic-driven fear of the future. One way to help such a person, then, would be through simple acts aimed at grounding him or her in the present: a walk in a park, the laughter of a child, a visit from a friend, a therapeutic massage—anything that will help the person let go of the obsessive mind and feel the groundedness of the body again. Eckhart recognizes the need to turn away from what is not (past, future), and open one's eyes to all that is (present). "When we are lifted above all things," he explains, "nothing can oppress us."[30] There is a way to be free from *samsara's* unending cycle. Freedom is available here and now, in the present moment. All we have to do is to allow ourselves to be "lifted above all things" and plunged into Ultimate Reality, into the reign of God.

Eckhart wants to give us some practical tools with which we can reach out to a person who is beginning the downward spiral into a dangerous emotional suffering rooted in attachment. Even more than that, though, is his interest in teaching us daily practice. How do we go about the daily detaching—keeping our minds focused, one-pointed, free from obsessive thinking? How do we begin the letting go now? For Thây, of course, we can begin with something as simple as the mindfulness bell: "When you hear the meditation bell, you stop your thinking. You stop what you are saying, and the bell rescues you and brings you back to your true home."[31] Thây might also invite us to touch a flower deeply, to eat a mango and let the juice roll down our chin, or simply to feel the warmth of the sun's rays on our face.

Eckhart summarizes his plan for teaching us to detach and let go as learning to "cleave entirely to God." It is a journey toward what the Meister calls the "de-forming" of the self, the detachment from the ego-driven mind. The task that he sets before us is to drop down into the Silent Desert of the soul where "God's ground is my ground and my ground is God's ground."[32] For Eckhart, one of the greatest aids in learning the art of detachment is the practice of interior silence, a silence that clears the mind and the heart of all clutter, preparing the way for God to speak in the temple of the soul. The silence leads us into "a forgetting and an unknowing. There must be a stillness and a silence for this Word [the voice of God] to make itself heard."[33] This "forgetting and unknowing" is important, says the Meister, because attachment, the great obstacle to spiritual freedom and the cause of much sorrow and suffering, is like inner noise that clouds the clarity of our mind.

Attachment often manifests itself as a kind of knowing—a secure certainty—that blocks the way for true knowing. It is born from the grasping need for spiritual security. Religious fundamentalism is nothing but attachment dressed in sacred garb. Though it uses a multitude of religious words, they are more like the noisy words of a television or radio blaring loudly in the background of daily life; they save one from having to face the terrifying silence of true spiritual encounter. When multiplied, of course, this type of inner noise can reach the level of the destructive mental obsession mentioned above.

Eckhart says, with advice reminiscent of that of a Zen master, that we must learn to "hide from the turmoil of inward thoughts, for they but create discord."[34] Anyone who has attempted sitting meditation or centering prayer in a serious manner knows that practicing mental stillness is no simple feat. The "turmoil of inward thoughts" can seem like a real monster at times. Inner silence and the quieting of the mind are necessary spiritual disciplines if we are to learn to counter our desperate attempts to fill the void with artificial relief. "It is a little difficult in the beginning in becoming detached," says Eckhart, "but when one has got into it, no life is easier, more delightful or lovelier."[35] Transformation takes time.

This temptation to grasp for anything that will fill up the deafening silence is very real for those on the spiritual path. For Eckhart, though, without the practice of contemplative silence there is no birth of God's Word within. One can speak many sophisticated, spiritualistic words without ever having had a true encounter with *the Word* that transforms one from within. Eckhart likens the grasping for artificial spiritual experience to the racketeering of the money changers whom Jesus confronted as they hawked their wares in the temple precincts (John 2:13-22). Their aim is to distract the disciple from entering into the deep recesses of the temple, the temple of the Spirit.

> See, those are all merchants who . . . wishing to be virtuous, do good works . . . in order that our Lord may give them something in return. . . . That is why God cast them out of the temple and drove them away. . . . When the temple is thus free of obstructions (that is attachment and ignorance), then it glistens with beauty, shining out bright and fair above all creation, and through all God's creation. . . . Be sure of this: if anyone else would speak in the temple (which is the soul) but Jesus, Jesus is silent, as if he were not at home. . . . But if Jesus is to speak in the soul, she must be alone, and she has to be quiet. . . . Then, in he comes and starts speaking.[36]

Eckhart, aware of how powerful is the pull to wander away from our center, filling the void with noise and cravings, gently invites us into the deep *inner dwelling place* where we learn to love the created world *in* the silent heart of God. The Meister knows that it is not an either-or situation. Detachment is not about choosing God over against the loud and busy world; that is dualism. Eckhart does teach, however, that it is a first this, then that situation. In other words, it is a question of priorities. A person must be willing to stop trying to solve life's aches and pains by placing one's trust in the gods of money, power, prestige, relationships, spiritual pleasure, and the like and plunge into the naked, silent Ground of God within.

It is by remaining rooted there, says Eckhart, in the interior "God-place," that we find the path that leads beyond suffering and into freedom. The path to freedom, like the kingdom, is within us. If we happen to wander and stray from our holy Ground, our God-centeredness, there *is* a way back home: we simply and humbly acknowledge that we are lost, *repent* (from the Greek word *apostrephō*, which literally means "I turn back on the road I have been traveling"), and come home.[37] Interior silence, which is the fruit of letting go of our inner noise and craving mind, helps us to know when we have wandered from the path. We "hear" in the silence of our own heart, the pain of separation. In a curious piece of a sermon, Eckhart makes the statement that "we learn more wisdom by hearing than by seeing." It is, of course, part of his call to inner stillness and silence. He goes on by saying that hearing is an act that draws a person inward, whereas seeing draws us outside of ourselves. "In hearing I am passive. . . . The act of hearing the eternal Word is within me."[38] The link with detachment is clear. By listening in the silence of the heart, we are drawn inward; we sink into the ground of God where we are free from all craving and attachment. This silent hearing is the first step on the journey back home.

For Thây, one of the first steps in letting go of attachment is through mindful breathing. In his early book *The Miracle of Mindfulness*, Thây reminds us of the importance of our breath in leading us back home from the wanderings of our craving minds: "[The] breath is the bridge which connects life to consciousness, which unites your body to your thoughts. . . . [It] is a natural and extremely effective tool which can prevent dispersion."[39] The breath and the silence work together; both serve as bridges that bring us back home. St. Catherine of Siena, cited in the previous chapter, spoke of Jesus as the bridge that brings us home to God. After his resurrection, Jesus breathed on the disciples the breath of the Spirit, the breath of peace—helping them come home to God in the midst of their suffering.

Only then were they able to let go of what was not to be (cf. Luke 24:20-21) and embrace what was: the unexpected gift of new life coming forth from death. The breath of the Spirit frees us to let go of writing our *own* ending to the story, opening us to the surprise of the present moment. Detachment, in the end, is the key to freedom and joy.

8

Compassion Born from Suffering

Looking Deeply

Thây's invitation to "look deeply" is like a wonderful compass, helping us navigate the path that leads beyond the suffering caused by attachment, back home to inner freedom. Succinctly put, the teaching goes something like this: Look deeply into *that* which has managed to lure you away from your true self. Listen to it. What is it? Where did it come from? How far down do the roots go? What is its name? Once we have acknowledged the dispersion, the suffering, the sorrow—and all their intertangled roots—then, says Thây, smile at it, embrace it, and let it go.

Looking deeply teaches us understanding. By dialoguing with the suffering and its causes, by really *listening* to the answers that come from the dialogue, we gain much insight. It is the insight and the understanding that help us navigate the way back home, from suffering to liberation. "Understanding is the process of looking deeply," says Thây. "A wave has to realize that there are other waves around her. Each wave has her own suffering. You are not the only person who suffers. Your sisters and brothers also suffer. The moment you *see* the suffering in them, you stop blaming them, and you stop the suffering in you. . . . If you touch suffering deeply in yourself and in the other person, understanding will arise."[1] Thây continues in another place to emphasize the need for understanding:

> Understanding is the key that can unlock the door to the prison of suffering. If we do not practice understanding, we do not avail ourselves of the most powerful instrument that can free us and other living beings from suffering. True love is possible only with real understanding. Buddhist meditation—stopping, calming and looking deeply—is to help us understand better. In each of us is a seed of understanding. That seed is God. It is also the Buddha.[2]

The Dalai Lama says almost the very same thing: "Genuine compassion . . . springs from a clear recognition of the experience of suffering on the part of the object of compassion, and from the realization that this creature is worthy of compassion and affection."[3]

Both of these contemporary Buddhist masters remind us of the importance of *looking deeply* and *seeing* with a contemplative and compassionate vision. This connects us very intimately with the Christian tradition. Often called *illumination* in the early church, part of the grace of baptism, as noted above, has to do with the healing of spiritual blindness. We are given eyes to see, to look deeply at reality. Not only do we begin to see ourselves in a new light, namely, in the light of God, but we begin to see others in that light, as well. Thây says that looking deeply is like "observing something or someone with so much concentration that the distinction between observer and observed disappears."[4] From this concentrated observation, this right vision, understanding is born. The blindness of deception, self-centeredness, and sin is gradually healed and we begin to open our eyes and hearts and see others in the brilliant light of God. We begin to understand and to respond to their suffering with love. St. Catherine of Siena, in a prayer written to encourage herself to more spiritual fervor, wrote, "Rouse yourself; open the eye of your understanding and look into the depth within the well of divine charity. For unless you see, you cannot love. The more you see, the more you love."[5] Like our Buddhist teachers, Catherine was aware of the close link between "looking into the depths" and a love born of understanding.

Friar Vincent de Couesnongle, former head of the Dominican order, gave a talk in Mexico in 1977 on the importance of practicing "contemplation of the street." He proposed that we practice a kind of walking meditation through the streets and public places of our world "with our eyes wide open." In this way, he said, we can cultivate compassion and love.

> It does not mean walking around distracted in the midst of the crowd, but an *attentive looking* at all that surrounds us: these persons, these faces, their way of walking, the poverty of their dress. . . . [It is] knowing how to look for and understand what cannot be seen: failures, suffering, hopes. . . . It means to always make present now the human and divine gaze of Christ upon the crowd, the sick, all who are possessed by the evil of money, injustice, hatred. . . . This contemplation should be the privileged point of union in our lives between faith and the world.[6]

Like Thây, de Couesnongle teaches a form of mindful seeing, a deep looking at the world that gives birth to understanding and love. This is a most helpful teaching for our times. We can turn every moment into a moment of mindful, contemplative seeing. Waiting in line at the supermarket, riding the subway train, walking through airports—the opportunities for this kind of contemplative, compassionate seeing are infinite. The simple fact that we choose to look at others with understanding and compassion is already the first step toward healing.

The wars and acts of violence that have plagued our world over the centuries, and especially in the past few years, are almost always the result of a lack of understanding, a failure to *see* the other person or the other country as one filled with the same divine spark as myself. Thây's teaching on the practice of *looking deeply* is directly connected to the practices of meditation and mindfulness. Through a symbolic "closing of our eyes," that is to say, a turning inward through meditative concentration (*samadhi*), our vision is made clearer. We actually see better. Says Eckhart, "Whoever would see God must be blind. . . . God is a light that shines in the darkness."[7] This is similar to his teaching on inner silence; there is no word unless there is silence. The discipline of meditation slows us down and trains us to look at the world with understanding and compassion. The result? We begin to *see* the world around us as it truly is.

In the 1500s, during the early years of the Spanish and Portuguese conquest of the Americas, Europe found itself embroiled in a theological debate on whether or not the conquered Indians (indigenous Americans) were fully human. As long as it could be stated that they were *not* fully human, they could be enslaved and worked to death. Another option was to save one's life by accepting mandatory baptism into the Christian faith. Luckily there were some who saw things differently. One such person was Dominican friar Bartolomé de Las Casas. Originally a land and slave owner himself, Las Casas gradually learned to see with the eyes of understanding and compassion. This contemplative vision, which rooted him in the truth of the Indians' human dignity, gave him the courage to unmask the lies of those who were becoming wealthy at the expense of the poor.

By *looking deeply* at the situation of suffering and oppression that surrounded him, Las Casas was able to see the indigenous inhabitants of the land as God saw them. "I began to consider the suffering and servitude of these people," he wrote many years later.[8] It was a seeing that led him to a deep understanding and, from there, to spend the next fifty years of his life working for the rights and freedom of the enslaved native Americans. Commenting on the gold-hungry bandits who profited by keeping their eyes closed to the truth, Las Casas said, "I see that some have written of Indian things, not those they witnessed, but rather those they heard about, and not too well. . . . They write to the detriment of truth."[9] As St. Catherine of Siena said, "Unless you see, you cannot love."

Another example of this kind of deep, contemplative seeing comes from the writings of Etty Hillesum, a Dutch Jew who was gassed to death at Auschwitz on November 30, 1943, at the age of thirty-nine. After spending some time in Westerbork, a Dutch processing camp that served as a collection point for Jews who were awaiting their final transport to Auschwitz, Etty wrote of her own looking into the face of suffering.

Nothing was alien to me, not one single expression of human sorrow. . . . I am not afraid to look suffering straight in the eyes. And at the end of the day, there was always the feeling: I love people so much. Never any bitterness about what was done to them, but always love for those who knew how to bear so much although nothing had prepared them for such burdens. . . . It still all comes down to the same thing: life is beautiful. And I believe in God. And I want to be right in the thick of what people call "horror" and still be able to say: life is beautiful.[10]

What all these people are saying is that the spiritual journey requires one to have the courage to look suffering in the face. Hidden in the suffering is truth, and as Jesus said, "the truth will make you free" (John 8:32). This kind of seeing requires introspection and tremendous honesty, for we must be willing to really see reality as it is, not as we would like it to be. I think, for example, of the white South Africans who were able to look deeply into the terrible suffering and injustice of apartheid and understand what needed to happen. This, of course, meant letting go of power and admitting the sins of their own privileged past and that of their ancestors. Looking deeply, then, is often painful, for it calls forth from us the letting go of our coveted attachments and self-righteous sufferings.

This practice of looking deeply, contemplatively, trains us to see the other without the emotionally colored lenses that taint our ability to see justly, from a stance of inner freedom and truth. The Dalai Lama offers a keen insight into how our way of seeing can affect how we love: "Genuine compassion . . . springs from a clear recognition of the experience of suffering on the part of the object of compassion, and from the realization that this creature is worthy of compassion and affection. . . . [It] can be extended even to one's enemies."[11]

When we open our eyes, and especially the inner eye of our heart, we see the suffering of the other person. This is the key to compassion, says the Dalai Lama. We also see that this person longs for happiness just as I do. The recurring question that echoed in the news media for months and months following the tragedy of September 11 was, "Why do they hate us?" Though many were willing to ask the question, few were willing to look deeply enough to find the answers. The answers were, and still are, too close to home. Only those who have the courage to look deeply into the suffering, asking the hard questions and waiting patiently for the answers to emerge, will experience the truth that sets us free.

One such person is Bill Pelke. Bill is a man who made his way through the painful tunnel of anger and the cry for vengeance into the lovely light of compassion. In 1985 Bill's grandmother was brutally murdered by four teenage girls who visited the elderly woman's house under the pretense that they wanted her to tell them some Bible stories. Bill was a firm believer in the death penalty at the time and felt vindicated with the news that the instigator of the murder, a fifteen-year-old girl, had been given the death penalty for the crime.

One night, while Bill was working the night shift at a steel mill in Pennsylvania, the face of his grandmother popped into his mind. He was surprised, he later remarked, that the face that came into his mind was not the bloodied face of his dead grandmother but her gentle, loving face—the face he had known all his life, the face of the grandmother known for teaching Bible stories to the children in her town. This *seeing*, this mental image, transformed Bill. By looking deeply at his grandmother's gentle, loving face, he somehow found himself looking into the suffering face of the young girl condemned to die. He *saw* the girl through the eyes of his grandmother. That night his whole life changed. He committed all his time and energy to saving the life of the girl sentenced to death for murdering his grandmother.

"I realized that night," Pelke said several years later during a prayer vigil in North Carolina calling for an end to the death penalty, "that my grandmother spent her whole life teaching children about God's love. If she were here today, she would want to reach out to this young girl and offer her God's love." His ability to *see* the young girl as one who, like his grandmother and like himself, was also suffering was the moment of breakthrough into a compassion-based consciousness. There was an experience of *interbeing* and solidarity within the suffering. As he said later in an interview, "I now believe that the answer is not the death penalty. The answer is love and compassion."[12]

To "look deeply at the suffering," as Thây teaches, is an invitation to befriend it, to listen to it, to learn from it. Suffering can be a great teacher. Surely we have all, at some point in our lives, made an important life-transforming decision as a result of dealing directly and honestly with some kind of existential angst. The key, then, is to learn the art of dialogue. How do we have a healthy and holistic "conversation" with our own pain and dis-ease? How do we do that with others? How might we do it on a societal level? Can a nation look at collective suffering—caused by things like corruption, abuse, war, poverty, discrimination, terrorism, etc.—and dialogue with it? What might we learn from this? As Thây reminds us so well, "Enlightenment and happiness and insight are only possible on the basis of suffering and confusion. The Buddha said it is because of the mud that the lotus can bloom. If you plant lotus on marble, the lotus cannot survive."[13] Detachment is not about annihilating suffering, but transforming it. To do that, we must sit down with it and listen to it.

Maybe there is good news in all this. Rather than seeing the mud in our lives as a problem to be solved (and getting attached to solving the problem!), maybe we can see it as a chance to cultivate a beautiful lotus. And if the lotus can bloom in the mud, maybe it can bloom in me, too—and in all of us. Maybe detachment means that we stop *worrying* about the mud and just take the risk of sinking our roots deep down into the dark un-knowing, and then wait for the miracle to happen, wait for the lotus to bloom. Maybe the kingdom really *is* here—right now—in the midst of our muddy world, if only we had eyes to see it. If that is the case, then my heart cries out with the blind man who was healed by Jesus, "Teacher, let me see" (Mark 10:51).

Compassion—The Risk of Loving

The relationship between suffering and love can be summed up in the word *compassion*. Compassion is love that is willing to run the risk of suffering *with* and *for* the beloved. For married couples, for parents with children, for people whose lives are oriented toward serving others, compassion is the stuff of everyday life. In fact, for anyone who really lives his or her life in mutual relationship with others, compassion is a way of life. Either we take the risk of living with and for others—paying the price that such a life entails—or we isolate ourselves and opt for a small, self-centered world made in our own image and likeness. That is to say, either we live for love or we die a spiritual death. Thây comments on this truth beautifully in *Going Home*.

> Love cannot exist without suffering. In fact, suffering is the ground on which love is born. If you have not suffered, if you don't see the suffering of people or other living beings, you would not have love in you nor would you understand what it is to love. Without suffering, compassion, loving-kindness, tolerance, and understanding would not arise. Do you want to live in a place where there is no suffering? If you live in such a place, you will not be able to know what is love. Love is born from suffering. . . . We need to touch suffering in order for our compassion to be born and to be nourished.[14]

The risky business of loving, of course, requires great patience. The two words *compassion* and *patience* both come from the Latin root *patior*, meaning "to suffer." It is as if even our language contains within it a great intuition, an important truth: to love another demands patience and the very real possibility of suffering. For Christians this is the basic insight that opens one up to a deeper understanding of the incarnation of the Son of God, culminating in the passion, death, and resurrection of Christ. If the relationship between God and the world is one of love, as the Christian scriptures claim ("God is love" [1 John 4:16]), then God must draw close to the universe and risk suffering in order to be true to the love that is at the core of who God is. God cannot love the world while remaining protected from suffering. God draws near to humanity through Jesus, who is the love of God made flesh, and with this loving come the consequences that such a love entails.

One of the world's great spokespersons on the theme of compassion is the Dalai Lama, and he also emphasizes the truth that real love, real compassion demands that we enter into relationship with others. Love is, by nature, communal.

> Compassion is impossible without the presence of others. Every aspect of your life—your religious practice, your spiritual growth, even your basic survival—is impossible without others. . . . It becomes impossible to believe that some people are totally irrelevant to your life or that you can afford to adopt an indifferent attitude toward them. There are no human beings who are irrelevant to your life.[15]

What powerful and penetrating words! "There are no human beings who are irrelevant to your life." Do we believe this? Do we live this? If we agree with these insights of the Dalai Lama, then we must go on to affirm that there can be no authentic spiritual life without being in relationship with other human beings and, in fact, with all beings. That is precisely what makes love so terribly risky, because it involves being in relationship, and being in relationship with others always opens us up to the possibility of suffering. Thây says it this way: "You love someone when that someone needs you. When that someone suffers, your love relieves his or her suffering. Your love is to bring happiness to him or her. That is the meaning of love. It is easy to understand that living beings around us who suffer need your love."[16]

As we saw in the previous chapter, the Christian community of the first century realized that love of God necessarily involves love of neighbor. "Those who say, 'I love God,' and hate their brother or sister are liars; for those who do not love a brother or sister whom they have seen, cannot love God whom they have not seen" (1 John 4:20). This pivotal text sets before us not a moral command to go around loving everyone we possibly can, so that we can "prove" to God how loving we are (and therefore get to heaven!). It is an invitation to simply become love. If we are waves riding upon the ocean of love, then we do not need to prove to the ocean that we are love. We just need to be love. Once we begin to be love, then, as the Dalai Lama pointed out above, no human being will be irrelevant in our lives. Love will be as natural to us as yawning when we are sleepy.

Ruben Habito, in his book *Living Zen, Loving God*, dedicates an entire chapter to Jesus' command to "love your neighbor as yourself." Commenting on the parable of the Good Samaritan, who stops to care for a wounded man on the roadside, Habito says, "What the Samaritan did was not some kind of . . . good deed, some type of voluntary action. . . . He merely did immediately the most natural thing to do in that situation. This 'most natural thing' is what we do spontaneously when we transcend duality, when we see 'the other' as not separate from our own self."[17] Love is not generic; we do not love "in general." Love is always concrete. It always involves real people. The same is true with God's love. We cannot really "love God." Where is God? The only way we have to love God is by loving *this* person *right here* and *right now*. I love God by helping an elderly man carry his sack of groceries to the car. There is not a lot of romance in loving God. It is pretty mundane actually. But if we really *do* believe that we live and move and have our being *in God*, then what difference does it make if I am loving God or loving my neighbor? Love just *loves*. To use Thây's phrase, these two dimensions to loving *inter*-are, that is, we cannot have one without the other.

Though most people know from personal experience that loving others almost always entails suffering—or at least daily sacrifices—there is often a subtle belief that there should be a way of loving that can skirt around all this unnecessary suffering. Maybe we all have this secret hope lurking around in our hearts somewhere! When this delusive desire becomes firmly rooted in our belief system, there is a possibility for real disaster. People caught in the addictive search for "the perfect relationship" often live out of this underlying belief without being aware of it. It is the cause of great emotional pain, always focused, of course, on the faults and mistakes of the other person. At some point one must begin the journey into healing, which means "looking deeply" at the cause of the suffering and realizing that the problem, the distorted belief, is not *out there* somewhere, but *in here*, in my own broken heart. Though the journey itself is often very painful, the discovery is liberating. The "perfect" relationship is *not* one that is free from suffering, but one that is full of compassion. Once we realize *that* truth, then there is only one real question to answer. It is the same one that Jesus asks when he tells the parable of the Good Samaritan (Luke 10:36). Am I willing to love this person? If the answer is *yes*, then compassion is born.

Once we choose to live our lives with compassion, we then live ready to embrace the probability that our loving will bring us face to face with suffering. This, of course, is not any great revelation to those who have raised children! It is just a fact of life. "Love is born from suffering," said Thây above. This is *not* some kind of religious masochism. It is the deep insight of all the great spiritual traditions. The Dalai Lama, in a seminar in which he reflected on several Christian scriptures from a Buddhist perspective, said the following about the Beatitudes which Jesus taught in his Sermon on the Mount:

When I read these lines from the Beatitudes, the first thing that comes to mind is . . . the simple fact that those who are willing to embark on a path and accept the hardships and the pain involved in it will reap the rewards of their commitment. When we speak of a kind of tolerance that demands that you accept the fact of hardships, pain and suffering, we should not have the erroneous notion that . . . suffering is beautiful, that suffering is what we all must seek. Needless to say, I do not subscribe to such a view.[18]

Suffering is part of loving; it just *is*. There is nothing romantic or heroic about it. Jesus' suffering and death was not based on some notion that this was an important spiritual practice, that by suffering he would prove to the world that he was a divine superhuman. And Jesus' suffering was certainly not because God the Father had a secret, predetermined plan that he carried out like some heavenly puppeteer. How could such a God be called a God of love? God does not *will* anyone to suffer. Jesus suffered because he took the risk to love, because he "embarked on a path and accepted the hardships," as the Dalai Lama says. Jesus loved because it was "the natural thing" to do. It was who he was. As Thây writes, "There was a person who was born nearly two thousand years ago. He was aware that suffering was going on in him and in his society, and *he did not hide himself from the suffering*."[19]

Thây's description of Jesus helps clarify the point that true compassion includes the possibility of suffering not because suffering is a good and noble thing, but because we choose to not hide ourselves from suffering. The suffering that is a consequence of loving is what compassion is all about. Jesus said, "Love one another as I have loved you" (John 15:12). Yet in case we get lost in a notion of love that is lofty and romantic, one that is free from suffering, Jesus tacks on the second part: "No one has greater love than this, to lay down one's life for one's friends" (John 15:13). This is love. We see it in action hundreds of times a day if we live with our eyes open. A mother "lays down her life" every time she wakes up in the middle of the night to nurse her newborn baby. A teacher "lays down his life" when he spends extra time tutoring the student who struggles with the demands of learning. A missionary sister in Brazil "lays down her life" by standing in solidarity with landless peasants struggling to reclaim their ancestral lands.

The young Chinese man who stood alone and unarmed before the approaching tank in Tiananmen Square in 1989 "laid down his life" most probably because he dreamed of a freer and more just world. In other words, there is no true love that does not include laying down our lives, setting aside our own agendas, giving away our time, sacrificing our security. These choices are integral to the spiritual path. Says Thây, "Love is a practice and unless you know what suffering is, you are not motivated to practice compassion, love and understanding."[20]

The Practice of Love

The relationship between suffering and love, between suffering and compassion, raises some interesting questions that are worth looking at. For example, how do these two realities interact with each other and with our own personal spiritual practice? Do they flow out of spiritual practice? Do they lead us to spiritual practice? Does it matter? I begin with a quotation from Thây: "It is because we are struggling to free ourselves from the grip of suffering and affliction that we learn how to love and how to take care of ourselves and others."[21]

This quotation is a gem of spiritual teaching, in part because it maps out the intimate relationship between our own spiritual practice and the lives of those around us. We do not practice spiritually in a bubble or on an island. My spiritual life and the world around me *inter*-are. We struggle to be free from suffering, says Thây, and in the process we learn how to love.

However, there is another reason why these words are important for me, as one raised in a Christian context. They help me to question the process in myself. What leads me to compassion? What does it mean to "love my neighbor as myself?" Does my being a Christian lead me to love, or does love lead me to be a Christian? I wonder if Buddhists approach this question in a way different from Christians? At this point, I do not know the answer to many of these questions, but I raise them as we search for common ground and understanding in our dialogue. Our differences add richness to our dialogue.

Let us return to Thây's words above: "It is because we are struggling to free ourselves from the grip of suffering and affliction that we learn how to love and how to take care of ourselves and others." If I were to reshape that statement into what I would call a more commonly "Christian" version, imagining the words coming from the mouth of Jesus, for example, it might sound something like this: "It is in our struggle to love and care for ourselves and one another that we learn how to be free from the grip of suffering and affliction."

One of the reasons why noting these gentle differences is of importance is that it can help us to understand the spiritual *praxis* of those whose path is different from our own. To illustrate the particular nuance between these two versions of the same quotation, I would like to offer an example. In July 1996, at the Abbey of Gethsemani in Kentucky, a Buddhist–Christian Dialogue on the Spiritual Life was held. Referred to as the "Gethsemani Encounter," it was held at the Cistercian Abbey where Thomas Merton lived his life as a monk.

The encounter was part of the celebration of the twenty-fifth anniversary of Merton's death and was organized primarily as a dialogue between Buddhist and Christian monastics.

As might be expected, the theme of suffering and compassion was one of the major themes treated at the gathering. At one point Cistercian monk Dom Armand Veilleux told the story of seven Cistercian monks who had been killed just two months before the encounter by a militant group of Muslim fundamentalists in Algeria. The tragedy had touched Christians and non-Christians across the globe and certainly was still very fresh in the minds of the Christian monks who were present for the dialogue at Gethsemani. The monasteries of Gethsemani and Algeria are sister monasteries, both belonging to the Trappist branch of the Cistercian order. The story of the Algerian martyrs raised very different reactions among Buddhists and Christians, and it is imperative that we grapple with those differences if we are to understand and grow in respect for each other's traditions. The two versions of Thây's statement from above come into play, I believe, in the different viewpoints that were voiced at the Gethsemani dialogue.

One of the encounter participants, Judith Simmer-Brown, a Buddhist and chair of the religious studies department at the Naropa Institute in Boulder, Colorado, had this to say:

> When I heard about your Algerian martyrs, I had a question about certain themes in Christianity—martyrdom, sacrifice, tragedy and transformation. . . . I can understand the personal transformation that the Algerian monks went through in deciding to stay [in Algeria, despite previous threats of death], but my question is how did their staying express compassion for the aggressors who, from a Buddhist point of view, will reap the karma for lifetimes for murdering them? . . . I find it very disturbing and troubling from a Buddhist point of view because compassion seems to be missing.[22]

I must admit that when my "Christian ears" hear Simmer-Brown's statement "compassion seems to be missing" it almost sounds like a foreign language to me, and I suspect that I am not alone in that sentiment. One journalist who was present at the encounter and remembers this particular exchange said, "For a shocked moment the Catholics looked blankly at one another, uncertain how to address this questioning of martyrdom, the supreme Christian gesture."[23] This "shock," which I must admit would have been my response as well, can only be understood if we recall that Jesus sums up his own teaching on compassion with a very succinct and clear statement: "This is my commandment, that you love one another as I have loved you. No one has greater love than this, to lay down one's life for one's friends" (John

15:12-13). Dom Armand responded to Simmer-Brown, "[The monks] did not desire to be killed. They desired to live and they loved life."[24] Their decision to stay was not based on a desire to die as martyrs, continued Dom Armand, but was a choice to remain as *witnesses*, followers of Jesus who, like their master, chose to remain present in loving solidarity with their many neighbors—both Muslim and Christian—who were suffering terribly from the ravages of war and violence. The choice of the monks to *remain even in the midst of the violence* sounds very similar to Thây's words about Jesus: "he did not hide himself from suffering." It is very much in that sense that Dom Armand responded to Simmer-Brown. In Christianity, the possibility of martyrdom is always one of the many dimensions of witnessing to the love of Jesus Christ.

What is so startling in this particular interreligious exchange is the realization that what for one person is a profound expression of compassion is, for another, almost the opposite. One realizes that such different understandings of compassion must be rooted in fundamentally different starting points. How do we join in the building of a more compassionate world when these differences seem so acute?

Let us go back and analyze a bit more deeply the two quotations that we compared above. Thây sees the relationship between suffering and compassion in this way: "It is because we are struggling to free ourselves from the grip of suffering and affliction that we learn how to love." Next to it we place the "Christian version" of the statement: "It is in our struggle to love and care for ourselves and one another that we are set free from the grip of suffering and affliction." At first glance it seems to be simply a question of sentence order, only a minor difference. I think, however, that the quotations truly do point to fundamentally different starting points. I would go so far as to say that Buddhists and Christians perhaps *do* have vastly different ways of understanding the relationship between suffering and love, between spiritual practice and compassion. Stating this fact is not about competing to see who has the truer truth. It is about honestly sharing our gifts and the insights from our respective traditions as a way of journeying together along the path of spiritual practice.

If it is true that Buddhism emphasizes the struggle to be free from suffering and affliction as the first half of the "spiritual equation," then any action that might allow suffering to happen, as in the case of the karmic effects of a murderer's actions, will be avoided at all cost. If this is so, then it could be that the choice of the monks to remain in Algeria might be seen as a lesser good, as it may not necessarily serve the spiritual interests of the Islamic fundamentalists. On the other hand, if it is true that Christianity emphasizes loving oneself and others as the starting point of the "equation," then the choice of a community of monks to stay in a war-torn country as a gesture of loving solidarity with those who are suffering would be considered to be of paramount spiritual value. In other words, the starting point of the equation directly affects the path of action taken.

In dialoguing on this particular topic, I find myself, not surprisingly, understanding and agreeing on a very deep level with the decision of the monks to remain in Algeria. On another level, a much more intellectual level I must admit, I *think* I understand the other side of the equation as well. Had the monks discerned, for example, that it was best for both themselves and the local Algerians that they return to France, that decision would have been equally important and loving. Their discernment, however, led to the communal choice to remain in the country, partly, it seems, because they did not want the local people to view a decision to leave as a sign of abandonment in their time of most need. What is vitally important for us, on the other hand, as we consider the relationship between suffering, compassion, and spiritual practice is that we listen deeply to one another and attempt to understand one another's spiritual motivations for acting in one way or the other. Growing in mutual understanding is already a step toward healing and peace for our world.

The dialogue at the Gethsemani Encounter continued, this time with a simple yet very important distinction by Dom Armand: "Christ saved us by his life, not by his death. But his death is part of his life."[25] This straightforward response helps clarify a frequently misunderstood idea in Christianity. It is not the death of Jesus that is the source of salvation, but his life. It is not what was done to Jesus that changed the world, but what Jesus did, how he lived and loved. During the writing of this book, the Mel Gibson film *The Passion of the Christ* has made its splash in every theater and newspaper and on every TV talk show in this country. It has been very interesting (and a bit disturbing) to me that so much of the film and almost *all* the talk about the film has focused on the violence done to Jesus, as if that were important information. I have heard almost no one talking about what *Jesus* did (or did not do) in the movie. One thing he did *not* do (and which the movie was faithful in portraying) was respond to the violence that surrounded him with violence. Not once did he cause another person to suffer through word or action. He responded with understanding, compassion, and love. *That* is the salvific message of Jesus' life. His violent death was but a consequence of a life founded on love.

Let us look at a more contemporary example, similar in some ways to the story of the martyred monks in Algeria. As we all know, many of the police and firefighters who rushed into the flame-engulfed World Trade Center in New York City on September 11, 2001, died in their attempt to save others' lives. Their deaths certainly brought increased suffering to a situation already numb with pain. Their spontaneous actions, based on the selfless love that characterizes those dedicated to public service, certainly flowed from the clear intention to help others whose lives were in danger. Love always involves risk. What is important in considering the suffering that might result from any loving action is the purity of intention. The intention *behind* the decisions of both the Algerian monks and the New York firefighters is the key. When love is selfless and pure (as much as possible, of course), seeking the well-being of the other, it is always a good.

Sr. Mary Margaret Funk, another participant at the Gethsemani Encounter, focused her comments on what is sometimes called the question of *right intention*: "It seemed to me from personally speaking with Fr. Christian from Algeria, that his staying there was both a fidelity to his commitment as a monk in the community, and also an expression of his deep trust in the best in the others. He believed in the others' goodness, maybe even more than they did. So I think from a Buddhist view, it might help to see that he knew they were good, and so he stayed to make that statement with his life."[26] Sr. Mary Margaret's words point to one possible affirmation that we might make, namely, that right intention is one of the elements necessary in the practice of authentic compassion.

As she reported, Fr. Christian (the prior of the community, and one of seven monks killed) hoped that their carefully discerned choice to remain with the people of Algeria would be seen as a gesture of good will and peace, as if to say, "We believe in your inherent goodness." He did, in fact, in a testament written several months earlier, state quite clearly that he hoped their staying would bring no harm to the Algerian people, the militant fundamentalists included: "I do not see, in fact, how I could rejoice if the people I love were to be accused indiscriminately of my murder. . . . [It] would be too high a price to pay for what will, perhaps, be called the 'grace of martyrdom.'"[27] Fr. James Wiseman, adding his voice to the discussion, expressed his hope that others who might be considering terrorist acts might actually be moved by the nonviolent witness of the monks to choose another path. "In that sense," he said, the fact that the monks remained "[would be] a very positive step— even from a Buddhist point of view."[28]

Present at the encounter was Maha Ghosananda, a Cambodian Buddhist monk who lived through the horrors of Cambodia's reign of terror. In the midst of all the back-and-forth, one of the Christian monks turned to the much-venerated Ghosananda and asked him if he could shed light on the discussion from his own experience of remaining in a country engulfed by unbelievable violence. "He was a tiny man, wizened and spotted with age and possessed of a tranquility born of suffering," noted a journalist who was present. "During the reign of the Khmer Rouge, some fifty thousand of his fellow monks had been murdered, along with countless [others]."[29] Perhaps there was no one as suited as he to add a voice of wisdom to the debate.

Ghosananda stood and addressed the Buddhists and Christians gathered, "In Cambodia, we say if you know suffering then you know the *Dharma*, because the Buddha teaches only one thing: suffering and the freedom from suffering."[30] Ghosananda's reference to *knowing suffering* rings true with Thây's words, "We need to *touch suffering* in order for our compassion to be born."[31] Maha Ghosananda has lived most of his life threatened by violence and death. He certainly embodies fidelity to the patient practice of nonviolence, as did Gandhi, who, like the Christian monks in Algeria, died as a martyr for compassion and nonviolence in his beloved India. The Dalai Lama, on the other hand, hemmed in by the communist invasion of Tibet, chose to go into exile in India, while remaining in close contact and solidarity with the many Buddhist monks and nuns who have chosen to stay in the country— many of whom have been imprisoned and killed.

So what exactly *is* compassion? What *is* the relationship between suffering, love and spiritual practice? What we have seen is that there are different responses, even though it is clear that the fundamental choices of all are fairly similar: a spiritual practice that combines inner freedom and compassionate action. We have seen that these elements flow in and out of each other differently for different people. Both traditions acknowledge the reality of suffering and the importance of compassion as part of the path that leads us out of suffering.

One final dimension in this discussion on compassion, one that is common to both Buddhism and Christianity, has to do with the love of our "enemies." This again connects us with the practice of detachment, for without the right vision that comes from detachment, it is very difficult to break through the dualism that separates us from our enemies. In his Sermon on the Mount, probably the most significant teaching in the Christian Gospels, Jesus also touches on the need for our love to be born from a free and detached heart.

> If you love those who love you, what credit is that to you? For even sinners love those who love them. If you do good to those who do good to you, what credit is that to you? For even sinners do the same. If you lend money to those from whom you hope to receive, what credit is that to you? Even sinners lend to sinners, to receive as much again. But love your enemies, do good, and lend, expecting nothing in return. . . . Be merciful, just as your Father is merciful. (Luke 6:32-26)

To love with a detached heart is not easy. We all know that. To love our enemies, we must do more than just change the way we act. It is not about biting the bullet and forcing a smile. It is a call to a total transformation of our minds. Commenting on the first of the Five Mindfulness Trainings, Thây says, "We see the suffering caused by the destruction of life, and we vow to cultivate compassion and use it as a source of energy for the protection of people, animals, plants and minerals."[32] The vow, though, goes beyond just our actions. By vowing to cultivate compassion one commits to reorienting one's entire life—heart, mind, body, and soul—in the direction of compassion. Says Thây, "We cannot condone any act of killing, even in our minds."[33]

Jesus taught this when he broadened the understanding of killing to include the anger of our hearts and minds. Again, from the Sermon on the Mount, "You have heard that it was said to those of ancient times, 'You shall not murder. . . .' But I say to you that if you are angry with a brother or sister, you will be liable to judgment" (Matt. 5:21-22). He continues the teaching with regard to adultery, making reference to "adultery in the heart" (5:28). This transformation of our minds (and our whole being) is what the New Testament calls *metanoia*, and what St. Paul means when he speaks of *having the mind of Christ* (1 Cor. 2:16). What happened to Bill Pelke the night that he saw in his mind his dead grandmother's gentle face was a total reorientation of his life in the direction of compassion, a complete *metanoia*. He vowed to save the life of a teenage girl condemned to die, a vow born of a compassion that *looks deeply* into the suffering of the other and chooses to enter into that suffering out of love.

The Dalai Lama says, commenting on the usual biased state of mind that robs us of the capacity for true compassion, "We have an attitude of distance from people we consider as unfriendly or enemies and a disproportionate sense of closeness or attachment toward those whom we consider to be our friends. . . . Until we overcome these prejudices, we have no possibility of generating genuine compassion."[34] Eckhart echoes a similar sentiment, "It is necessary that you should make no distinction in the [human] family, not being closer to yourself than to another. You must love all equally, respect and regard them equally. . . . In the love that one gives there is no duality."[35]

The Dalai Lama continues, "If you carefully examine the nature of compassion, you will also find that genuine compassion can be extended even to one's enemies, those whom you consider to be hostile towards you. In contrast, compassion mixed with attachment cannot be extended to someone whom you consider to be your enemy."[36] It is clear that for both traditions, genuine compassion cannot be separated from the practice of *mindful seeing*.

Thây shows how this mindful seeing, this contemplative vision, leads us down the path of compassion: "When you look deeply into your anger," he says, "you will see that the person you call your enemy is also suffering."[37] There are few teachings that are more important than this one for the present situation of conflict, violence, and war that grips our world. Unless we are able to develop the capacity of understanding our enemy's suffering, we cannot possibly begin to build a world of peace. We must be willing to "look deeply" and contemplatively into the face of the *other*, the one who is unique, the one who believes differently than I, and even the one who might do us harm. For Christians, as noted above, this *other person* is, in the end, Christ himself (Matt. 25). In his final testament, Fr. Christian, the prior of the Algerian Trappist monks, addressed his would-be assassin with these words: "And also you, the friend of my final moment, who would not be aware of what you are doing, yes, I also say this *Thank You* and this *A-Dieu* to you *in whom I see the face of God.*"[38]

The nuances and connections between spiritual practice, suffering, and detachment are many, and perhaps what our dialogue helps us to affirm is the fact that the prism of compassion is made up of many different colors. There is no *single* answer, no *single* path. Learning to love carries with it the risk of suffering, and freeing ourselves from suffering teaches us to love. The many colors only make the light more radiant.

9

The Tree of the Cross

The Cross: Path to Freedom

There is no way to touch on the theme of suffering and compassion in a dialogue between Buddhists and Christians without looking deeply into the crucifixion of Jesus. It is an image that cannot be overlooked, a symbol that defies all pious explanations. For Christians, the journey into the mystery of the cross is at the very essence of discipleship, but in no way is it an easy journey. On one hand, the follower of Jesus is faced with the sufferings and uncertainties that form part of any human life, while at the same time grappling with the paradoxical, almost scandalous sayings from St. Paul, such as "May I never boast of anything but the cross of our Lord Jesus Christ" (Gal. 6:14). The cross is much more than a historical event for Christians; it is a spiritual path that leads through the fire of suffering into the freedom of the children of God. What, though, does all this mean, especially in the context of interreligious dialogue?

Though Eckhart speaks frequently about suffering, he says almost nothing about the historical crucifixion of Jesus. Because of his primary interest in the mystical dimension of the Christian life, Eckhart does not focus much on Jesus' human death on the cross. He is much more interested in how the death of Jesus becomes a pathway that leads to life—not only for Jesus but for us as well. Says Eckhart, "We must take suffering upon ourselves and follow the lamb [of God—Jesus] in sorrow as in joy."[1] Eckhart's teachings are meant to awaken us to the spiritual value of the cross, namely, learning to embrace with inner freedom and detachment the pain and sufferings of life. The cross, seen from this perspective, is more of a path to follow than something we are encouraged to imitate.

A healthy spirituality of the cross leads us not into a glorification of suffering but into the paschal journey of Jesus Christ, which passes through death into the fullness of life in the resurrection. The cross, for Eckhart, is important inasmuch as it leads us to a freer and more faithful following of Jesus. In other words, it is not the carrying of the cross in and of itself that is of special spiritual value for Eckhart, but doing so with faith, detachment, and inner tranquility. Commenting on Jesus' words, "If any want to become my followers, let them deny themselves, and take up their cross and follow me" (Matt. 16:24), Eckhart says, "[This] is not merely a commandment, as is commonly said and thought: it is a promise and a divine prescription for a [person] to make all his suffering, all his deeds, and all his life happy and joyful. It is more a reward than a commandment."[2]

The "way of the cross" for Eckhart is the path of detachment that leads us to true joy. This is why he can call it a "reward." We recall here that the Meister defines detachment as a mind that stands unmoved by joy, sorrow, honor, shame, and disgrace "as a mountain of lead stands unmoved by a breath of wind."[3] So for Eckhart, it is when life's sufferings are embraced with abandonment, standing steadfast and with deep trust in God's faithfulness, that a person is led to true happiness and joy. Jesus' words from the cross, "Father, into your hands I commend my spirit" (Luke 23:46), are an expression of what Eckhart might call liberating abandonment—the utter freedom and joy that is born from the embrace of that kind of suffering which the Dalai Lama calls "inevitable suffering."

Jesus' willingness to embrace the "inevitable suffering" that came upon him is an expression of his deepest freedom. Detachment finds no greater expression for Christians than in the icon of the cross. To embrace the cross means to live life fully and freely, trusting that in the deepest realms of life, where we dwell *in* and *with* God, all is well, even in the midst of life's pain and suffering. Eckhart, with a bit of humor, encourages us down this path of inner freedom. Keep God alone in your mind, he says, and "forge ahead without qualms. . . . If a painter had to plan every brush-stroke with the first, he would paint nothing. . . . So, follow the first step and continue: you will get to the right place, and all is well."[4] In other words, live this moment freely and fully, even when it brings with it a sharing in the suffering of the world. Trust the inner strength that is available in the present moment; all shall be well. Not bad spiritual advice, actually. It is precisely what Jesus did. He forged ahead in his mission of love, step by step, not worrying too much about the possible consequences. Death, after all, is part of life. Thây says, in a similar vein, "Go back to yourself and dwell in mindfulness. [This] is the best practice in difficult moments. Mindfulness of breathing is your island, where you can be safe and happy, knowing that whatever happens, you are doing your best. . . . You can take refuge here and now. You only need to dwell in the present moment."[5]

The embrace of the cross as a source of liberating joy is a principal theme in the Gospels, especially in the Gospel of John. Facing his impending death, Jesus says with true single-mindedness, "I lay down my life in order to take it up again. No one takes it from me, but I lay it down of my own accord. I have power to lay it down, and I have power to take it up again. I have received this . . . from my Father" (John 10:17-18). This free embrace of the inevitable, the laying down of his life, is not something that happens to Jesus only on the cross; it is part of his entire life. It is the fruit of a freedom born in love, and it is as available to all of us as it was for Jesus. Jesus chooses this path of loving freedom throughout his life. When he sits at table to eat with sinners and tax collectors, in order to express to them God's unconditional love (Matt. 9:11), he lays down his life, aware that such choices will bring with them serious repercussions. When Jesus enters into dialogue with the Canaanite woman who begs him to heal her daughter, he lays down his life, opening himself up to a new risk, to a new and more profound understanding of himself and his mission (Matt. 15:21-28). When Jesus looks down from the cross upon his enemies to speak his final words of healing and peace, "Father, forgive them: for they do not know what they are doing," he lays down his life out of love (Luke 23:34). This inner freedom, born of love and self-giving, is expressed in an ancient Christian hymn found in St. Paul's letter to the disciples in the city of Philippi: "Let the same mind be in you that was in Christ Jesus, who, though he was in the form of God, did not regard equality with God as something to be exploited, but emptied himself, taking the form of a slave . . . and became obedient to the point of death, even death on a cross" (Phil. 2:5-8).

The cross can be "understood" only when it is seen as the culmination of the freely embraced *laying down of life* that marked Jesus' entire existence. His choices flowed from an inner freedom that transcended any attachment to self-preservation. His love was a continual self-emptying, a self-emptying that was brought to a tragic fulfillment on the cross. It is this free embrace of a love that transcends death that is at the core of the Christian devotion to the cross. This is not to deny in any way the ugliness of the historical crucifixion of Jesus; it is instead a profound intuition that only in the act of self-giving are we fully liberated.

The Cross as Tree of Life

There is a *koan* from the ancient Zen collection of *koans* called the *Mumonkan*, or *Gateless Gate*, that is entitled "Kyogen's Man Up a Tree." It goes like this:

Master Kyogen said, "It's like a man up a tree, hanging from a branch by his mouth; his hands cannot grasp a branch, his feet won't reach a bough. Suppose there is another man under the tree who asks him, 'What is the meaning of Bodhidarma's coming from the west?' If he does not respond, he goes against the wish of the questioner. If he answers, he will lose his life. At such a time, how should he respond?"[6]

As is true with all Zen *koans*, there is no correct answer to the question or situation presented. The task of the *koan* is to help move us beyond our dualistic thinking mind, so as to enter into the spacious mind of nonduality and freedom. Commenting one day on this particular *koan*, Zen teacher Ruben Habito said, "Kyogen's man up in the tree is not so different than Jesus on the cross." The statement at first struck me as strange, but I have found it to be a statement of great wisdom. The man hanging in the tree by his mouth is faced with the same fundamental questions of life and death, of inner truth and freedom, that Jesus was faced with. Jesus' whole life, in a sense, is a lived response to *the great question* of life and death and inner freedom. This is true with our lives, as well. Do we answer the question and speak the truth—ready to pay the consequences—or do we remain silent and immobile, paralyzed and enslaved by fear? Jesus, like the Buddha and many other great teachers, chose to speak the truth.

The *koan* of the man in the tree calls to mind the beginning of the Judeo-Christian story; it is a story that begins symbolically in a garden full of trees, including one tree that is the "tree of the knowledge of good and evil." *This* tree, however, is also a tree of death (Gen. 2:17). It is the tree where we learn humility and respect for the Great Mystery, the Ultimate Reality we call God. It is the tree where the wave learns that she is water, but where she also learns that she is not "the" Water. The garden, complete with the tree of the knowledge of good and evil, is the place where we learn that we are born *of God*, but where we also learn that we are *not God*.

For Christians, the garden, with its tree of life and death, appears again in the story of the crucifixion of Jesus. John's Gospel says, "Now there was a garden in the place where he was crucified" (19:41). The death of Jesus, according to John, happens symbolically "in the garden" where the story of creation began. This time, though, the tree of death—the cross—does not have the final word in the story. The resurrection of Jesus is a symbolic retelling by John of the story of the tree of death in the Book of Genesis; this time, though, it blossoms into the tree of life. Jesus' self-emptying on the cross announces the dawning of a new creation.

> Then I saw a new heaven and a new earth. The former heaven and the former earth had passed away. . . . The angel showed me the river of the water of life. . . . On either side of the river is the tree of life with its twelve kinds of fruit, producing its fruit each month; and the leaves of the tree are for the healing of the nations. Nothing accursed will be found there anymore. (Rev. 21:1; 22:1-3)

The scriptural symbols of the tree of life and death invite us into the paradox of the cross, which is the paradox of the paschal event of Jesus' death and resurrection. Like the man hanging in the tree by his mouth, looking death in the face, so too did Jesus also live his life looking death in the face. He embraced his suffering and the suffering of the world in the depths of his compassionate heart, freely choosing to *stand with* all who suffer. As Thây said earlier, Jesus "did not hide from suffering." His death and his life were his answer to the *great question*; they were his very being lived as truth. In the end, his truth was his death, and his death was no-death; it was life. Says St. Paul: "This perishable body must put on imperishability, and this mortal body must put on immortality . . . then the saying that is written will be fulfilled: Death has been swallowed up in victory. Where, O death, is your victory? Where, O death, is your sting?" (1 Cor. 15:53-55).

To embrace the cross means to answer the great question that is posed to us as we hang in the tree of life and death. It is to speak the truth in its fullest sense, and this only happens when one's entire life *becomes truth*. This is what Eckhart calls plunging into the naked being of God.[7] When this happens, there is perfect freedom—the beginning of eternal life. The man hanging in the tree answers the great question, and the dead tree blossoms into fullness. "I am the way, and the truth, and the life," Jesus said (John 14:6). What Jesus speaks and what he *is* are one and the same; his whole life is a speaking of the truth. "Whoever has once been touched by truth," says Eckhart, "though it entailed all the pangs of hell, that one could never turn from [it] for an instant."[8] In 1980, in the small country of El Salvador in Central America, Archbishop Oscar Romero was assassinated while celebrating the Eucharist in the chapel of a small hospital for persons with cancer. His great "crime" was to speak the truth in the midst of a world of oppressive lies. Not long before his death, aware that his life was in danger, Romero noted that even though a prophet may be killed, "no one can kill the voice of justice."[9]

Jesus also spoke the truth, the truth of his very being. His being and his truth were but a manifestation of the very being and truth of God. For that reason, his death is not death in the ultimate sense; it is life. "Our whole life ought to be *being*," continues Eckhart. "So far as our life is being, so far it is in God."[10] The tree can be cut down, but the ultimate source of the life of the tree is eternal; it embraces both death and life. Once we touch deeply this ultimate dimension of reality, as Thây says so frequently, we are set free. Death is swallowed up forever. "Once you are capable of touching the water, you will not mind the coming and going of the waves. You are no longer concerned about the coming and going of the wave. You are no longer afraid."[11]

Since Jesus' life is lived *in God*, immersed in the Ultimate Reality, his embrace of death is an expression of perfect freedom; it is the culmination of a life lived freely and fully in the present moment, the eternal *Now* of God. In Jesus, death and life are one. The tree of death is the tree of life. His truth—

his *being in God*—expresses itself as fully in life as in death. This is what we, his disciples, are invited to taste as well. We are invited into the radical freedom and truth of Jesus. His death, embraced as the freedom to be in God, is our path of life. By our abiding in Christ (John 15:6-10), what our Buddhist brothers and sisters would call "taking refuge in Christ," we, too, walk his path of liberating truth. The cross is not the end of the journey, however. For Christians, it is in a very real way only the beginning. It is where freedom and truth blossom into fullness. This is why St. Paul can say so boldly, "May I never boast of anything except the cross of our Lord Jesus Christ" (Gal. 6:14). The cross of Jesus can be "understood" only in this way, in the way a Zen *koan* is understood. It must be embraced as a paradox. The cross is the tree of violence and death. The cross is also the tree of freedom and life. As Master Mumon himself said many centuries ago in commenting on the *koan* of the man in the tree, "If you can respond to [this *koan*] fittingly, you will give life to those who have been dead, and put to death those who have been alive."[12]

The *koan* of the man up in the tree is similar to the contemporary parable of the person who falls over the cliff and who, just before plunging to his death in the ravine below, grabs onto a branch. Left dangling over the precipice, he cries out, "Is there anyone up there?" As his hands begin to slip, he hears an answer, "This is God. I am here. Just let go and I will catch you." A few seconds pass by, and the man cries out again, "Is there anyone *else* up there?" He, like all of us, quickly shies away from having to answer the *great question*, for it may require the death of his self-sufficiency. It is only by letting go that we experience the fullness of freedom. We learn this step by step, breath by breath, in our daily lives.

Jesus, like the Zen masters, leads his disciples along the path of dying to the self-sufficient ego. This path is the way of the cross: "If any want to become my followers, let them deny themselves and take up their cross daily and follow me" (Luke 9:23). Jesus lives his freedom and his truth—that oneness with God that is stronger than death—and he invites us to do the same. He calls us to die to the illusion that we are separate from God, that death has any ultimate power over us. In *Living Buddha, Living Christ*, Thây tells the story of St. Francis of Assisi asking the almond tree to tell him about God. "It was winter. There were no leaves, flowers, or fruits. . . . In just a few seconds the tree was covered with beautiful flowers. We are entirely capable of touching the ultimate dimension."[13] We are never separated from God. The wave is never separate from the water. "We suffer if we only touch the waves, but if we learn how to stay in touch with the water, we feel the greatest relief. Touching nirvana, touching the kingdom of God, liberates us."[14] We too are able to say with St. Paul, "Where, O death, is your sting?"

To live this liberating truth of our oneness with the Ultimate Dimension is to experience the resurrection—the dead tree blossoming into the fullness of life. It is what St. Paul calls "putting on imperishability." This is the ultimate expression of Eckhart's teaching on detachment. Do we really believe that letting go of our lives is the key to living life in abundance? This is not a question to be asked just at the end of our lives. It is *the question* of our lives. Eternal life, as we saw early on in this book, is not something that happens in some distant future. Eternal life is here and now, and we enter into it to the extent that we answer the question posed to us as we hang by our teeth from the tree of death and life.

In the foreword to *Living Buddha, Living Christ*, Brother David Steindl-Rast speaks of Thây's life from this perspective, namely, that of living *the great question* of life and death. Steindl-Rast, Fr. Dan Berrigan, and Thây met in New York City in 1968, an encounter that culminated with the celebration of the Eucharist—the supreme sacramental expression of Jesus' own lived response to *the great question*. Brother David remembers the day well:

> It was April 4, 1968. How could I forget that date! Afterwards we went to listen to a lecture by Hans Küng, but the event was interrupted by the shattering news that Dr. Martin Luther King, Jr., had been assassinated [King had nominated Thây for the Nobel Peace Prize]. The [eucharistic] ritual we celebrated earlier that evening had once again been reenacted in history: "Greater love no one has but to lay down one's life for one's friends" (John 15:13). Jesus had done this 2,000 years ago; Martin had done it today; and Thây, in risking his own life to *speak out uncompromisingly for peace in Vietnam*, was allowing himself to walk in the same direction. "Nhat Hanh is a free man who has acted as a free man in favor of his brothers [and sisters], moved by the spiritual dynamic of a tradition of religious compassion," Thomas Merton wrote.[15]

What these words convey to us is quite simple: Thây's entire life has been lived as an answer to *the great question*. He has touched the tree of death, he has walked the *way of the cross*, and he stands among us today as a living embodiment of the tree of life, the tree of compassion. In Thây, we glimpse anew the lives of Jesus and the Buddha and all the great saints and enlightened beings who have lived the truth of their lives with freedom and compassion. They stand among us like giant trees whose branches stretch out beyond space and time, beyond death into life. They are like the tree in Jesus' parable of the mustard seed: "It is the greatest of shrubs and becomes a tree, so that the birds of the air come and make nests in its branches" (Matt. 13:32). Many of us have found in these teachers a home, a place to rest and to be nourished by the ancient wisdom of these venerable spiritual traditions.

The Icon of the Cross

In *Going Home* Thây says of the image of the crucified Christ, "This is a very painful image for me. It does not convey joy or peace, and this does not do justice to Jesus. I hope that our Christian friends will also portray Jesus in other ways, like sitting in the lotus position or doing walking meditation."[16] Thây's words are understandable and have been echoed by other people. D. T. Suzuki writes, "Whenever I see a crucified figure of Christ, I cannot help thinking of the gap that lies deep between Christianity and Buddhism."[17] No one, not even Christians, can deny the fact that the cross of Jesus Christ is ugly and painful. But that is not all it is. It is also, for most Christians, an icon of love. Much of what follows in this chapter is a response to Thây, a response born of my own struggle, prayer, and reflection, my own attempt to discover in the cross of Jesus a path to life. I appreciate Thây's honest acknowledgment of pain with regard to the image of the cross, and, as a brother, I offer my own insights so as to help bridge the "gap" that lies between us.

Thây continues his brotherly critique by wishing that Christians might find "other ways" to portray Jesus, other than the image of the crucified Christ. Christian art has, in fact, produced over the centuries a remarkable array of images of Jesus, frequently portrayed in ways particular to the different cultures where Christianity is practiced. One of the most common is that of Jesus, the Good Shepherd. Based on the Gospel story of a shepherd who leaves behind his ninety-nine sheep in search of the one lost sheep (Luke 15:1-6), the Good Shepherd is a lovely image, a favorite among Christians, one often used in teaching children about the love of God. We are all that lone sheep at one time or another in our lives, and it is comforting and healing to know that the shepherd risks losing all the other sheep just to find the lost one. The image of Jesus walking along, carrying the lost sheep on his shoulders, expresses the abundant mercy and compassion of God.

Other depictions of Jesus in Christian art include many murals and paintings of Jesus eating the Jewish Passover meal, the Last Supper, with his disciples, as well as the scene of his baptism by John in the Jordan River. Da Vinci's *Last Supper* is one of the most famous depictions in the world. There are images of Jesus healing the sick, the lame, and the blind. African Christian artists often portrays Jesus with an African face, and in Latin America there abound scenes of the birth of Jesus surrounded by indigenous peoples bearing gifts common to their local culture. At the Jeevan Dhara ashram, where Sr. Vandana lives near the banks of the Ganges River in India, there is a striking painting of Jesus sitting in the lotus position, offering living water to the Samaritan woman (John 4). A similar sculpture of Jesus, seated in the lotus position and looking out into the four directions, graces Saccidananda ashram in southern India, where Fr. Bede Griffiths lived for many years.

One of the most well known images of Jesus is that of the Sacred Heart. This very popular depiction of Jesus usually shows a very peaceful face of Christ, with a heart that is both wounded and aflame with love. One of the reasons why this image of Jesus might be so dear to many is that it brings together in one image both the reality of Jesus' passion and death and the consoling peace of his mercy and all-embracing love. The image of the Sacred Heart attempts to convey the message that "God is love," but it does so from the uniquely Christian perspective of a God who, through his Son, risks suffering with us through faithful and unconditional solidarity.

It is this dimension of unconditional solidarity that, perhaps more than any other aspect, points to a particularly Christian understanding of compassion. Solidarity, a term that has been used frequently in Catholic social teaching, might best be defined as the choice to *stand with* those who suffer. His Holiness Pope John Paul II calls it "a firm and persevering determination to commit oneself to the common good."[18] Solidarity is part of what motivated the Trappist monks to remain in Algeria, in spite of the danger and violence. John Paul II goes on to say that "it is the unity of the human race which must ultimately inspire our solidarity," and this unity is expressed in love for one's neighbor, even when the neighbor is an enemy. Solidarity requires readiness "for sacrifice, even the ultimate one: to lay down one's life for one's brethren."[19]

Solidarity reminds us that we do not walk the path alone, but together. This is why Pope John Paul II speaks of it in connection with "unity . . . expressed in love for one's neighbor." As Thây mentioned in the previous chapter, "You are not the only person who suffers. Your sisters and brothers also suffer. . . . If you touch suffering deeply in yourself and in the other person, understanding will arise."[20] For Christians, the icon of the cross sacramentalizes and makes tangible the solidarity of Jesus, his choice to *stand with* us in our suffering. Suffering is part of the common ground we share, and therefore it is a source of hope and healing that Jesus stands with us in this dimension of our lives.

It is not uncommon to hear of people who, because of some deep suffering in their own lives, experience a dramatic spiritual transformation, a mystical breakthrough, which gives birth to compassion and solidarity toward suffering people all over the world. Some of these people dedicate the rest of their lives to alleviating the sufferings of others, based on this experience of *oneness-in-suffering*. As St. Paul reminded the community of Corinth: "If one member [of the body] suffers, all suffer together with it" (1 Cor. 12:26). Suffering serves as a teacher, showing us the way into solidarity and love, opening our hearts to a deeper insight into the interconnectedness of all beings. To use one of Thây's phrases, through suffering we *inter*-are.

A Presbyterian pastor in New York, Thomas Tewell, writing recently in a journal, recounts the story of two friends, Don and John, both of whom had to face unexpected tragedies in the midst of what had been, up until then, very healthy and successful lives. It began when Don suffered a sudden stroke a few years ago, one that left him almost completely paralyzed, capable of only minimal speech. Don's friends, including John, remained committed companions, however, meeting every Tuesday morning with Don for prayer and support.

One Sunday night, the other friend, John, received a phone call that launched him into his own dark night of tragedy. His daughter had been found under a tarpaulin in the woods—murdered with a single bullet in her head. Crushed by the tragedy, John called his friends from the support group the following Tuesday morning to say that he would not be able to make the weekly meeting; he did not have the strength to join the others that day. They understood and were about to hang up when Don spoke haltingly from his wheelchair, "Tell John I want to see him." Tewell recounts that John, much to the group's surprise, showed up, only to find a house full of "sophisticated people [who] were all at a loss as to what to say after such a tragedy. They were standing around, hemming and hawing, when Don slowly wheeled his chair over to John and just put out his arms. John knelt down and sobbed in Don's arms."[21] Don's embrace was a gesture of compassionate solidarity, as if to say to John, "I cannot take your pain away from you, but I can be with you in the midst of it."

Tewell says, reflecting on the story, "God doesn't cause all suffering. But . . . out of it God can bring good. How do I know? The cross is empty. God raised the one who was crucified from the dead and he now lives. He can comfort us in our suffering."[22] This story is an example of the way Christians experience the cross of Christ as a source of the kind of solidarity that is born when we are not afraid to touch our own and others' suffering. The result of this solidarity is that it evokes in us an experience of nondual *oneness-in-suffering*. Don's outstretched arms, into which John buried his head and wept, were the arms of one who had touched suffering deeply in himself. Looking at this scene from a Christian perspective, one can say that Don's outstretched arms are also the outstretched arms of the crucified Christ. The icon of the cross becomes the lens through which Tewell sees the salvific embrace of Christ reaching out, through Don's arms, to embrace and heal our suffering world.

As Tewell's comments show, we Christians speak from a lived experience of nonduality in suffering, almost without realizing it. We say, "God comforts us in our suffering," even though we know that the arms which reach out to communicate that comforting love are our very own arms. Don's embrace of his friend John is Christ's embrace; it is God's loving embrace flowing through us. Don, reaching out awkwardly from the confines of his wheelchair, is but one manifestation of the eternal embrace of God, made flesh in history through the crucified Christ's embrace of the suffering of the world. The practice of Christian solidarity awakens us to our *being* the body of Christ. Though we do not always have the words to express the reality, we know intuitively that we are the arms with which God embraces the world: "I was hungry and you gave me food. . . . I was sick and you took care of me" (Matt. 25:35-36). We are Christ's body, and the compassion that flows from the collective body is nothing less than the compassion of Christ himself.

The first of the *Four Great Vows* of the Bodhisattva states, "Sentient beings are numberless; I vow to free them." As Ruben Habito points out, "The central characteristic of a sentient being [is the] capacity to suffer. Not only the *capacity*, but the actuality of *being in suffering*. . . . If one has glimpsed that world of nonduality in an experiential way . . . [then] one must become fully at one with" those who suffer.[23] The *vow* of the bodhisattva is rooted in the experience of nonduality; it is oneness-in-suffering. For Christians this is *the key* to the practice of compassion. It is the willingness to lose one's separate self through communion with another's suffering. In the words of Jesus, "No one has greater love than this, to lay down one's life for one's friends" (John 15:13).

One of the reasons why the icon of the Sacred Heart of Jesus is so popular is that it portrays the human solidarity of Christ who draws near to us in love, to communicate his oneness with us in our suffering. The human face and heart of Jesus offer us a glimpse of who God is. It is through this contemplative *glimpse* of the compassionate face of God, reflected in the human face of Jesus, that we are touched by a spiritual energy capable of transforming us into persons who radiate the love of God to others. The heart of Christ points us simultaneously to the heart of God and to our own human heart. Or to say it in a different way, the Sacred Heart of Christ awakens us to the presence of God who dwells in loving solidarity within our own human heart. In a deeply mystical way, what we are drawn toward is the nondual awakening to the truth that there is, in the end, simply *one heart*, aflame with compassion for the world.

Commenting on the image of the Sacred Heart, Beatrice Bruteau draws our attention to the mystical dimensions of this popular devotion by recalling a particular moment in the Gospel of John's story of the Last Supper (John 13:23-25). The Gospel recounts the scene of one of Jesus' disciples, the one called the "beloved disciple," reclining back against Jesus to ask him a question. Says Bruteau:

> When John wished to move closer to Jesus . . . he just leaned back toward him. We do a similar thing in our consciousness. . . . In order to move closer to the heart of Jesus, we "lean back toward" him by sinking

down toward the center of being. . . . Each deeper level that we sink to, position our sense of "I" in, brings us closer to the heart or center of Jesus, because it is bringing us closer to our own center. . . . We are *backing up into each other.* . . . Were we to face him we would always remain outside him. We do not look *at* him. . . . [We] have to enter inside the subject, enter into that subject's own awareness. . . . The consciousness of Jesus, the interior of his heart, is becoming more "available" to us, "known" to us, "familiar" to us—because our own heart is sharing those same dispositions. We are coming to know the Sacred Heart from the inside, inside his consciousness and inside our consciousness. And our "inside" is coming to be more and more coincident with his "inside." His heart is becoming the heart of our heart.[24]

Bruteau artfully paints for us a picture of mystical union, nonduality. The power of a holy icon lies precisely in its capacity to evoke in the viewer, in the one who "prays the icon," an experience of his or her essential oneness with God.

As we can see, the artistic and devotional portrayals of Jesus are rich and varied, and they focus on many different aspects of his life and his message. Most of these depictions of Jesus focus predominantly on some aspect of his mission of love. What is important in all of them, however, is their capacity to evoke in us that same oneness in love, that same capacity for solidarity and communion-in-suffering.

He Did Not Hide from Suffering

Returning to Thây's earlier statement about the painful symbol of the cross, why then do we not hold onto all the life-giving and peaceful portrayals of Jesus and deemphasize the artistic depiction of the crucified Christ? Why, ask our Buddhist brothers and sisters, do we persist in venerating such a sad and painful image? First of all, we Christians do ourselves no favor by denying the fact that Jesus died a very ugly and violent death. Whether we like it or not, this too is part of the life of Christ. In fact, it is precisely his death on the cross that shows us, albeit in a paradoxical way, his most profound act of loving-kindness. As he said, "No one has greater love than this" (John 15:13). It is only from the perspective of a love that *remains with* the beloved—no matter what happens—that one can understand the centrality (dare I say "the beauty?") of the cross of Christ.

Jesus is the one who shows us what it means to *stands with* the other person, willing to suffer out of love for him or her. "I am the good shepherd," says Jesus. "The good shepherd lays down his life for the sheep. The hired hand, who is not a shepherd and does not own the sheep, sees the wolf coming and leaves the sheep and runs away" (John 10:11-12). Jesus does not run away. He *stays with* us in our suffering. The cross is not a glorification of suffering per se, but an icon of that kind of love that is willing to *stand with* those who suffer. Eckhart says that God is the one who "stands by us, and remains standing by us, constant and unmoved."[25] Parents live this great truth every single day of their lives, in one continual act of solidarity—standing with and silently laying down their lives for their children. Jesus calls this laying down of one's life the greatest expression of love. As Thây said earlier, "You love someone when that someone needs you. When that someone suffers, your love relieves his or her suffering. . . . That is the meaning of love."[26]

What is important to underscore at this point, for it is something that at times gets in the way of Christian–Buddhist dialogue, is that the God of Christians is *not* a God who is fascinated with suffering. To *stand with* one who suffers is not the same as agreeing with or condoning that suffering. This is not to deny the fact that there have been at different times in the church's history unhealthy forms of idealization and exaltation of suffering. This is *not*, however, sound Christian theology.

Most Jewish and Christian theologians agree that suffering is a manifestation of evil; it is the result of sin, greed, and the selfish attachment to one's ego. It is the consequence of turning one's back on God and God's presence in the world. The reality of the millions of people who suffer each day from hunger, for example, is directly connected with the sin of greed. People in Africa die of hunger while people in Europe and the United States control the world markets and throw away tons of food each day. An unhealthy theology might say, "This is God's will. The wealthy nations have been blessed with abundance from God. This is just the way it is." This simply is not true. God does not give a few people food in abundance, while leaving the multitudes hungry. Hunger is a direct consequence of human greed, and greed is sin. It is to turn our backs on God, who is present in our hungry neighbor. "I was hungry," said Jesus, "and you gave me food" (Matt. 25:35). Suffering is *not* part of God's plan. There is no place in Christian theology for a morose understanding of a God who wills suffering. Having said this, though, we must acknowledge that suffering *is* a reality that we must face; we cannot run away from suffering. For a Christian, though it is true that Jesus' life takes him into the fire of suffering, this is only a small part of his greater mission: to help all beings "have life, and have it abundantly" (John 10:10).

So, what do we do with the "painful image" of the cross? First of all, it is important to affirm that this is *precisely* what it is: a painful image. Did God condone the suffering of Jesus, standing back at a distance while the beloved son was murdered? If our image of God is of some eternal being "up there in heaven" who watches us from afar, then perhaps this is the only conclusion that is possible. But if God is closer to us than we are to ourselves, as Eckhart teaches, then there is no such thing as being distant from God. The wave cannot exist apart from the water. God is not far from Jesus on the cross. God is the breath of Jesus' every breath.

Was Jesus' life *supposed* to end this way? No. Did it *have* to end this way. No. But it did. Jesus was a man aflame with the love of God, whose message and actions in favor of the poor, the dispossessed, and the unwanted got in the way of those who were drunk with religious and political power in his day, so they killed him. Jesus' death, seen from a sociopolitical perspective, is no different from the death of Buddhist monks and nuns in Tibet or of Mahatma Gandhi or Martin Luther King, Jr. People who practice universal love in a world that is not ready to embrace this way of life are considered obstacles to the status quo. In the mind of those obsessed with holding onto power, all obstacles that get in the way of their perverse plans must be removed. Jesus was a man of humble origins, a faithful Jew, whose great "sin" was that he "did not hide himself from suffering."[27] He felt and touched the suffering of those around him. He embraced those who were rejected. Because of this, he was considered an obstacle to the status quo. The obstacle had to be removed.

When we read in the New Testament phrases such as, "The Son of Man *must* undergo great suffering, and be rejected by the elders, chief priests, and scribes, and be killed" (Luke 9:22), we must be very careful not to read into those words the idea that this terrible death was in some way part of a great plot, dreamed up by a Wizard-of-Oz-type God who controls the destiny of the world by pulling levers and pushing buttons. To see the life and death of Jesus through this lens is terribly flawed, not to speak of the distorted image of God that such an interpretation portrays.

As Dom Armand so clearly stated in the previous chapter, "Christ saved us by his life, not by his death. But his death is part of his life."[28] Jesus did not *have* to suffer and die because it was part of some morbid plan of God. He suffered and died because of the way he lived. He *knew* that to embrace lepers, to forgive prostitutes and adulterers, and to eat with sinners and gentiles was against the law. He also knew—deep within his heart of hearts—that to act in this way was part of God's law of love. Jesus was humble, but he was not naïve; he knew that if he broke the laws, he would be considered an obstacle to the status quo and that therefore he would have to "undergo great suffering, be rejected and killed." He chose the path of God's law of love and freely embraced the consequences that such a choice entailed.

Archbishop Oscar Romero, the martyred archbishop of San Salvador, also knew that he very likely would have to *undergo great suffering* in order to be faithful to his mission of solidarity with and compassion for the poor. In the three years prior to his death, many priests, religious sisters, and community leaders had already been killed. Aware of the danger, he made a choice to

stand with his people, rather than "hide from suffering." He said in one sermon, "I was told this week that I should be careful, that something was being
plotted against my life. I trust in the Lord."[29] Several months later, when the
country's military leaders offered him an armed bodyguard, he replied, "I
want to repeat to you what I said once before: the shepherd does not want
security while they give no security to his flock."[30] Again, just four months
before his assassination, he said, "I want to assure you—and I ask for your
prayers to be faithful to this promise—that I will not abandon my people, but
that together with them I will run all the risks that my ministry demands."[31]
Finally, just minutes before his death, Romero spoke the following words in
his homily, "God's reign is already present on our earth. . . . That is the hope
that inspires Christians."[32] God's reign surely was present, and it was made
manifest in Romero and in the gift of his life, poured out in love for his
people. Once again the tree of death blossomed into the fullness of life.

I share these words from Archbishop Romero not only because I think that
his untimely death shows us what "not hiding from suffering" might mean for
us today, but also because it serves as an example of what the New Testament
is attempting to communicate when it says that Jesus had to suffer. Romero
knew that he would have to suffer, not because God had whispered in his ear
and warned him ahead of time but because of the simple fact that he lived
with his eyes open to what was happening around him. When Buddhist nuns
in Tibet openly speak of their allegiance to the Dalai Lama and call for just
policies to be enacted by the Chinese government, they do so obviously aware
that they will very likely "have to undergo great suffering." To practice love in
a world still bound by hatred brings with it the inescapable reality of suffering, but it is this kind of love that bears the fruit of peace.

When Jesus says to the heartbroken disciples on their way to Emmaus,
"Was it not necessary that the Messiah should suffer these things and then
enter into his glory?" (Luke 24:26), he is not just trying to convince them that
"this is the way it *had* to happen." He is showing them the kind of love that is
born from a heart that is free. His *knowing* is not some kind of fringe benefit
that comes as part of the package of being God's beloved son. We belittle the
story of Jesus' life by making him into a magician and a soothsayer. Jesus
knew he had to suffer because he was attentive to all that was going on around
him; it was this that allowed him to intuit the very real possibility of an
untimely death. His death on the cross was not part of God's plan; it was the
result of fear—a fear that crippled a small group of people who became
threatened by a man whose heart was free enough to love all people equally.
As Gandhi's life and practice of *ahimsa* show,[33] such love is the status quo's
most hated enemy.

The icon of the cross is *not*, then, an image of a distant and indifferent
God. It is, in fact, an icon through which we glimpse the face of a God who is

love. This "glimpse" is only possible, however, if we are able to look deeply enough into the cross and see it as the fruit of Jesus' entire life, lived as an expression of the loving solidarity of God. The cross is *ugly* because it happened; it is *beautiful* because of *why* it happened. It happened because of one man's faithfulness to love.

How can we see the cross as an expression of God's love for us today? If we accept that Jesus died two thousand years ago on the cross as a consequence of his compassion and love, what about today? Would it not be better to move on and find a more positive, life-giving symbol?

The First Noble Truth: suffering exists. Suffering is as much a reality today as it was in Jesus' day. We may wish it were otherwise, but it is not. Those of us who live in the more developed first world are not always comfortable with this First Noble Truth. When, we wonder, will we be able to erase suffering from the list of things we have to do and get on with a normal life? Says Thây:

> We tend to believe that there is a place where we can go by abandoning, or leaving behind, this world of suffering. . . . The pollutions that afflict us are anger and hatred, despair, sorrow and fear. When you suffer so much, the tendency to want to leave it behind becomes very strong. I don't want to be here anymore, I want to get out. "Stop the world, I want to get off."[34]

This sentiment is understandable. We all know it well. Suffering sometimes seems unbearable. For Christians, the cross can sometimes make us very uncomfortable; it makes the temptation to "hide from suffering" more difficult. The cross reminds us that *suffering is*. It happens. It is part of life, and there is no getting around it. The only true spiritual path is the one that passes *through* suffering. By looking at the cross (sometimes it feels more like the cross is staring into us), we are given the courage to face our suffering and the suffering of others. The cross is the Christian version of the Buddha's Four Noble Truths.

Many years ago, one of my Dominican brothers, Fr. Jim Campbell, OP, was sitting in a Zen-Christian meditation hall in Japan, trying to do *zazen*[35] while suffering from excruciating back pain, for which he ultimately underwent surgery. Feeling he could go on no longer, he was about to abandon the practice when he glanced up and saw a small wooden cross on the wall. He said years later, "It all made sense—the cross, the pain, the promise of liberation. I knew then why I was a Christian."

It is certainly possible that another person might have had an entirely different experience upon looking at the cross on the wall of the zendo. However, for many Christians down through the centuries, the cross has served as a kind of gentle mirror[36] that helps us to see our sufferings and to touch

them—not in a way that overwhelms us and leaves us feeling abandoned—
but a seeing and touching that happen in and through and with our teacher,
Jesus. By "watching him" embrace his suffering with patience and love, we see
the path by which we too can journey forward. In contemporary psychological language, it is akin to "making friends with our shadow," embracing a neg-
ative that becomes a positive. The cross can only be approached as a
paradoxical symbol—one that confounds and offers untold hope. St. Paul
had the following to say:

> For the message of the cross is foolishness to those who are perishing,
> but to us who are being saved it is the power of God. . . . For Jews
> demand signs and Greeks desire wisdom, but *we proclaim Christ cruci-
> fied*, a stumbling block to Jews and foolishness to Gentiles; but to those
> who are called, Jews and Greeks, Christ, the power of God and the wis-
> dom of God. For God's foolishness is wiser than human wisdom, and
> God's weakness is stronger than human strength. (1 Cor 1:18-25)

There is no logical way to explain St. Paul's words; they can only be experienced as a deep and liberating reality. All that St. Paul can do is to state the
paradox. The cross is both foolishness and wisdom. It is both death and life.

Before continuing, I feel a need to state very clearly that I do not write
these words about the cross of Jesus unaware of the abuse of the symbol of
the cross at different periods of Christianity's two thousand years of history.
There are some episodes that stand out as particularly brutal, which leave a
Christian with no option but to bow one's head and ask God and our sisters
and brothers for mercy and forgiveness.

Having worked many years in Latin America, I am not naïve regarding the
abusive history of the cross throughout the continent. The poverty and cultural violence so widespread in Latin America today are not disconnected
from its history of political and religious domination by European colonial
powers. Baptism was frequently used in the years of colonial rule not as an
introduction into the mystery of the indwelling of God through the paschal
death and resurrection of Christ, but as a weapon of coercion and control.
This unfortunate legacy has snaked its way down through five centuries of
failed democracy, political corruption at all levels, ecological devastation and
the ongoing selling of the continent's collective body and soul to the highest
international bidder. Little has changed today, except that the highest bidder
is now the United States.

In other parts of the world, there have been Crusades, Inquisitions, and the
burning at the stake of scores of holy women and men—all fueled by a distorted idolatry of the cross. Nazism and fascism have fed their furnaces of
Aryan supremacy with language taken from the Christian Bible. In the south-

ern United States where I grew up, African Americans have awakened many a night to hooded perpetrators of hatred burning crosses in front of their houses and bombing their churches—all in the name of some idol called "god." All of these atrocities have their roots in fear and the abuse of power. There have been some apologies and public expressions of repentance, though not enough.[37] When the Catholic bishops of Latin America and the Caribbean gathered in Santo Domingo in 1992 to commemorate five hundred years of Christianity's arrival in the Americas, a statement was made "giving thanks to God for the many and great lights [during these five hundred years] and asking forgiveness for the undeniable shadows that have covered this period."[38] More reflection on the violent past and more public apologies will be necessary for the healing to take effect, but some initial steps have been taken.

Having said this, though, I think it is important to distinguish between those segments of Christianity that have chosen to be aligned with the powers of domination, and the life and teachings of Jesus. All religions have to deal with abuses and fanatics. Fundamentalist ideologies can seep into even the most venerable traditions. But like Moses and Buddha, like the Hindu saints and Muhammad, Jesus was a man of integrity, a man of God, whose life continues to stand out as a timeless manifestation of compassion and love. The cross is a living icon of the consequences stemming from Jesus' option for a life rooted in the practice of nonviolent love and mercy. Any manipulation of the icon of the cross into an instrument that justifies the use of violence or religious coercion is an insult to all who genuinely attempt to follow the life and teachings of Jesus.

All of us who have chosen a spiritual path have, at one time or another, fallen short of the goal. We are all human beings in process, learning day by day to be more human. The errors and shortcomings of those of us who sometimes stumble along the various spiritual paths should not overshadow the enlightened teachings of those who bequeathed these sacred paths to us. Recognizing our limitations and those of our forebears, we have no choice but to continue forward. The *Way* is eternal, without beginning and end, as new and as fresh as when our teachers walked it themselves. We learn from the mistakes of the past, so that today we can say *yes* once again to the journey.

10

Love in Full Bloom

Touching the Body of Christ

Since the "wisdom of the cross" is not something that can be easily explained or grasped, as St. Paul said, I find it necessary to include in this reflection a few examples of people who have *touched* the crucified Christ and, in so doing, have touched the liberating power of God. These people and their stories have taught me much. Like the young sister in the previous chapter who radiantly told Mother Teresa that she had been "touching the body of Christ" in the man to whom she ministered in the streets of Calcutta, such is the courage with which many people have looked upon and touched the suffering Christ by touching the suffering of the world with mindful compassion. Through the witness of these people, we understand more than ever that the crucified Christ is indeed the living Christ.

Many years ago I met a woman in El Salvador named Sara, whose son had been abducted in the middle of the night by government security forces, tortured, and killed. For over two years following the tragedy, Sara suffered from severe depression. She had lost all desire to live. One day, as she stood in the street in front of her house, a neighbor with whom she had not spoken since the onset of her depression walked past and greeted Sara. Surprisingly, Sara responded, asking how the neighbor was doing. The neighbor's eyes quickly filled with tears and she began to cry. After a few moments, she was able to share with Sara that two of her sons had recently been kidnapped and killed. This is what Sara told me the day she recounted the story:

> That very moment my depression lifted. I do not know exactly how it happened. All I know is that I realized in that very instant that my neighbor needed me. She was suffering twice as much as I was. Since that day, for the past several years now, I have been helping to organize the families in our neighborhood who have been through this tragedy. My life has meaning once again.

Though Sara did not use sophisticated theological language to speak of her mental healing and transformation, she recognizes that it was only her faith in Christ and his sacrifice on the cross that got her through so dark a night.

162

She experienced a rebirth, a movement "from death to life." Sara recognizes that something profound happened within her the moment she saw and touched her neighbor's suffering. She was able to enter into the paschal mystery of Christ, sharing intimately in both his death and his resurrection. In encountering her neighbor that day, she *touched the body of Christ*—crucified and risen from the dead. Says St. Paul, "Do you know that all of us who have been baptized into Christ Jesus were baptized into his death? Therefore we have been buried with him by baptism into death, so that, just as Christ was raised from the dead by the glory of the Father, so we too might walk in newness of life" (Rom. 6:3-4). This was precisely Sara's experience. Her encounter with death awakened within her, after a period of germination, the baptismal experience of her sharing in the resurrection of Christ. She was able to rise with Christ from the dead and "walk in newness of life."

In the mid-1980s, I spent a year studying theology in Lima, Peru—the same country that had received me as a teenage foreign exchange student. It was a year that opened my eyes to many new realities, one of which was what I first defined (in my narrow-mindedness) as "the Peruvian people's unhealthy fascination with bloody crucifixes." Even though I was raised as a Catholic, the crucifixes of my childhood were extremely "domesticated" compared to the ones I found hanging in all the churches in Lima. The crucifixion, as depicted in most North American Christian churches, has been properly "sanitized"—more a reflection of our own denial of suffering than anything else. I was a product of my culture. The bloody corpses hanging on crosses in every dark corner of Lima seemed to me nothing but a self-fulfilling prophecy: "These people are obsessed with suffering," were the words I heard coming from deep within my own heart. "Where is the hope, the life, the resurrection? If all they think about is blood and death, then no wonder the situation is so bad!" My haughty first world theological speculation was just that: haughty and speculative.

That year, one of my Dominican brothers and I were asked to help with the Good Friday service at the Church of St. Dominic in the center of the city. Our task, as part of the solemn remembrance of the day Jesus died on the cross, was to hold an almost-life-sized crucifix in our arms so that the people (thousands of people, or so it seemed!) could approach and venerate the crucified Christ by kissing the cross. It was "interesting" for the first ten minutes, but the lines of people seemed endless, and soon our arms and backs began to ache. I think we stood there for a couple of hours, but it seemed like days!

Little by little, though, I began to let go of my judging mind and simply watch the people, mostly women dressed in black, as they approached with tears streaming down their faces. Many of them bent down and kissed the bloodied corpse of Jesus, wiping his body with a handkerchief or tissue which they then took home as a holy relic that would console and strengthen them in their trials and sufferings in the coming year. I became transfixed as I watched these women kiss and "wash the body" of Christ with the passion and love of a mother preparing the body of a dead son for burial. Many of them *had*, in fact, already buried several of their own children. I cannot explain the effect that this experience had on me. My neat, tidy theological world began to crumble before my very eyes.

What I realized that day, as I held the tortured, crucified body of Christ in my arms, was that this was *not* just a religious ritual for these people. This was their life. Unlike my life, lived in the safety and comfort of middle-class North America, their lives looked a lot like that bloody body on the cross. This was no self-fulfilling prophecy. This was the real thing. The body on that cross was not religious art for them. It was their own dead son; it was their three or four children who had died from malnutrition as infants; it was their neighbor dying of cancer with no medicine and no hope. The beaten, bloodied corpse of Jesus was their country's slow, agonizing death—the result of centuries of poverty, corruption, military coups, foreign debt, and civil war. With so little real political power, so few options, there was one thing that they could do, and that was to kiss this broken body of humanity, wash the blood from its face, and pray to the God who raised Jesus from the dead.

As the scales fell from my eyes in the days and weeks and years following this Good Friday experience, I began to *see* with new eyes. For the poor of Latin America, the crucified Christ is their greatest source of hope. They know what suffering is. Suffering is their daily bread. For that reason, a pretty cross, decorated with a sanitized, bloodless corpse, or with no corpse at all, is simply not their world. It is not *real*. The poor believe deeply in the resurrection of Jesus from the dead, in the path that leads from suffering to liberation, but the only way they have for touching the new life of the risen Christ is by first touching the cross. Any shortcut to new life is false.

For the people of Latin America, the bloody Jesus on the cross is the icon of a God who knows what suffering is and who has not turned away from their pain. On the contrary, God has chosen to draw near to them in their suffering. As Eckhart says, we suffer *in God* and "God is *with us* in [our] suffering."[1] The crucified Christ is *Emmanuel*: "God with us" (see Isa. 7:14; Matt. 1:23). For the poor, a God who would "hide from suffering" is *not* "God with us." God's name throughout the Judeo-Christian tradition—from Moses' encounter with the burning bush to the paschal death and resurrection of Jesus—has been in one way or another an echo of that one great truth: "I am with you always, to the end of the age" (Matt. 28:20). Only a God who becomes vulnerable, who risks walking the path of that kind of love that could end in a shameful, violent death, has the credibility to say to the poor and brokenhearted, "I am with you." Any other god is a false god.

The Cross of Nonviolent Love

The cross is not an exaltation of suffering. It is the price paid for the vulnerability of loving. In the first pages of *Living Buddha, Living Christ*, Thây relates the pain of the years of social unrest and war in Vietnam. "During the war in Vietnam," he says, "I saw communists and anti-communists killing and destroying each other because each side believed they had a monopoly on the truth. . . . I wrote a booklet entitled "Dialogue: The Key to Peace," but my voice was drowned out by the bombs, mortars, and shouting."[2] The title of Thây's book reminds me of a peasant farmer in Honduras, a man named Don Felipe Huete, who was gunned down in 1991 along with several co-workers and family members, as they tried to protect their land. Unarmed, Don Felipe stood peacefully before the armed thugs who had come in the middle of the night to run the families from their land. Don Felipe made one request, "Let us dialogue." As with Thây's booklet, Don Felipe's hope for dialogue was also drowned out by violence. One cannot help wondering why simple, respectful dialogue is looked upon with such fear and contempt.

Thây goes on to tell the story of an American soldier in Vietnam who, while sitting on top of a military truck, spit onto the head of one of Thây's disciples, Nhât Trí. "Brother Nhât Trí became so angry that he thought about leaving the monastery and joining the National Liberation Front," recounts Thây. "I urged Brother Nhât Trí to remember that the G.I. was also a war victim, the victim of a wrong view and a wrong policy, and I urged him to continue his work for peace as a monk. He was able to see that, and he became one of the most active workers in the Buddhist School of Youth for Social Service."[3]

Brother Nhât Trí was spit at and humiliated in the midst of a situation of violence. Jesus was also spit upon, beaten, and humiliated in a very similar context. For both men, though, the suffering they endured was intimately connected with their choice to act out of compassion and in a spirit of reconciliation and loving-kindness. By choosing not to react to the violence with more violence, they made themselves vulnerable, opening their hearts up to the difficult task of understanding and forgiving their enemies. Like Don Felipe and Thây, they wanted to establish a dialogue rooted in love. Both Nhât Trí and Jesus were able to look deeply enough into the suffering of their aggressors that they glimpsed the human faces and human dignity hidden beneath the anger and violence. For Christians, to contemplate the crucified Christ is at the same time an invitation to contemplate the dignity and divine image hidden in those who carried out such a terrible act. We cannot look upon the crucified Jesus without hearing the words of forgiveness that he spoke from the cross, "Father, forgive them; they do not know what they are doing" (Luke 23:34). The crucified Christ is the same Christ who shows us the path to nonviolent love. Do we follow that path today?

"The Buddha always resisted violence and immorality," writes Thây. "Are our sanghas doing the same—opposing social injustice and violence—or are we blessing wars and sending priests with our armies to support the efforts of war? With utmost courage, Jesus taught a gospel of nonviolence. Is the church today practicing the same by its presence and behavior?"[4] Thây's questions are challenging; they may very likely make us uneasy. In one way or another, though, we must have the courage to answer them. To not answer them is to live shackled by fear. We may not be living the challenge of nonviolent love perfectly yet, but even the honest recognition of our shortcomings can be part of the vulnerability that comes with learning to love.

We do ourselves no spiritual favor by ignoring the difficult questions. We do ourselves no spiritual favor by turning our backs on the ugliness of the cross. We must be willing to look into the eyes of the soldier who spits on us, for his eyes are also the eyes of the crucified Christ. It is precisely there—in that particular gaze and at that very moment—that our spiritual practice becomes authentic. It is in that moment that we have the opportunity to choose love over hatred. Says Eckhart, "You must love all people equally, respect and regard them equally."[5] The cross is a school of nonviolent love. The Dalai Lama says, "If you can cultivate the right attitude, your enemies are your best spiritual teachers because their presence provides you with the opportunity to enhance and develop tolerance, patience, and understanding."[6]

On the one hand, the cross is the enemy, the tree of death; on the other hand, the cross is our teacher, the one who leads us to the tree of life. To hide from the cross, to sanitize it and make it look more respectable, is to cover over the truth. It is to miss the central message of the life of Jesus. Only by touching the wounded, crucified Christ can we touch the living Christ of nonviolent love. This touching leads us to true peace, but not a peace that is removed from all suffering; such a world does not exist. The peace of the cross is the peace that stands unmoved in the midst of suffering. This peace is what is also known as equanimity.

Equanimity: What Is, Is

As we have seen, suffering exists. This truth, articulated by the Buddha in the Four Noble Truths and symbolized in Jesus' embrace of the cross is a truth that we all know—not from books or from religious teachings but from the inside-out, from our own lives and experiences. What we choose to *do* with suffering, how we live with it and move toward overcoming it, is an important dimension of the spiritual journey. Though it may be true that Buddhism places more emphasis on overcoming suffering by following the Eightfold Path,[7] while Christianity stresses the redemptive value of suffering in itself, there is, I believe, more in common among the two traditions than first meets the eye.

Both Buddhism and Christianity teach in different ways that suffering is overcome not by avoiding it, but by going through it—by facing it, touching it, and moving beyond it. As Thây mentioned above, "We are all tempted to go to a place where there is no suffering. . . . Happiness and well-being [however] cannot be separated from suffering and ill-being."[8] In other words, the only way beyond suffering is *through* it. The only way to experience the resurrection is by walking the way of the cross. In the Hebrew scriptures, the same insight is symbolized in the ancient story of the exodus, the journey of the people of Israel from their slavery in Egypt to the "land flowing with milk and honey" (Lev. 20:24). This story, important to Jews and Christians alike, reminds us that the only way to the Promised Land, to the Pure Land, is by risking the perilous journey through the desert.

Almost seven centuries ago, Eckhart addressed the spiritual challenge of "walking through the desert" in his own particular way. He states very clearly, in one of his more famous sermons, based on the gospel story of Jesus' visit to the house of Mary and Martha (Luke 10:38-42), that the spiritual life is lived *not* by avoiding the desert of suffering but by going through it in such a way that it does not disturb our fundamental dwelling in the presence of God:

> Good people declare that we must be so perfect that no joy can move us, we must be untouched by weal and woe. They are wrong in this. . . . I declare that no saint ever lived or ever will attain to that state where pain cannot hurt him nor pleasure please. . . . Yet on the other hand I hold that it is possible for a saint, even in this life, to be so that nothing can move him [or her] to turn from God. . . . Whatever then occurs cannot impede eternal bliss, so long as it does not invade the summit of the soul up yonder where it is at one with God's sweet will.[9]

Eckhart's words about living life—even when touched by pain and suffering—in such a way that we are able to dwell in an interior place of peace and tranquility, firmly grounded and anchored in God, is a timeless teaching common to Buddhism, Christianity, and most of the great world religions. Called *equanimity* in most spiritual traditions, it is fundamental in the teachings of both Eckhart and Thây. There are few areas, in fact, where the teachings of Eckhart so closely resemble basic Buddhist teaching as this one. Though the term *equanimity* is much more familiar to Buddhists than Christians, it is a rich spiritual treasure that, through fruitful dialogue, can bring us more closely together, while enriching us in the unique practices of our different traditions. To live with equanimity in the face of either suffering or pleasure is one of the great gems of the spiritual life, yet it is a discipline learned only through patient practice. Once "learned," though, it has the capacity to lead one into an interior landscape of "eternal bliss" as Eckhart promises. If the cross of Christ can be likened to a tree of life, then equanimity is one of its choicest blossoms.

In one sermon Eckhart defines equanimity as, "Being equable in joy and in sorrow . . . in bitterness and [in] sweetness."[10] We might define it as: *the calm, peaceful acceptance of the way things are in the present moment*. Again in the words of Eckhart: "For [someone] to have a peaceful life is good, but for [that person] to have a life of pain in patience is better; but . . . to have peace in a life of pain is best."[11] Equanimity is not about romanticizing suffering; it is about embracing life one moment at a time. It is learning to find the peace in the midst of the pain. As my dear and wise friend, Sr. Priscilla Trost, OSB, is fond of saying, in her three-word summary of all of Eckhart's teachings: "What is, *is*." To discover the *is-ness* of God in all that *is* truly opens up for us the door to a life of inner peace. It is perfectly normal to hope that the day will be bright and sunny for the year's first springtime picnic, but when the rain comes down in torrents, equanimity invites us to walk through the park "singing in the rain." Equanimity is the inner calm that one discovers in accepting that what is, *simply is*. As one popular saying goes, "If life hands you lemons, then make lemonade."

In a question-and-answer session at Plum Village in France in 1996, someone asked Thây to shed some light on the suffering brought on by Alzheimer's disease and the painful loss of memory that accompanies it. Thây's response, based on an experience from his own life, is a very fine and honest example of what living with equanimity means in daily life: "I used to have a very good memory, and the first time I noticed my memory betraying me, I suffered. You realize that you are no longer young, and you don't believe it. You find that you are no longer bright, remembering everything, and you feel hurt. It can be difficult to accept the fact that you are growing old. *But we have to accept the situation as it is*. . . . Now, if I can't remember something, if I cannot do something as well as I used to, I just smile."[12] What is, is.

Once again Thây offers us insight into a spiritual practice that is simple and tangible. Equanimity teaches us to smile and to laugh at life. We learn to accept each and every situation *just as it is* and, to the best of our ability, to do so with a sense of humor. Thây does not prescribe running from the pain or wishing it away with some form of meditation that constructs an illusory world in our minds. Says Thây, "Mindfulness does not regard pain as an enemy that needs to be suppressed. . . . It knows the pain is part of us. It is like a mother embracing her baby. The mother knows the baby is part of her. The crying baby is our pain, and the mother is our tenderness. There is no barrier between our tenderness and our pain."[13] This is a teaching so needed in our world today, a world so torn apart by pain and suffering. Hidden within the suffering itself are the seeds of tenderness, well-being, and peace. As Thây says frequently, all we have to do is to water them. The suffering we experience is only one part of the reality. Beneath it all, to use Eckhart's language, we realize that our pain is *in* God; in fact, our pain *is* God.

In his series of talks to novices entitled *The Talks of Instruction*, Eckhart uses language very similar to that of the Buddhist masters to talk about the practice of equanimity. "The most powerful prayer," says the Meister, "is that which proceeds from a *bare mind*. The more bare it is, the more powerful, worthy, useful, praiseworthy and perfect the prayer and the work."[14] For Eckhart, a *bare mind* frees us to pray and work without expecting the results to be this way or that way. It is a path leading to inner calm and freedom. As Sr. Priscilla says, whatever is, simply *is*. Eckhart continues, "What is a bare mind? A bare mind is one which is worried by nothing and is tied to nothing, which has not bound its best part to any mode, does not seek its own in anything, that is fully immersed in God's dearest will and gone out of its own."[15]

A bare mind is worried by nothing and tied to nothing. There is no predetermined outcome to which one is attached. The bare mind is free to embrace reality as it is. This is equanimity. Eckhart goes on to place the cultivation of *bare mind* and the practice of equanimity within the larger context of what Christian theology calls "doing the will of God." The language of "doing God's will" can be somewhat confusing to understand, especially if one is not familiar with what Eckhart and the scholastic theologians of his time mean by the phrase. Though there is not time here to delve into such a topic extensively, a few words of clarification are needed.

If we want to understand Eckhart's teaching on the relationship between suffering and equanimity, it is essential to understand that when he speaks of "God's will" he is not using the phrase to say, "This is what God *wants* to happen" or "This is what God *has planned* to happen." Our modern ear, of course, tends to hear the phrase in this way. A better way for us to hear the phrase "God's will" would be: "This is what happens *in God*." Or perhaps an even more helpful translation might be: "This is what *happened*, and all that *happens*, happens in God."

Following up on the previous chapter's treatment of suffering, it is important to understand what Eckhart and other Christian theologians are saying when they speak of taking suffering "in God's will." What they are *not* saying is that God wills suffering. Who would want to follow a God who *wills* for people to suffer? This is just another version of the Wizard-of-Oz God who is "out there" somewhere, arbitrarily pulling the strings of history. Such an image of God is hardly a reflection of a mature spirituality. God is not "out there" *anywhere*. God is the *is-ness* that flows through all that is. When a person suffers, the person suffers *in God*, and therefore, God is *in* the suffering. The suffering happens within God. To awaken to this profound insight, says Eckhart, is to discover a oneness with God that transcends all suffering. Says the Meister, "God's being with us in suffering means that [God] suffers with me. . . . If my suffering is in God and God suffers with me, how then can my suffering be painful when my suffering loses its pain, and my pain is in God and my pain *is* God? . . . Whenever I find pure suffering in God and for God, there I find God."[16]

Equanimity has to do with standing with our feet firmly rooted in God, in the Ground of all being—not untouched by pain but rooted in such a way that our truest, deepest self, the self who is one with God, is unmoved, even in the midst of suffering. The pain is *in* God and the pain *is* God. Living this mystery deeply, freed from attachments, is what Eckhart calls "bare mind." It is to be empty of any mental expectations of how this moment should be and to be open to the fullness of God's presence in the way things are. This inner tranquility is the key to a life of freedom and peace.

This inner tranquility, the fruit of embracing suffering *in God*, can be understood only in connection with what Christian theology calls "free will." God's will is not coercive; God always permits us to make free choices. To do God's will is to choose to act freely *within* God. Both our choices and the consequences of those choices happen within God. In a way similar to the Eastern understanding of karma, Christianity recognizes that all our free choices produce their subsequent effects. So, for example, if I smile at the ticket agent at the airport and greet her with a friendly "Good morning," it is very likely that my pleasant attitude (the fruit of daily spiritual practice) will encourage the agent to respond kindly to my request for an aisle seat. If, however, I arrive late to the airport and impatiently demand that the agent change the claustrophobic middle seat that I have been assigned to a more comfortable aisle seat, there is a greater possibility that I will "suffer" through the long flight stuck between two screaming children in a middle seat. As the plane takes off with me squeezed miserably into seat 32B, do we dare to say that this is "God's will?" The answer is an unequivocal yes. And not only is it God's will, but it is an opportunity to practice equanimity. Equanimity blossoms when I embrace the situation *as it is* and begin planning a way to entertain the two screaming kids! Eckhart says it this way in one of his sermons: "Now you might want to ask, 'How do I know if it is God's will?' I reply, 'If it were *not* God's will for a single instant, it would not be—it *must* always be God's will.'"[17] God, of course, is not to blame for either my late start or my impatience with the ticket agent. Those choices were mine. God permits the "suffering" to happen, though, for it is nothing more than the natural consequence of my own actions. This is the will of God.

What happens, though, if I arrive with plenty of time to the airport, with an abundance of patience, only to find that the ticket agent is already in a bad mood? This time it seems completely out of my control. She refuses to negotiate, assigning me middle seat 32B, even though I go out of my way to be kind and courteous? For Eckhart, *this* is where the practice of equanimity is really put to the test. *This* is where Thây's practice of mindful breathing is a life saver. Let us listen to what Eckhart himself says, commenting on the time that *he* was assigned seat 32B:

> I accept and take the suffering in God's will and from God's will. *Such* suffering alone is perfect suffering, for it arises and springs from pure love of God's sheer goodness and joy. . . . If God wills [i.e., 'permits'] to give me what I want, then I have the pleasure of it; if God does not will to give it to me, then I get by doing without, in God's same will. . . . So what do I lose?[18]

"What do I lose?" asks Eckhart. Through the practice of equanimity, we lose nothing. What we gain, though, in inner peace and tranquility, is immeasurable. What the spiritual masters are teaching us is that there is a way to remain *grounded* in the inner place of calm no matter what happens. Life itself becomes a win-win situation. Eckhart goes on to say in his treatise *The Book of Divine Comfort*:

> I say then: when outward ills befall the good and just [person], if she remains in equanimity with the peace of her heart unmoved, then it is true, as I have said, that nothing that happens to her can disturb the just. . . . Therefore a [person] should strive earnestly to de-form herself of herself. . . . Then nothing will be able to afflict or sadden her . . . all her being, life, knowledge, wisdom and love will be from God and in God, and *be* God.[19]

The practice of equanimity reminds us (i.e., brings to *mindfulness*) that the spiritual life is a life not of freedom *from* suffering but of freedom *in* suffering. Equanimity opens us up to an inner freedom that remains calm and peacefully detached in the midst of suffering. Suffering is no longer experienced as some kind of "spiritual exile" that leaves us completely isolated and separated from God. It is an illusion to think that only by overcoming the suffering will we be able to return to being with God. This dualistic thinking, as the Buddha taught so wisely, actually *causes* suffering. We are invited to awaken to the profound spiritual truth that liberation happens *within* the suffering, not somewhere else. If it is true, as St. Paul said, that "in God we live and move and have our being" (Acts 17:28), then even the suffering and the brokenness, the violence and the sin of our world are in a mysterious way held in the very heart of God. Our spiritual practices of mindfulness and equanimity teach us to "be not afraid." We learn to walk calmly and courageously *into* the furnace of suffering, trusting that we do so while remaining in the merciful heart of God. "Then nothing will be able to afflict or sadden [us]," says Eckhart, for everything "will be from God and in God, and *be* God."[20]

Using a lovely metaphor, Thây encourages his monks and nuns to discover the gift of equanimity—even in the midst of suffering:

> Suffering is always there, around us and inside of us, and we have to find ways that alleviate the suffering and transform it into well-being and peace. Monks and nuns in both their traditions practice prayer, meditation, mindful walking, silent meals, and many other ways to try to overcome their suffering. It is a kind of luxury to be a monk or nun, to be able to sit quietly and look deeply into the nature of suffering and the way out. Sitting and looking deeply into your body, your consciousness, and your mental states is like being a mother hen covering her eggs. One day insight will be born like a baby chick. If monks and nuns do not cherish their time of practice, they will have nothing to offer the world.[21]

The simplicity of Thây's image will, we hope, encourage us in the practice of equanimity, helping us to see it as a path to freedom and not as a burden that weighs us down and interrupts our daily life. At the same time, though, it is important to remember that equanimity requires a serious dedication to living in the present moment, within the unfinished-ness of daily life. Equanimity helps us to let go of having to force the future into happening before its proper time. It may sound very simple, but most of us know that learning this art takes great effort and patience. It would probably do us all some good to spend some time contemplating a roosting hen, as she waits day and night in her quiet immobility for the new life of her chicks to come forth. Equanimity is born in this way. The image, of course, gives sitting on a meditation cushion a whole new perspective!

Equanimity and the Cross

Julian of Norwich, an English mystic who wrote about fifty years after Eckhart, sought to understand the reality of suffering and sin, wondering aloud in her writings why God, in designing and creating the universe, did not prevent such unfortunate realities from entering into the world. Why do people have to suffer? We have *all* asked this question at one time or another. Julian received a revelation in which Jesus spoke to her, inviting her to let go of her mental struggle and trust in the providential love of God: "Sin is necessary," Jesus told her, "but all will be well, and all will be well, and every kind of thing will be well."[22] Through her mystical encounter with the living Christ, Julian came to understand that "this pain is something for a time, for it purges and makes us know ourselves and ask for mercy. . . . Because of the tender love which our good Lord has for all who will be saved, he comforts readily and sweetly, meaning this: it is true that sin is the cause of all this pain, but all will be well, and every kind of thing will be well."[23]

Though Julian does not use the term *equanimity*, she discovers that even in the midst of suffering there is a groundedness in God. The suffering itself, in fact, purges us and prepares us for this deeper communion with God. Julian's repetition of the phrase *all will be well* sounds forth like a mantra to guide us in the practice of equanimity. It is a phrase that gently roots us in the present moment, calling us to greater trust, balance, and peace. Julian is like the mother hen who understands that she is to sit and wait with utmost patience, confident that new life will break through in due time.

Julian's words are reminiscent of the words scribbled by St. Teresa of Avila into her prayer book: "Let nothing trouble you; let nothing frighten you. The one who has God lacks nothing. God alone suffices." The mystical insights of both of these women point us down the path of equanimity. They remind us that even in the midst of suffering, God is present to comfort us—sturdy and steadfast as a Rock (Ps. 31:4). The kingdom is here and now, and because that is true, we know in the depths of our being that "all will be well."

It is precisely this steadfast trust in God that finally transforms the crucified Jesus from a suffering victim of hatred and violence into an icon of peace and well-being. The Good News of his loving-kindness is hidden deep within his very own pain. The cross is the story of his faithful journey through the desert of suffering into the peace of the kingdom of God. There is no doubt that the crucified Jesus was touched by unbearable suffering and pain. This is vividly clear in his cry from the cross, "My God, my God, why have you forsaken me?" (Mark 15:34). At first, though, this cry sounds like anything but an expression of equanimity. Thây reacts to such a "distressing" cry, and understandably so.[24] Did Jesus actually think that God had abandoned him? As always, it is important to hear these words in their proper context. Jesus' cry from the cross is not a theological statement; he is not saying that God abandons people in the midst of their worst suffering. This is impossible, for all that happens—even suffering—happens within the very heart of God, the Ground of all being. No matter how much the wave suffers, she is always grounded by the ocean's steadfast presence. Nothing can separate us from the love of God (see Rom. 8:39).

Jesus' cry from the cross is the cry of all who have found themselves alone in the dark night of existential suffering. There are few experiences more terrifying. It is a very real human cry. It is heard millions of times a day throughout the world. Does this mean that God abandons us in the midst of suffering? No. But it does mean that there are experiences of suffering that are so painful that one is left with nothing but the sense of total abandonment. Jesus shares in that most desolate of human experiences. But that is not the end of the story. Even in the midst of his cry, Jesus remains *grounded* in God. His truest, deepest self, the self grounded in the Ultimate Reality of God's love, hands back to the Father, in utter trust and tranquility, the gift of his very life: "Father, into your hands I commend my spirit" (Luke 23:46). In that very moment, that moment of darkest night, Jesus finds himself in the gentle hands of God. He knows once again that he is home, and that he has always been home—in God. *This* is perfect equanimity.

This breakthrough into equanimity and peace is available to all of us. It is what the spiritual journey is all about. Recently, while facilitating a spiritual retreat, I met a woman named Susanna, who has lived for many years with a disease that has left her increasingly crippled. Even though Susanna has suffered much both physically and emotionally, each time I looked at her during the days of the retreat, I continually found myself surprised by her smiling, luminous face. I was curious to know what allowed her to shine with such peacefulness.

When a chance to talk came around, Susanna told me her story. She had suffered from the disease for much of her life, always hoping that God would heal her; her hopes, however, were never realized. The previous year, though, during a similar spiritual retreat, she chose to take part in a prayer service for healing, during which she received the sacramental anointing of the sick. "I had always hoped for a physical healing," she told me, "but then something happened that was totally unexpected. When the priest touched my hand with the blessed oil I was completely healed—spiritually and psychologically. No physical healing could ever come near to the healing which I received." The smile on her face had given her secret away long before she ever told me her story. She now lives with remarkable equanimity in the midst of her physical suffering. At the end of our conversation she laughed and said, "I still walk funny, but that doesn't matter anymore. I am whole." She has found true peace and liberation, even in the midst of her physical suffering.

What struck me in my conversation with Susanna was that in many ways her healing and the gift of her profound equanimity and peace have much to do with a healing of how she views both herself and life in general. She has been given a new perspective, a new outlook on life. Her experience of wholeness seems to stem from seeing herself now as one with God. *In God* she is complete, whole, free. She knows this truth in a very deep and real way.

Thây touches on this interrelationship between *seeing* and *equanimity* in a

Dharma talk on the Buddha's teaching of the "Four Immeasureable Minds," a teaching offered as part of the training for younger monks. Thây, noting first that equanimity is one of the "four aspects of true love," goes on to point out that the word equanimity comes from the Sanskrit word *upeksha*, meaning "nonattachment," "even-mindedness," or "letting go." What is especially insightful is Thây's explanation of the two Sanskrit words that make up the word *upeksha*. Says Thây, "*Upe* means 'over,' and *ksh* means 'to look.' You climb the mountain to be able to look over the whole situation, not bound by one side or the other."[25]

Thây's relating of *upeksha*—equanimity—to love seems to me to be a profound insight. Love needs the practice of equanimity in order to, first of all, see clearly and, second, to develop freely. To grow in love, says Thây, requires that we develop the spiritual capacity to rise above the fray of life, to be able to observe any given situation without being attached to either *this* side or *that* side. Susanna, I realize now, has been able to *rise above* her situation and *see* herself as complete in God. This has won for her a new and lasting sense of freedom—and a sense of humor to go along with it!

"Blessed are the pure in heart," said Jesus, "for they will see God" (Matt. 5:8). *Seeing* and *loving*, as we have considered in previous chapters, always go hand in hand in the spiritual life. As St. Catherine of Siena said earlier, "If we do not see, we cannot love." Equanimity, as a spiritual practice, helps us to see clearly, to have a deeper insight into life. It would follow, then, that *right viewpoint*, part of the Buddha's Eightfold Path which orients a person on the journey from suffering to freedom, would profit much from the practice of equanimity. In other words, the way we look upon a particular situation, upon another person, or upon the world in general would directly affect the way we act and, therefore, the way we love. For people struggling with relationships, for nations engaged in negotiations and conflict resolution, the practice of equanimity—seeing clearly and justly—cannot help serving as a wise guide along the way toward balance, understanding, mutuality, and peace.

The practice of equanimity, along with its sister practice, mindfulness, teaches us how to face our own suffering, as well as the world's, without being swallowed by it. We can stand in the midst of a fragile situation, see it clearly and touch it deeply, without drowning in it. Equanimity teaches us to look into the wounded heart of the other person with tranquility and patience, until we are able to see the rays of light shining through the cracks. It is a practice that helps us to love.

In helping us to love more authentically, equanimity is also one of the keys that opens up the door of forgiveness—such an important dimension in all relationships. What often makes forgiveness so difficult is the feeling of being overwhelmed by the faults—imagined or real—of the other. As Thây said above, equanimity helps us to climb to the top of the mountain and see the situation from a more objective viewpoint. We are able to see the other's goodness, his or her acts of loving-kindness, even within the midst of the suffering that is at the root of the difficult relationship. Such a seeing, a calm and just seeing, is essential if we are to move beyond the paralysis of judgment and into the freedom of reconciliation.

Equanimity is the school where we learn to love our enemies. How greatly is our world in need of this precious gift today. Those Palestinians and Israelis who are still shackled by fear and hatred, for example, could begin see one another as brothers and sisters through this practice. The same is true with violent criminals and the victims of violent crime, as we saw in the case of Bill Pelke, who was able to *see* the young teen who killed his grandmother with the eyes of compassion and love. In place of wars based on preemptive strikes, we might be preemptive in our practice of looking upon our enemies with patience, equanimity, and compassion. The Dalai Lama says, "The precondition for genuine compassion is to have a sense of equanimity toward all sentient beings. . . . As long as [compassion] is not based on profound equanimity, [it] will remain biased, for it is mixed with attachment."[26] Thây touches on the same theme by posing a question: "How can we love our enemy? There is only one way—to understand him. . . . Understanding a person brings us the power to love and accept him. And the moment we love and accept him, he ceases to be our enemy."[27] A world that begins to *see* the enemy with equanimity will be a world filled with peace and joy. That world is here and now; we need only to open our eyes.

The Horizontal Buddha

There is one final image that may help us as we reflect on the role that equanimity plays in our spiritual journey. It is an image that comes from Buddhist master D. T. Suzuki's very insightful book *Mysticism: Christian and Buddhist*. In this book, Suzuki compares the symbol of the vertical, crucified Christ with that of the horizontal or seated Buddha. "Verticality suggests action, motion, and aspiration," he says, describing what he calls the "almost unbearable" sight of the crucified Christ.[28] "Horizontality, as in the case of the lying Buddha, makes us think of peace, satisfaction or contentment. A sitting figure gives us the notion of solidity, firm conviction and immovability . . . [a] symbol of peace, tranquility and self-assurance."[29] Though I cannot say that I agree wholeheartedly with Suzuki's conclusions—especially regarding the cross (which, in fact, is both vertical *and* horizontal)—the image he paints of the Buddha lying down or seated on the ground in meditation is both striking and appealing.

What Suzuki is inviting us to, and for this reason his words are of great importance, is a practice of equanimity that can lead us from a life of aspiration and active pursuit (what we might call a "conquering" mentality), to an attitude of tranquility and acceptance of life as it comes to us day by day. According to Suzuki, horizontality symbolizes a noncompetitive approach to life, an embrace of each moment *as it is*, whereas verticality is a symbol of one who *grasps* life, trying to control the outcome of each and every moment. Suffering, in the Buddha's teaching, is the result of a grasping attitude. If we want to live a life of tranquility and peace, we must learn to let life come to us gently, accepting it as a gift, rather than "tackling" life as an obstacle that we aspire to overcome.

There is a story in the Gospels that tells of Jesus falling asleep while crossing the Sea of Galilee in a boat with his disciples. A violent storm suddenly comes up, tossing the tiny boat and filling it with water. In an almost humorous, *koan*-like way, Jesus remains asleep on a cushion—horizontally—throughout the raging storm. The disciples, of course, panic and finally wake Jesus up, "Teacher, do you not care that we are perishing?" Jesus calms the winds with the words, "Peace! Be still!" Then he turns to his disciples and asks them, "Why are you afraid? Have you still no faith?" (Mark 4:35-41). This story attempts, in a very simple way, to teach us something about the practice of equanimity. Jesus' rebuke of the violent winds can be heard as words addressed to us, "Peace! Be still!" Equanimity is about living with inner stillness in the midst of life's storms; it is the fruit of mindfulness and contemplative prayer. We do not have to flee from the violent storms of life or pretend that they do not touch us with suffering. Instead, we can learn the art of remaining calm and peaceful, practicing equanimity in the midst of the storm. In so doing we, like Jesus, can offer our own peace to others around us. The possibilities of extending one's own peaceful practice of equanimity out into the world are endless. This is certainly the territory of the saints and the bodhisattvas.

The Gospel story of Jesus' peaceful sleep in the storm-tossed boat in the company of his disciples reminds me of pictures that I have seen of statues of reclining Buddhas, what Suzuki refers to as the "horizontality" of the Buddha. As with the horizontal Buddha, the sleeping Jesus is a symbol of perfect equanimity, "a symbol of peace, tranquility, and self-assurance." Jesus invites us to rest in his loving presence, to trust that "all will be well."

Thomas Merton, writing in his *Asian Journal* during his trip to the East, which was the last trip of his life, was completely captivated and transformed by the immense statues of the reclining Buddha at Polonnaruwa in Sri Lanka. As one reads of what was for Merton a transforming encounter, there is a sense that a very deep part of Merton's psyche and soul was finally able to rise into a new level of enlightened consciousness. It is as if at last he found the Buddha reclining within himself.

I am able to approach the Buddhas barefoot and undisturbed, my feet in wet grass, wet sand. Then the silence of the extraordinary faces. The great smiles. Huge and yet subtle. Filled with every possibility, questioning nothing, knowing everything, rejecting nothing, the peace not of emotional resignation but of Mudhyamika, of sunyata. . . . For the doctrinaire, the mind that needs well-established positions, such peace, such silence, can be frightening. I was knocked over with a rush of relief and thankfulness. . . . Looking at these figures I was suddenly, almost forcibly, jerked clean out of the habitual, half-tied vision of things, and an inner calmness, clarity, as if exploding from the rocks themselves, became evident and obvious. . . . I know I have seen what I was obscurely looking for. I don't know what else remains but I have now seen and have pierced through the surface and have got beyond the shadow and the disguise. This is Asia in its purity.[30]

A week later, on December 10, 1968, Thomas Merton died in Bangkok—electrocuted while taking a shower. He had delivered a conference at ten o'clock that morning on Marxism and monasticism. Sometime around noon that day he wrote a letter to his fellow monk and close friend Brother Patrick Hart, back home at the Abbey of Gethsemani in Kentucky. The letter ended with these words, "I think of all of you on this Feast Day and with Christmas approaching I feel homesick for Gethsemani. . . . No more for the moment. Best love to all."[31] Patrick Hart writes in the Postscript to Merton's journal, "By Christmas he was, after all, back at Gethsemani, *lying buried* alongside the Abbey church overlooking the wooded knobs that had become so familiar to him during his twenty-seven years of monastic life in Kentucky."[32]

So Thomas Merton ended his earthly life reclining like the Buddha, asleep with Christ in the darkness of the earth, *back home* where it all began. The "half-tied vision of things" was suddenly and definitively set free by the inner clarity. He had finally tasted perfect equanimity: "I don't know what else remains but I have now seen and have pierced through the surface and have got beyond the shadow and the disguise."[33] Equanimity is what leads us "beyond the shadow and the disguise," beyond that suffering which deceives us into thinking that we are separated or distant from God. Equanimity helps us savor life *just as it is*—no frills, no masks, no yesterday, no tomorrow. Equanimity is life lived in its fullness, free from this and that, free to trust that, in the end, "all will be well."

CONCLUSION

A Journey and a Begging Bowl

During my stay at Deer Park Monastery in early 2004, I had the privilege of participating in a formal, ceremonial meal one day with Thây and the monastic community. With begging bowls in hand, we walked meditatively in procession to the newly completed Ocean of Peace Meditation Hall where, after a period of silence and chanting, we ate our meals in mindful attentiveness. The event brought to mind many similar solemn processions and liturgical celebrations that have been so much a part of my life as both a Catholic and a Dominican friar. I was reminded of the importance of ritual, symbol, and liturgy in the spiritual life of the world's different religious traditions. There will always be a dimension of the spiritual life that can only be expressed properly through the profound, pregnant silence of ritual. Today, as I look back on the experience of the formal meal, I smile in gratitude as I again realize how much our two traditions have in common.

We are all on a journey—a spiritual journey—whether we acknowledge it in those terms or not. We are all part of a great procession, walking together toward a future that unfolds as we go along. Thomas Merton wrote a prayer many years ago that expresses his own experience of life as a spiritual journey:

> My Lord God, I have no idea where I am going. I do not see the road ahead of me. I cannot know for certain where it will end. . . . I know that . . . you will lead me by the right road, though I may know nothing about it. Therefore I will trust you always though I may seem to be lost and in the shadow of death. I will not fear, for you are ever with me, and you will never leave me to face my perils alone.[1]

Spiritual processions and walking meditation are both outward practices that reflect the inward journey of our hearts. These practices invite us to live more mindfully of our journey with God, our communion with the Ultimate Reality of life. The ability to enjoy a quiet, meditative stroll in a forest, along the bank of a river, or even down the sidewalk of a busy city street is a good sign that our spiritual life is "on track." As Thây teaches with beautiful simplicity, when we treat ourselves to a quiet walking meditation, we are inviting our frantic, busy hearts to come back home and rest in the present moment.

179

This practice allows us to "catch our breath" again, and, as Merton points out, it frees us from the paralysis of fear, teaching us the art of living with trust. There are resting spots along the journey of life where we can look back at the winding path that we have left behind us and give thanks for the inner and outer journeys that have gone into bringing us to *this place* where we stand today. If we are fortunate enough, we can breathe deeply and say, as Thây reminds us, "I have arrived; I am home."

When St. Dominic, the founder of the Dominicans, gathered together his first disciples in the early 1200s, he took them atop a small hill in southern France and sent them out in pairs and small clusters to different cities in Europe to preach the Good News of Jesus. They were to be both itinerant and mendicant—wandering beggars—men and women called to walk in the footsteps of Jesus, trusting in the providential love of God and the goodness of others along the way. Though they did not have the exact equivalent of a Buddhist monk's or nun's begging bowl, the mendicant way of life they adopted has much in common with the Buddhist monastic tradition. Dominic made it clear that his disciples were to walk in complete trust, living fully each step of the journey, certain that God was with them at all times. Dominic's decision to send the brothers forth as mendicant preachers was based on a pivotal teaching of Jesus found in the Gospels:

> The Lord appointed seventy others and sent them on ahead of him in pairs to every town and place where he himself intended to go. . . . "Carry no purse, no bag, no sandals. . . . Whatever house you enter, first say, 'Peace to this house!' And if anyone is there who shares in peace, your peace will rest on that person; but if not, it will return to you. Remain in the same house, eating and drinking whatever they provide. . . . Whenever you enter a town and its people welcome you, eat what is set before you; cure the sick who are there, and say to them, 'The Kingdom of God has come near to you.'" (Matt 10:1-9)

Many centuries have passed since Jesus spoke these words, and today Dominican friars and Buddhist monastics have had to learn to accommodate their ancient practices to modern times. The begging bowl used today by Buddhists monks and nuns and the vow of poverty taken by Catholic friars, monks, and nuns may not be exactly what they were a few centuries ago, but these symbolic practices can still offer us an insight into a way of living in the present moment with trust, inner freedom, and gratitude. What is important, then, is that we learn to look deeply into the spiritual practices of our ancient traditions and discover the value that lies in them for spiritual seekers today.

It may still be possible today for a Hindu *sannyasi* in India or a Buddhist nun in Vietnam to go out each day to beg for his or her daily sustenance, but as a Westerner living in the twenty-first century, I want to discover new ways to incorporate these ancient practices into a modern spiritual journey. For example, in a world where millions of people are *really starving* each day, it may be that begging today means committing part of my weekly energy toward alleviating the poverty and hunger of the world. In this way, the begging bowl and the vow of poverty become tools for uniting me more mindfully with others. As a Christian, then, part of my spiritual "homework" is to look back at the story of Jesus sending his disciples out two-by-two to walk from town to town, begging for their daily bread, staying wherever they were offered a place to stay, curing the sick, and announcing that the reign of God is near, and I ask myself, "So, how do I remain faithful to that today?" How do I live a life of simplicity, itinerancy, and mindful awareness today, showing through my words and actions that in this very moment, and in this very place, we can touch the Ultimate Reality of the reign of God.

There is great spiritual depth in these ancient practices, and it seems that we do ourselves no favor if we simply bypass them as outdated and unrealistic for these modern times. As a way of concluding the reflections of our two great spiritual teachers, Meister Eckhart and Thich Nhat Hanh, I would like to propose that the image of the wandering, mendicant monk or friar can be of great value for those of us who wish to live a daily spiritual practice that is both refreshing and transforming in our world today. The ancient practices of our different traditions still have much to offer us, and though it is true that we must translate them into a language that is understandable today, we must not simply dismiss them as a kind of irrelevant romanticism of ages past.

As spiritual practitioners of the twenty-first century, we, like our ancestors, are on a journey, walking a path that unfolds in each and every step. The practice of mindfulness teaches us to savor each step, to live the present moment in all its fullness, aware that the kingdom is either now or never. Sometimes the spiritual path can seem rather dark, and we can wonder if we are headed in the right direction. As Merton says in his prayer to God, "I will trust you always though I may seem to be lost." The image of the spiritual life as a road that unfolds as we walk is an invitation to live life with deep trust. We are challenged to let go, to be detached from the obsessive worries that tempt us to spend our energies fretting about the road that lies ahead, searching for security in a future that is not yet real. This is a very important spiritual lesson for our world today. We live in an age in which security—both personal and national—has become a type of idolatry; we worship all that makes us feel safe and secure. To embrace life in the spirit of a wandering beggar, one who journeys one day at a time, fully immersed in the present moment, with no need to secure the future, is to live with freedom. By attempting to practice this kind of spiritual mendicancy and trust we can help to bring well-being and peace to our security-obsessed world.

Jesus said to his disciples, "Carry no purse, no bag, no sandals. . . . Whatever house you enter, first say, 'Peace to this house!' And if anyone is there who shares in peace, your peace will rest on that person." The person who journeys through life unburdened and uncluttered by the worries of the world is naturally a person of peace. Such a person does not have to *do* anything extraordinary to communicate peace to a neighboring house or nation; that person *is* peace. The wandering beggar's heart will naturally radiate peace to the heart of his or her neighbor. This peace is the fruit of the poverty of spirit proclaimed by Jesus in the Beatitudes (Matt 5:3). Because it is poor and trusting, the wandering beggar's heart has the capacity of sowing seeds of well-being, harmony, and peace in our world, what in Hebrew is called *shalom*. It is the peace that many of us have seen enfleshed in the lives and teachings of Thây, the Dalai Lama, Mother Teresa of Calcutta, Peace Pilgrim, Gandhi, and many other spiritual teachers of our day.

Jesus directs his disciples to stay in whatever house opens its doors to them, eating the food that is set before them. In our day, if we were to knock on a stranger's door and seek shelter for the night, it may be that we would end up spending the night in jail! Times have changed. These words of Jesus, though, are filled with profound wisdom, especially for those of us who have embarked on the journey of interreligious dialogue. Jesus' invitation forces us to ask certain questions, difficult questions that we are not always comfortable asking. What does it mean, for example, to journey forth as a pilgrim into the spiritual world of a tradition other than my own, where I am welcomed as a brother or a sister and fed spiritually from my host's table of ancient wisdom and truth? It may be a food that I have never before tasted. Likewise, what does it mean to invite the *other* into the home of my own faith tradition—that most intimate of sacred places—and to feed him or her with the spiritual bread that has been passed down by our ancestors through the centuries? Are we willing to take this risk, knowing that it will probably require a rethinking of some of our own ancient teachings? Hospitality, after all, is never a one-way street. Do we dare risk practicing communion before we fully understand what it might mean or look like?

Jesus seems to have wanted his disciples to take this risk into the unknown, to share daily life and daily bread with people who were very different from the disciples themselves. They were sent *empty handed*; this is so very important if true dialogue is to happen. We do not enter the other's house with the truth already tattooed onto the tip of our tongues, just waiting for the chance to reveal it to our neighbor. We enter as poor beggars, open to the sharing of word and bread, attentive to the gift and the truth of the present moment. When the door is opened and our dusty feet are washed in the cool waters of our host's hospitable heart, all we have to say at that moment, says Jesus, is, "Peace be on this house. The kingdom of God has come near to you." These words *are* the great revelation. These words are the words of communion that can bring healing to our fragmented world. Once we find ourselves seated at the table together—Buddhists and Christians, Hindus and Untouchables, Muslims and Jews—then we will not have to say too many words, for gratitude will fill our hearts. Meister Eckhart once said that if he had to summarize the entire spiritual life into a single word or phrase, it would be "Thank you." When we are able to look into each other's eyes and smile, receiving the gift that each has to offer, we will spontaneously want nothing more than to give thanks, using our diverse gestures and languages, for we will know without any doubt that the kingdom of God has come near. We will know that, though far away from the place where our journey began, we are finally home. The journey, though different and unique for each practitioner and each tradition, is one, and the great joy is the discovery that we walk the path together.

The spiritual pilgrim sets off on the journey of life as a wandering beggar for no other reason than to finally come home. This is beautifully portrayed in the celebrated Ox-Herding pictures from the Zen tradition. The end of the spiritual journey, as portrayed in these pictures, is not geographically different from the starting place. The inner landscape, however, has changed drastically. Says Ruben Habito:

> The tenth [and final] stage is the fullness and completion . . . the return to the market place. We are back in the concrete struggles of daily life. And yet, we are now able to live them, live right in the midst of them, with a sense of playfulness. We transcend our struggles not by escaping them, but by plunging ourselves right into them with a new sense of freedom and a sense of humor and a sense of acceptance.[2]

Interreligious dialogue offers us the opportunity to experience this wonderful truth. I speak from my own experience in this regard. I see my mendicant wanderings into the world of Buddhist and Hindu mysticism as an essential part of my Christian discipleship. It is Jesus himself who has sent me out empty handed, a poor beggar in the spiritual tradition of St. Dominic. I have been invited into homes and temples, mosques and synagogues where I have heard stories and languages very different from my own. I have sat at tables and been invited to eat food that, until then, was unknown to my palate. I have prayed and chanted with brothers and sisters whose spiritual world is expressed in rituals as beautiful as those from my own tradition. I have shared the scriptures and the music of Jesus with these newly found friends, and they have done the same with me. I have heard in the depths of my heart the harmony that springs forth from these blessed encounters. I am beginning to discover that the more my heart becomes a begging bowl, the more wonderfully do I experience the gratuitousness of life.

I would venture to say that I am a better disciple of Jesus because of this journey into the world of interreligious dialogue. Perhaps *better* is not the right word. It is as if I can see Jesus—the living Christ—more clearly now, as he is reflected through the teachings and practices of other spiritual traditions. I am still a wandering pilgrim, and sometimes I feel that the road is as dark and uncertain as the day I began. But I walk with a sense of *presence*, the presence of Jesus, the presence of God, the presence of the Buddha and many other holy men and women throughout the ages. This *presence* becomes more real each time I am able to dwell fully in the present moment. No one has helped me to learn the art of dwelling in the present moment as much as Thây. Because Thây has opened the door of his heart and his spiritual tradition to me, I have been able to come home more fully in my own spiritual journey.

> When we say, "Home sweet home," where is it? When we practice looking deeply, we realize that our home is everywhere. . . . "Listen, listen. This wonderful sound brings me back to my true home." The voice of the Buddha, the sound of the bell, the breath of the Holy Spirit, the sunshine, everything is calling us back to our true home. Once you are back in your home, you'll feel the peace and the joy you deserve. If you are a Christian, you feel that Jesus Christ is your home. It's very comfortable to think of Jesus as your home. If you are a Buddhist, then it's very nice to think of the Buddha as your home. Your home is available in the here and now. Christ is there, the Buddha is there. The practice is how to touch them, how to touch your home.[3]

As I bring these pages to an end, I can say with deep gratitude, "I have arrived; I am home." But perhaps more than ever, I sense that I must now say those words in the plural: *We have arrived; we are home.* In no way does this mean that the journey is over. It has only begun. Today is the day of salvation. This moment is the eternal Now. Life is a great gift, a great surprise. At the same time, though, gratitude energizes us to continue the journey with a sense of commitment and hope. Yes, we are home, and yet there is a long road ahead, as well. For this reason we take a step—one step—and we smile and give thanks. Today the journey continues to unfold—with Jesus and the Buddha, with Eckhart and Thây, and with so many others along the way, for we walk the path together.

Notes

Introduction

1. Thich Nhat Hanh, *Going Home: Jesus and Buddha as Brothers* (New York: Riverhead Books, 1999), 202.

2. For a concise and insightful look at the spiritual movements and milieu of Eckhart's day, see Richard Woods, OP, *Eckhart's Way* (Wilmington, Del.: Michael Glazier, 1986), chs. 1, 3.

3. Thomas Merton, as quoted by Frank X. Tuoti, "Thomas Merton: The Awakening of the Inner Self," *MONOS* [Tulsa, Okla.] 10, no. 1, ed. Patrick Eastman (January/February 1998): 1.

4. One of the more famous mystics of the time, and one who clearly influenced Eckhart, was Marguerite Porete, author of *The Mirror of Simple Souls*. She was condemned and executed in Paris in 1310. See Woods, *Eckhart's Way*, 75.

5. Not only was Eckhart not condemned as a heretic, but the Dominican order has officially called for the opening of the Meister's process of beatification and canonization.

Chapter 1: Magnanimity

1. Thich Nhat Hanh, *Living Buddha, Living Christ* (New York: Riverhead Books, 1995), 118-19.

2. Timothy Radcliffe, OP, "Vowed to Mission: A Letter to the Order" (Rome: General Curia of the Order of Preachers, 1994), 6.

3. Nhat Hanh, *Living Buddha, Living Christ*, 9.

4. Meister Eckhart, OP, *Meister Eckhart: Sermons and Treatises*, 3 vols., ed. and trans. Maurice O'C. Walshe (Shaftesbury: Element Books, 1979), #22: p. 177. All subsequent references to the sermons of Meister Eckhart from the Walshe collection will appear as *Eckhart*, followed by the sermon # and page.

5. Plum Village is the Buddhist monastery and spiritual practice center founded by Thich Nhat Hanh in the south of France.

6. Thich Nhat Hanh, *Touching Peace: Practicing the Art of Mindful Living* (Berkeley, Calif.: Parallax Press, 1992), 3-4.

7. *Eckhart*, # 22: p. 179.

8. From the *Acts of the General Chapter of the Order of Friars Preachers*, Caleruega, Spain, 1995.

9. Shunryu Suzuki, *Zen Mind, Beginner's Mind* (New York: Weatherhill, 1970), 21.

10. "Declaration on the Relation of the Church to Non-Christian Religions," in *Documents of the Second Vatican Council,* proclaimed by His Holiness Pope Paul VI, October 28, 1965, no.2.

11. His Holiness Pope John Paul II, "A Message for World Mission Sunday," Society for the Propagation of the Faith (October 20, 2002), 7-8.

12. Chrys McVey, OP, in a talk given at the Conferencia Interprovincial Dominicana en America Latina y el Caribe in Santiago, Chile, February 2, 2004.

13. Message from the participants of the Interfaith Congress for Dominicans, Bangkok-Bang Na, Thailand, February 7-12, 2001. Cited in Chrys McVey, OP, Conferencia Interprovincial Dominicana en America Latina y el Caribe, 2004.

14. Nhat Hanh, *Living Buddha, Living Christ,* 6-7.

Chapter 2: Mindfulness and the Eternal Now

1. Thich Nhat Hanh, *Going Home: Jesus and Buddha as Brothers* (New York: Riverhead Books, 1999), 84.

2. "The Eightfold Path is the Middle Way followed by the Buddha in his own search for enlightenment. It is a code for living as a Buddhist." This path includes right viewpoint, right intention, right speech, right action, right work, right effort, right mindfulness and right meditation, as cited in *The Usborne Encyclopedia of World Religions* (London: Usborne Publishing, 2001), 39. In the words of Thich Nhat Hanh, "The Five Wonderful Precepts (also called the Five Mindfulness Trainings) of Buddhism—reverence for life, generosity, responsible sexual behavior, speaking and listening deeply, and ingesting only wholesome substances—can contribute greatly to the happiness of the family and society," as cited in Thich Nhat Hanh, *Living Buddha, Living Christ* (New York: Riverhead Books, 1995), 91. See also Thich Nhat Hanh and the Dharmacarya Council of Plum Village, *The Revised Pratimoksha* (San Jose: Unified Buddhist Church, 2004) and Thich Nhat Hanh, *Stepping into Freedom: An Introduction to Buddhist Monastic Training* (Berkeley: Parallax Press, 1997).

3. Nhat Hanh, *Living Buddha, Living Christ,* 113-14.

4. Nhat Hanh, *Going Home,* 84.

5. St. Irenaeus, *Against Heresies* 4.20.5-7, as cited in *The Liturgy of the Hours* (New York: Catholic Book Publishing, 1975), 3:1499.

6. Thich Nhat Hanh, *Touching Peace: Practicing the Art of Mindful Living* (Berkeley, Calif.: Parallax Press, 1992), 1-2.

7. Thomas Philippe, *The Fire of Contemplation* (New York: Society of St. Paul, 1981), 47.

8. Brother Lawrence of the Resurrection, *The Practice of the Presence of God,* trans. John J. Delaney (New York: Doubleday, 1977), 61-68.

9. Nhat Hanh, *Going Home,* 194.

10. Meister Eckhart, Sermon Pr. 4, cited in Bernard McGinn, *The Mystical Thought of Meister Eckhart* (New York: Crossroad, 2001), 132.

11. Meister Eckhart, *The Talks of Instruction,* cited in McGinn, *Mystical Thought,* 132.

12. Meister Eckhart, OP, *Meister Eckhart: Sermons and Treatises,* 3 vols., ed. and trans. Maurice O'C. Walshe (Shaftesbury: Element Books, 1979), #8: 74.

13. *Eckhart*, #93: p. 319.

14. See *Eckhart*, #49: pp. 38-39.

15. *Eckhart*, #25: p. 198.

16. Nhat Hanh, *Going Home*, 9-10.

17. Ruben L. F. Habito, *Healing Breath: Zen Spirituality for a Wounded Earth* (Dallas: Maria Kannon Zen Center Publications, 2001), 124.

18. *Eckhart*, #8: pp. 72-73.

19. Thich Nhat Hanh, "The Essence of the Records of Master Lin Chi." These unpublished notes were written by Thây and circulated among his monastic community during the winter retreat, Jan–Mar 2004.

20. Nhat Hanh, *Going Home*, 38.

21. Richard Woods, OP, "Recovering Our Dominican Contemplative Tradition" (talk given at the Southern Dominican Provincial Assembly in San Antonio, Texas, May 28, 2002), 11.

22. Meister Eckhart, *Talks of Instruction*, p. 19, as cited in ibid., 11-12.

23. *Eckhart*, #50: p. 46.

24. Meister Eckhart, cited in McGinn, *Mystical Thought*, 134-35.

25. *Eckhart*, #79: p. 230.

26. Nhat Hanh, *Going Home*, 155-56.

27. Habito, *Healing Breath*, 125.

28. Nhat Hanh, *Going Home*, 40-41.

29. Ibid.

30. David Wagoner, *Poetic Medicine*, ed. John Fox (New York: Tarcher-Putnam, 1997), 192.

31. His Holiness Pope John Paul II, "A Message for World Mission Sunday," The Society for the Propagation of the Faith (October 20, 2002), 8.

32. Thomas Merton, *Life and Holiness* (New York: Image Books, 1962), 12.

33. Nhat Hanh, *Going Home*, 136-37.

34. Ibid., 42.

35. St. Augustine of Hippo, *The Confessions* (#27), cited in *Light from Light: An Anthology of Christian Mysticism*, ed. Louis Dupré and James A. Wiseman, OSB (New York: Paulist Press, 2001), 62-63.

36. *Eckhart*, #69: pp. 165, 169.

37. Thich Nhat Hanh, *Call Me by My True Names: The Collected Poems of Thich Nhat Hanh* (Berkeley, Calif.: Parallax Press, 1999), 118-19.

38. Nhat Hanh, *Living Buddha, Living Christ*, 22.

39. Henry David Thoreau, *Walden Or, Life in the Woods* (Boston: Shambhala, 1992), 72.

40. Nhat Hanh, *My True Names*, 183.

41. Cardinal Basil Hume, OSB, cited in a talk given by Timothy Radcliffe, OP.

42. St. Augustine of Hippo, *The Confessions*, in *Light from Light*, ed. Dupré and Wiseman, 58.

43. Thomas Merton, OCSO, *Thoughts in Solitude* (Boston: Shambhala, 1993), 43.

44. *Avatara* refers to the historical or, at times, mythical incarnation of a god or goddess in Hinduism. "In Krishna, Vishnu takes human form to bring righteousness to the earth. The *avatara* descends from heaven, from the higher consciousness, into our level of

consciousness, in order to raise us to the higher level of consciousness" (Bede Griffiths, *A New Vision of Reality* [New Delhi: Harper Collins, 1992], 141).

45. Nhat Hanh, *Living Buddha, Living Christ*, 166.

46. Anthony DeMello, unable to confirm source.

47. *Eckhart*, #32b: p. 241.

48. Ibid.

49. Meister Eckhart, *Talks of Instruction*, cited in Walshe, vol. 3, #7: p. 20.

50. Nhat Hanh, *Going Home*, 41.

51. Ibid., 36.

52. Woods, "Recovering Our Dominican Contemplative Tradition," 5.

53. Jan van Ruusbroec, *The Spiritual Espousals*, cited in *Light from Light*, ed. Dupré and Wiseman, 199.

54. Master Hakuin Zenji, cited in Ruben L. F. Habito, *Living Zen, Loving God* (Boston: Wisdom Publications, 2004), 51. The translation of Hakuin's song has been slightly revised, based on a version that Habito and his students use in chanting at the Maria Kannon Zen Center in Dallas, Texas.

55. St. Irenaeus, *Against Heresies* 4.20.4-5, cited in *Liturgy of the Hours*, 1:288.

56. *Tathagata* comes from two words: *tatha*, which means "thatness" or "suchness," and *gata*, which means "gone." "*Tathagata* is the one who has gone to 'that,' the one who has gone to the reality, who knows the reality, who knows the truth. . . . The Buddha was the one who discovered this reality" (Griffiths, *New Vision of Reality*, 138).

57. Nhat Hanh, *Living Buddha, Living Christ*, 180-81.

58. Nhat Hanh, *Going Home*, 33.

59. Ibid., 35.

60. *The Prayers of St. Catherine of Siena*, ed. Suzanne Noffke, OP (New York: Paulist Press, 1983), Prayer #19: p. 180.

Chapter 3: The Breath of the Holy Spirit

1. Thich Nhat Hanh, *Living Buddha, Living Christ* (New York: Riverhead Books, 1995), 15-16.

2. Thich Nhat Hanh, *Going Home: Jesus and Buddha as Brothers* (New York: Riverhead Books, 1999), 48.

3. Ruben L. F. Habito, *Healing Breath: Zen Spirituality for a Wounded Earth* (Dallas: Maria Kannon Zen Center Publications, 2001), 38.

4. Nhat Hanh, *Living Buddha, Living Christ*, 16.

5. Bede Griffiths, *Return to the Center* (Springfield, Ill.: Templegate, 1976), 129.

6. Nhat Hanh, *Living Buddha, Living Christ*, xvi.

7. Ibid., 20.

8. "Giver of Life" is one of the titles of the Holy Spirit in the Nicene Creed.

9. Jean-Pierre Lintanf, OP, cited in *Dominican Ashram* (Nagpur, India: Seminary Hill, 1993-94).

10. St. Dominic de Guzmán, founder of the Dominican order, said in one of his sermons, "The seed which is hoarded rots, while the seed which is planted bears much fruit."

11. Nhat Hanh, *Living Buddha, Living Christ*, 21.

12. Nhat Hanh, *Going Home*, 69.

13. Meister Eckhart, OP, *Meister Eckhart: Sermons and Treatises*, 3 vols., ed. and trans. Maurice O'C. Walshe (Shaftesbury: Element Books, 1979), #23: p. 181.

14. *Eckhart*, #62: p. 111.

15. Nhat Hanh, *Going Home*, 5.

16. Thich Nhat Hanh, "The Essence of the Records of Master Lin Chi." These unpublished notes were written by Thây and circulated among his monastic community during the winter retreat, January-March 2004, p. 3.

17. Ibid., 194.

18. *Eckhart*, #66: p. 144.

19. The phrase "born again" is based on the biblical phrase "born from above," from the Gospel of John (3:1-10). It has been used frequently by some Christian denominations to refer to the choice to accept Jesus Christ and become a Christian. This particular interpretation sees being "born again" as a once-in-a-lifetime event. But another way of understanding the text would be as an invitation to live each and every moment with the newness of life that comes from Christ. One way that this is incorporated into the mindful living of Thây's disciples is through the practice of *beginning anew*, which involves a time set apart for renewal and reconciliation, not so unlike a time for spiritual rebirth.

20. *Eckhart*, #1: p. 1.

21. Nhat Hanh, *Living Buddha, Living Christ*, 181.

22. David Steindl-Rast, OSB, cited in Nhat Hanh, *Living Buddha, Living Christ*, xiii.

23. Thây's teaching on *interbeing* will be looked at more in detail in chapter 5.

24. Nhat Hanh, *Going Home*, 5.

25. *Eckhart*, #70: pp. 174-75; #83: pp. 252-53.

26. *Eckhart*, #65: p. 135.

27. Thomas Merton, *Conjectures of a Guilty Bystander* (New York: Doubleday, 1966), 142.

28. Thich Nhat Hanh, *Touching Peace: Practicing the Art of Mindful Living* (Berkeley, Calif.: Parallax Press, 1992), 8.

29. Nhat Hanh, *Living Buddha, Living Christ*, 112-13.

30. Ibid., 10.

31. Meister Eckhart, OP, *The Talks of Instruction*, in *Meister Eckhart: Sermons and Treatises*, ed. and trans. Walshe, 3:20.

32. Nhat Hanh, *Going Home*, p.194.

33. Nhat Hanh, *Living Buddha, Living Christ*, 155.

34. *Eckhart*, #12: p. 103.

35. See also John 5:42; 15:9, 13, 17, 19, 26; 21:15; and 1 John 2:5; 3:1, 11, 16; 4:8, 10, 16, 18-19.

36. Bede Griffiths, taken from an audio cassette of a talk entitled "Eastern Mysticism and Christian Faith," given at Deaken University in Australia, May 1985.

37. Nhat Hanh, *Going Home*, 155-56, 158, 160.

38. Ibid., 67-68.

39. Ibid., 68.

40. *Eckhart*, #5: p. 50.

41. *Eckhart*, #12: p. 103.

42. Meister Eckhart, *Of the Nobleman*, in *Meister Eckhart: The Essential Sermons, Commentaries, Treatises and Defense*, trans. and intro. by Edmund Colledge, OSA, and Bernard McGinn (New York: Paulist Press, 1981), 242.

43. Nhat Hanh, *Going Home*, 68, 70.

44. *Eckhart*, #62: p. 113.

45. Meister Eckhart, OP, *The Book of Divine Comfort*, in *Meister Eckhart: Sermons and Treatises*, ed. and trans. Walshe, 3:78.

Chapter 4: The Water and the Waves

1. Thich Nhat Hanh, *Going Home: Jesus and Buddha as Brothers* (New York: Riverhead Books, 1999), 138.

2. Ibid., 103-4.

3. St. Seraphim of Sarov, *St. Seraphim of Sarov*, ed. Valentine Zander, trans. Sr. Gabriel Anne, SSC (Crestwood, N.Y.: St. Vladimir's Seminary Press, 1999), 92.

4. Meister Eckhart, OP, *Meister Eckhart: Sermons and Treatises*, 3 vols., ed. and trans. Maurice O'C. Walshe (Shaftesbury: Element Books, 1979), #88: p. 282 and #60: pp. 104-5.

5. *Eckhart*, #60: p. 105.

6. *Eckhart*, #31: p. 229.

7. *Eckhart*, #19: p. 160.

8. Bernard McGinn, *The Mystical Thought of Meister Eckhart* (New York: Crossroad Publishing Co., 2001), 44. In this fine English-language overview of the latest scholarship on Eckhart's mystical writings, Bernard McGinn categorizes Eckhart's unique brand of mysticism under the title "mysticism of the ground." Says McGinn, "*Grunt* is employed by Eckhart in a rich variety of ways, but the basic intention of the semantic field of ground-language is always geared to one goal: achieving indistinct identity of God and human in what Eckhart calls the 'simple One'" (p. 47).

9. Meister Eckhart, from Sermon Pr. 15, cited in McGinn, *Mystical Thought*, 45.

10. The Buddha, *Udana* viii, 3, quoted in Thich Nhat Hanh, *Living Buddha, Living Christ* (New York: Riverhead Books, 1995), 138-39.

11. Richard Woods, *Eckhart's Way* (Wilmington, Del.: Michael Glazier, 1986), 44.

12. *Eckhart*, #2: p. 16.

13. *Eckhart*, #94: p. 323.

14. Nhat Hanh, *Going Home*, 9.

15. *Catechism of the Catholic Church* (Washington, D.C.: U.S. Catholic Conference, 1994), no. 2009, p. 487. Whereas the West tends to speak of "created grace," and the divinizing effect of "sanctifying grace," the East focuses on "uncreated grace," or "indwelling." Both traditions, however, speak of *divinization*. "The grace of Christ is the gratuitous gift that God makes to us of his own life . . . *sanctifying* or *deifying grace*" (no. 1999, p. 484).

16. Nhat Hanh, *Living Buddha, Living Christ*, 123.

17. *Eckhart*, #47: pp. 27-29.

18. John Meyendorff, *Byzantine Theology: Historical Trends and Doctrinal Themes*, 2nd ed. (New York: Fordham University Press, 1983), 164-65.

19. *Eckhart*, #70: p. 173.

20. Meister Eckhart, *Of the Nobleman*, in *Meister Eckhart: The Essential Sermons,*

Commentaries, Treatises and Defense, trans. and intro. Edmund Colledge, OSA, and Bernard McGinn (New York: Paulist Press, 1981), 241.

21. Juan G. Arintero, OP, *The Mystical Evolution in the Development and Vitality of the Church*, 2 vols., trans. Jordan Aumann (St. Louis: B. Herder Book Co., 1949), 1:7. Meyendorff stresses the same point as Arintero, saying that a deified humanity "does not in any way lose its human characteristics. Quite to the contrary. These characteristics become even more real and authentic by contact with the divine model according to which they were created," in Meyendorff, *Byzantine Theology,* 164.

22. *Eckhart*, #20: p. 164.

23. *Eckhart*, #88: p. 283.

24. From a *dharma* talk given at Deer Park Monastery in Escondido, California, on March 14, 2004.

25. Meister Eckhart, from Sermon Pr. 15, cited in McGinn, *Mystical Thought*, 45.

26. *Eckhart*, #7: p. 66.

27. *Tao Te Ching*, a new English version by Stephen Mitchell (New York: Harper & Row, 1988), no. 25.

28. *Eckhart*, #94: p. 323.

29. Nhat Hanh, *Going Home*, 148 and 6-7.

30. Frank Kacmarcik, Obl.S.B., and Paul Philibert, OP, *Seeing and Believing: Images of Christian Faith* (Collegeville, Minn.: Liturgical Press, 1995), 42. See also Thomas Aquinas, *Summa Theologiae* II, 1.3.4.c.

31. See *Eckhart*, Sermons 43 and 49.

32. Nhat Hanh, *Living Buddha, Living Christ*, 142.

33. *Eckhart*, #30: p. 227.

34. *Eckhart*, #33: p. 247.

35. Nhat Hanh, *Going Home*, 99.

36. Ibid., 43.

37. Ibid., 146.

38. Nhat Hanh, *Living Buddha, Living Christ*, 138.

39. Meister Eckhart, *Of the Nobleman*, in *Meister Eckhart*, ed. Colledge and McGinn, 243 (language adapted).

40. Nhat Hanh, *Going Home*, 90.

41. Swami Abhishiktananda, in Odette Baumer-Despeigne, "The Lord's Prayer as a Way of Initiation," cited in *Swami Abhishiktananda: The Man and his Teaching*, ed. Vandana (New Delhi, ISPCK, 1986), 54.

42. St. Catherine of Siena, *The Dialogue*, trans. and intro. Suzanne Noffke, OP (New York: Paulist Press, 1980), 211 n. 112.

43. *Catechism of the Catholic Church*, nos. 1997-98, pp. 483-84.

44. Eckhart, from the *Commentary on the Gospel of John* (no. 117), cited in McGinn, *Mystical Thought*, 117.

45. *Eckhart*, #6: p. 55.

46. *Eckhart*, #6: p. 61.

47. *Eckhart*, #45: p. 15.

48. *Eckhart*, #14b: p. 127.

49. *Eckhart*, #4: p. 45.

50. *Eckhart,* #69: p. 165.

51. Nhat Hanh, *Going Home,* 44.

52. *Eckhart,* #21: p. 172.

53. Nhat Hanh, *Going Home,* 11.

54. Ibid., 158.

55. McGinn, *Mystical Thought,* 128.

56. Ibid.

57. Nhat Hanh, *Living Buddha, Living Christ,* 88.

58. Ibid., 28-29.

59. Nhat Hanh, *Going Home,* 5.

60. Taken from the "Five Mindfulness Trainings Recitation Ceremony"; see Nhat Hanh, *Going Home,* 133-34.

61. Nhat Hanh, *Going Home,* 158.

Chapter 5: Jesus and God

1. Meister Eckhart, OP, *The Book of Divine Comfort,* in *Meister Eckhart: Sermons and Treatises,* ed. and trans. Maurice O'C. Walshe (Shaftesbury: Element Books, 1979), 3:76.

2. Ibid., 77.

3. Meister Eckhart, Latin Sermon XLIX.3, n. 511, cited in Bernard McGinn, *The Mystical Thought of Meister Eckhart* (New York: Crossroad, 2001), 72.

4. Fr. Bede's use of the word *differentiation* will be key to understanding much of what is to follow in this chapter. It is one way of speaking of *otherness* within the *oneness* of God.

5. Bede Griffiths, taken from an audio casette of a talk, entitled "Eastern Mysticism and Christian Faith," given at Deaken University in Australia, May 1985.

6. Though other medieval theologians, such as Aquinas and Albert the Great, as well as other mystics, such as Marguerite Porete, also used these terms in their writings, "none of these authors developed the all-important relation between Trinitarian divine *bullitio* (God's inner boiling) and creative *ebullitio* (the boiling over)... [This was] Eckhart's new 'explosive metaphor' for presenting the metaphysics of flow" (McGinn, *Mystical Thought,* 74).

7. *Eckhart,* #12: p. 106.

8. *Eckhart,* #29: p. 221.

9. *Eckhart,* #60: p. 105.

10. Eckhart, *Divine Comfort,* in *Meister Eckhart,* ed. and trans. Walshe, 3:76.

11. The use of measurements of time in this discussion is only for the sake of clarity. Richard Woods, OP, commenting on Eckhart's distinction between the undifferentiated Godhead and the differentiated Trinity, says that, for Eckhart, the Godhead is not prior to God *in time,* but simply "logically prior." He then quotes Eckhart on this important distinction: "Everything that is in the Godhead is one, and of that there is nothing to be said. God works, the Godhead does no work" (*Eckhart* #56: p. 81). See Richard Woods, *Eckhart's Way* (Wilmington, Del.: Michael Glazier, 1986), 46.

12. *Eckhart* #56: p. 81.

13. Griffiths, "Eastern Mysticism and Christian Faith." See also Bede Griffiths, *A New Vision of Reality* (India: Indus and Harper Collins, 1992), 158-59. For more on D. T.

Suzuki's teaching on the Buddhist doctrine of *sunyata,* refer to D. T. Suzuki, *Mysticism: Christian and Buddhist* (New York: Harper & Row, 1957), 6, 29-38. *Nirvana* is the freedom of enlightenment, which is attained when one passes beyond the endless cycle of unenlightened existence known as *samsara.* The dynamic emptiness of *sunyata* lies beyond the apparent opposition between *nirvana* and *samsara,* where all is one.

14. Thich Nhat Hanh, *Living Buddha, Living Christ* (New York: Riverhead Books, 1995), 41-42.

15. The Dalai Lama says, "In Buddhism it is thought that there is a special relationship between the emanation and the emanating force, and that an emanation comes to an end when it has fulfilled its destiny. There is an idea that the emanation is reabsorbed into its source, although in some cases the emanation disappears of its own accord." Cited in *The Good Heart: A Buddhist Perspective on the Teachings of Jesus* (Boston: Wisdom Publications, 1996), 120.

16. *Eckhart,* #33: p. 247.

17. *Eckhart,* #6: p. 66.

18. *Eckhart,* #56: p. 82.

19. *Chandogya Upanishad* 6:12, cited in Griffiths, *New Vision,* 64.

20. St. Thomas Aquinas's *Summa Theologiae* "is structured according to the way that leads from God to the world (*exitus*) and the way that leads from the world back to God (*reditus*)" (cited in Robert Barron, *Thomas Aquinas: Spiritual Master* [New York: Crossroad, 1996], 25). Marie-Dominique Chenu, OP, is acknowledged to be the one responsible for discovering and highlighting the Neoplatonic movement of emanation and return—*exitus* and *reditus*—at the heart of the *Summa Theologiae's* structure. See M.-D. Chenu, OP, *Aquinas and His Role in Theology,* trans. Paul J. Philibert, OP (Collegeville, Minn.: Liturgical Press, 2002), ch. 5.

21. Griffiths, "Eastern Mysticism and Christian Faith."

22. Griffiths, *New Vision,* 172-74.

23. Robert Barron, "The Christian: Missionary of Hope," *Chicago Studies* 33 (August 1994): 140. The reference to "Balthasar" is to the theologian Hans Urs von Balthasar.

24. John Tauler, OP, "Sermon One—Christmas," in *Johhanes Tauler: Sermons,* trans. Maria Shrady (New York: Paulist Press, 1985), 36-37.

25. Nhat Hanh, *Living Buddha, Living Christ,* 70.

26. *Eckhart,* #22: pp. 177-79.

27. Nhat Hanh, *Living Buddha, Living Christ,* 42.

28. St. Catherine of Siena, *The Dialogue,* trans. and intro. Suzanne Noffke, OP (New York: Paulist Press, 1980), ##21-22, pp. 64-65.

29. St. Catherine of Siena, "Letter to Thomas della Fonte" in *Catherine of Siena: Passion for Truth, Compassion for Humanity,* ed. Mary O'Driscoll (New York: New City Press, 1993), 24. "Recognizing that we are nothing," wrote Catherine, "we are humbled, and so we are able to enter into the blazing, fiery, open heart [of Christ] . . . which is never closed."

30. A slightly altered version of a line from the First Eucharistic Prayer of Reconciliation in the Roman Catholic sacramentary.

31. Griffiths, *New Vision,* 173.

32. T. S. Eliot, *Four Quartets,* "Little Gidding" (San Diego: Harcourt Brace Jovanovich, 1943), 58-59.

33. Bede Griffiths, from a *satsang* talk given at Shantivanam Ashram in India in 1989. The cassette from this talk was shared by Sr. Pascaline Coff, OSB, who lived with Fr. Bede for a time in his ashram.

34. Swami Abhishiktananda, taken from reflections on the Lord's Prayer, cited in an interview with Odette Baumer-Despeigne, which was conducted by Sr. Pascaline Coff, OSB, *Bulletin of Monastic Interreligious Dialogue* 51 (October 17, 1994): 20.

35. Eckhart, *Divine Comfort*, in *Meister Eckhart*, ed. and trans. Walshe, 3:76-77.

36. *Eckhart, #69: p. 165.*

37. Thich Nhat Hanh, *Going Home* (New York: Riverhead Books, 1999), 98.

38. Nhat Hanh, *Living Buddha, Living Christ*, 36. Thây says later in the book, "According to the teaching of the Trinity in the Orthodox church, the Father is the source of divinity who engenders the Son. With the Word (*Logos*), He brings about the Spirit that is alive in the Son. This is very much like the nondual nature of Buddha, Dharma, and Sangha" (pp. 123-24).

39. Cyprian Smith, *Meister Eckhart: The Way of Paradox* (New York: Paulist Press, 1987), 61.

40. *Eckhart, #13a: pp. 110-11.*

41. *Eckhart, #96: p. 334.*

42. Eckhart, *Divine Comfort*, in *Meister Eckhart*, ed. and trans. Walshe, 3:77.

43. Nhat Hanh, *Going Home*, 9-11.

44. *Eckhart, #1: p. 1.*

45. Nhat Hanh, *Going Home*, 146.

46. Ibid., 138.

47. Ibid., 104-5.

48. Ibid., 155.

49. Smith, *Way of Paradox*, 76.

50. "We confess one Christ, one Son, one Lord. In accordance with this union without confusion, we profess the holy Virgin to be Mother of God (*theotokos*), for God the Word became flesh and was made human and from the moment of conception united to himself the temple he had taken from her." Taken from the documents of the Council of Ephesus, as cited in Richard P. McBrien, *Catholicism* (Minneapolis: Winston Press, 1980), 453.

51. *Eckhart, #1: p. 5; #2: p. 15.*

52. *Eckhart, # 90: p. 301.*

53. *Eckhart, #88: p. 281.*

54. Bernard McGinn carefully points out Eckhart's subtle distinction between "*grunt* as precondition (i.e., pure possibility) for emanation and the Father as actual source for the God who becomes" (*Mystical Thought*, 82). Eckhart says in the *Commentary on Exodus*, "The potentiality of begetting in the Father is in the essence rather than the Paternity" (82). For this present discussion we will use Father and *grunt* interchangeably (as Eckhart himself does often), in other words, as referring to the *essential Father*, the undifferentiated Father or Godhead. This is not to deny that Eckhart frequently distinguishes between the Godhead and the trinitarian differentiation of the divine persons.

55. Eckhart's "silent desert" is one of the many ways he uses to speak of the *grunt*. "The true word of eternity is spoken only in solitude, where man is a desert" (*Eckhart, #4: p. 42*). "It is the light (in the soul) which lays straight hold of God . . . it catches Him in the act of

begetting . . . it wants to get into the silent desert into which no distinction ever peeped" (#60: pp. 104-5). See also McGinn, *Mystical Thought*, 35-52.

56. *Eckhart*, #70: p. 175. McGinn dedicates an entire chapter to what he calls Eckhart's "Metaphysics of Flow" (*Mystical Thought*, 71-113). Beginning with the scholastic notion of *exitus-reditus*, or the flowing-out from God and the flowing-back-into God, Eckhart further develops the idea that the flowing-out that happens eternally within the inner dynamic of the Trinity is re-presented or concomitant with the flowing-out that happens in creation. This will be discussed more fully later in this chapter.

57. *Eckhart*, #1: pp. 3, 5; #3: p. 33. It is important to note that at times Eckhart refers to the birth of the *Word* in the soul, and at other times he speaks of the birth of the *Son*. It is one and the same. As he says in one sermon, combining the two, "When the Word speaks in the soul and the soul replies in the living Word, then the Son is alive in the soul" (#36: pp. 265-66).

58. *Eckhart*, #88: p. 279.

59. Nhat Hanh, *Living Buddha, Living Christ*, 40.

60. The birth of the divine Word in the ground of the soul is God's action at work in the human person. "Buddhists regard the Buddha as a teacher and a brother, not as a god," recognizes Thây (*Living Buddha, Living Christ*, 40). Though both are pointing to the meeting of the ultimate and historical dimensions, it is important for the sake of the ongoing interreligious dialogue to note that the two traditions are not saying exactly the same thing.

61. *Eckhart*, #19: pp. 157-58.

62. *Eckhart*, #77: p. 220.

63. *Eckhart*, #80: p. 237.

64. McGinn, *Mystical Thought*, 57.

65. Suzuki, *Mysticism: Christian and Buddhist*, 17.

66. Ibid., 18.

67. *Eckhart*, #2: p. 20.

68. *Eckhart*, #2: p. 15.

69. *Eckhart*, #1: p. 3.

70. *Eckhart*, #2: pp. 16-17.

71. *Eckhart*, #96: p. 333.

72. Timothy Radcliffe, OP, "Letter to Our Brothers and Sisters in Initial Formation" (May 1999). Written as a pastoral letter to the different branches of the Dominican family.

73. *Eckhart*, #2: p. 15.

74. Nhat Hanh, *Going Home*, 66-67.

Chapter 6: Christ

1. Meister Eckhart, OP, *Meister Eckhart: Sermons and Treatises*, 3 vols., ed. and trans. Maurice O'C. Walshe (Shaftesbury: Element Books, 1979), #54: p. 72 and #14b: p. 124.

2. Donald Goergen, OP, *Jesus, Son of God, Son of Mary, Immanuel* (Collegeville, Minn.: Liturgical Press, 1995), 27.

3. Christian theology, as articulated by the metaphysics of St. Thomas Aquinas and other scholastic theologians, distinguishes between the *necessary being* of God (a verb: *esse*) and the contingent being of creatures (a noun: *ens*). In other words, God cannot *not be*,

whereas creatures receive their being from the *is-ness* of God. Eckhart's doctrine follows directly from St. Thomas on this point. See *Summa Theologiae* II, 1.3.4.c.

4. *Eckhart*, #79: p. 232.

5. Meister Eckhart, OP, *The Book of Divine Comfort*, in *Meister Eckhart: Sermons and Treatises*, ed. and trans. Walshe, 3:80-81.

6. Meister Eckhart, *Commentary on the Prologue of the Gospel of John* (no. 106), cited in Bernard McGinn, *The Mystical Thought of Meister Eckhart* (New York: Crossroad, 2001), 117.

7. Meister Eckhart, Proc. Col. II, cited in McGinn, *Mystical Thought*, 117.

8. *Eckhart*, #20: p. 166.

9. Meister Eckhart, *Of the Nobleman*, in *Meister Eckhart: Sermons and Treatises*, ed. and trans. Walshe, 3:241.

10. Thich Nhat Hanh, *Going Home: Jesus and Buddha as Brothers* (New York: Riverhead Books, 1999), 9.

11. Thomas Merton, *New Seeds of Contemplation* (New York: New Directions Books, 1961), 2-3.

12. Nhat Hanh, *Going Home*, 149-51.

13. *Eckhart*, #18: p. 148.

14. Cyprian Smith, OSB, *The Way of Paradox: Spiritual Life as Taught by Meister Eckhart* (New York: Paulist Press, 1987), 62-63.

15. Merton, *New Seeds*, 3.

16. *Eckhart*, #22: p. 179.

17. Nhat Hanh, *Going Home*, 137.

18. "Morning Has Broken," text by Eleanor Farjeon, (1881-1965), *The Children's Bells* (London: Oxford University Press, 1957). Music: Bunessan, Gaelic: Arr. by Marty Haugen (b. 1950) (GIA Publications, 1987).

19. *Eckhart*, #14b: p. 127.

20. *Eckhart*, #22: pp. 177-79.

21. Joseph Milne, "Eckhart and the Word," *Eckhart Review* [Oxford: The Eckhart Society] no. 11 (Spring 2002): 11.

22. Thich Nhat Hanh, *Living Buddha, Living Christ* (New York: Riverhead Books, 1995), 34.

23. Ibid., 35.

24. Ibid.

25. Nhat Hanh, *Going Home*, 152-53.

26. Mother Teresa of Calcutta told this story at the Eucharistic Congress in Philadelphia, Pennsylvania, in 1976. Cited from a cassette produced by Servant Cassettes.

27. Though there is not sufficient space to pursue the theme in this book, the writings of Pierre Teilhard de Chardin, S.J., were some of the first to delve deeply into the implications of a cosmic Christology.

28. Bede Griffiths, *The Marriage of East and West* (Springfield, Ill.: Templegate Publishers, 1982), 195.

29. *Eckhart*, #33: pp. 247-49.

30. *Eckhart*, #51: p. 49.

31. Nhat Hanh, *Going Home*, 153-54.

32. Bede Griffiths, 1989 *satsang* talk.

33. Laurence Freeman, OSB, in His Holiness the Dalai Lama, *The Good Heart: A Buddhist Perspective on the Teachings of Jesus* (Boston: Wisdom Publications, 1996), 121.

34. Dalai Lama, in *Good Heart*, 119.

35. Griffiths, 1989 *satsang* talk.

36. *Eckhart*, #53: p. 64.

37. Nhat Hanh, *Going Home*, 145.

38. Ibid., 107.

39. From a conversation with Paul Philibert, OP, in May 2004.

40. *Eckhart*, #49: p. 37 and #77: p. 220.

Chapter 7: Suffering

1. Thich Nhat Hanh, *Living Buddha, Living Christ* (New York: Riverhead Books, 1995), 48.

2. An essential teaching of the Buddha, the Four Noble Truths are (1) All life involves suffering. (2) The cause of suffering is desire and attachment. (3) Desire and attachment can be overcome. (4) The way to overcome them is to follow the Eightfold Path. Taken from Susan Meredith and Clare Hickman, *The Usborne Encyclopedia of World Religions* (London: Usborne Publishing, 2001), 38.

3. His Holiness the Dalai Lama, *The Good Heart: A Buddhist Perspective on the Teachings of Jesus* (Boston: Wisdom Publications, 1996) from the glossary of Buddhist terms, 181.

4. Thich Nhat Hanh, *Going Home: Jesus and Buddha as Brothers* (New York: Riverhead Books, 1999), 124-25.

5. Ibid., 125-26.

6. Dalai Lama, *Good Heart*, 54.

7. Meister Eckhart, OP, *The Book of Divine Comfort*, in *Meister Eckhart: Sermons and Treatises*, 3 vols., ed. and trans. Maurice O'C. Walshe (Shaftesbury: Element Books, 1979), 3:64.

8. Ibid., 71.

9. Ibid., 66.

10. Elizabeth Barrett Browning, from "Aurora Leigh," book vii, cited in *America* (December 7, 1996): 9.

11. "When is God your God?" asks Eckhart. "When you desire nothing but Him, for you find Him so tasty. But if you desire anything that entices you anywhere out of Him, then he is not your God" (*Eckhart* #74: p. 203).

12. *Eckhart*, #22: p. 177.

13. Bernard McGinn, *The Mystical Thought of Meister Eckhart* (New York: Crossroad, 2001), 133. Eckhart uses several different words to refer to detachment: leaving, letting go, detaching, resigning, un-forming, de-forming, un-becoming, etc.

14. Eckhart, *On Detachment*, in *Meister Eckhart*, ed. and trans. Walshe, 3:120-21.

15. *Eckhart*, #3: p. 33.

16. Eckhart, *Divine Comfort*, in *Meister Eckhart*, ed. and trans. Walshe, 3:70.

17. *Eckhart*, #13a: p. 112.

18. Nhat Hanh, *Going Home*, 153.

19. *Eckhart*, #49: p. 37.

20. *Eckhart*, #77: p. 220.

21. *Eckhart*, #87: p. 271.

22. *Eckhart*, #13b: pp. 117-18.

23. *Eckhart*, #12: p. 104.

24. *Eckhart*, #74: p. 204.

25. Eckhart, *Divine Comfort*, in *Meister Eckhart*, ed. and trans. Walshe, 3:67.

26. Ibid., 65-66.

27. Thich Nhat Hanh, "Liberation from Suffering," *The Mindfulness Bell* no. 19 (May-August 1977): 1.

28. *Eckhart*, #2: p. 17.

29. Eckhart, *Divine Comfort*, in *Meister Eckhart*, ed. and trans. Walshe, 3:66-67.

30. *Eckhart*, #68: p. 158.

31. Nhat Hanh, *Going Home*, 91.

32. Meister Eckhart, Sermon Pr. 5b, cited in McGinn, *Mystical Thought*, 45.

33. *Eckhart*, #2: pp. 20-21.

34. *Eckhart*, #1: p. 7.

35. *Eckhart*, #69: p. 169.

36. *Eckhart*, #6: pp. 56-59.

37. As noted in earlier chapters, this is the motif of the parable of the prodigal son in Luke 15:11-32. For more on the meaning of the words *repent* and *penance,* see *The New World Dictionary-Concordance to the New American Bible* (New York: World Publishing, 1970), 520.

38. *Eckhart*, #2: p. 21.

39. Thich Nhat Hanh, *The Miracle of Mindfulness: A Manual on Meditation* (Boston: Beacon Press, 1975), 15.

Chapter 8: Compassion Born from Suffering

1. Thich Nhat Hanh, *Going Home: Jesus and Buddha as Brothers* (New York: Riverhead Books, 1999), 36-37.

2. Thich Nhat Hanh, *Living Buddha, Living Christ* (New York: Riverhead Books, 1995), 84.

3. His Holiness the Dalai Lama, *The Good Heart: A Buddhist Perspective on the Teachings of Jesus* (Boston: Wisdom Publications, 1996), 68.

4. Nhat Hanh, *Living Buddha, Living Christ*, 10-11.

5. St. Catherine of Siena, in *Catherine of Siena: Passion for the Truth, Compassion for Humanity*, ed. Mary O'Driscoll, OP (New York: New City Press, 1993), prayer no.19, p. 83.

6. Vincent de Couesnongle, OP, former Master of the Order of Preachers, in a talk given on the occasion of the reception of the habit by a group of Dominican novices at the Convento de San Luís Beltrán, Amecameca, Mexico, August 4, 1977.

7. Meister Eckhart, OP, *Meister Eckhart: Sermons and Treatises*, 3 vols., ed. and trans. Maurice O'C. Walshe (Shaftesbury: Element Books, 1979), #95: p. 328.

8. Bartolomé de Las Casas, *History of the Indies*, trans. and ed. Andrée Collard (New York: Harper & Row, 1971), book III, ch. 129, p. 257.

9. Ibid., prologue, p. 5.

10. Etty Hillesum, *An Interrupted Life and Letters from Westerbork* (New York: Henry Holt and Co., 1996), 226-27.

11. Dalai Lama, *Good Heart*, 68.

12. Bill Pelke, quoted in "Group Travels to Speak against the Death Penalty," by Khalid Moss, *Dayton Daily News*, May 16, 2001.

13. Nhat Hanh, *Going Home*, 73.

14. Ibid., 164.

15. Dalai Lama, *Good Heart*, 68.

16. Nhat Hanh, *Going Home*, 32.

17. Ruben L. F. Habito, *Living Zen, Loving God* (Boston: Wisdom Publications, 2004), 77.

18. Dalai Lama, *Good Heart*, 53-54.

19. Nhat Hanh, *Going Home*, 37.

20. Ibid., 165.

21. Ibid.

22. *The Gethsemani Encounter: A Dialogue on the Spiritual Life by Buddhist and Christian Monastics*, ed. Donald Mitchell and James Wiseman, OSB (New York: Continuum, 1997), 231.

23. Fenton Johnson, *Keeping Faith: A Skeptic's Journey* (Boston: Houghton Mifflin, 2003), 19.

24. *Gethsemani Encounter*, 232.

25. Ibid.

26. Ibid.

27. Ibid., 132. Taken from a talk by Dom Armand Veilleux, OCSO.

28. Ibid., 233.

29. Johnson, *Keeping Faith*, 19.

30. *Gethsemani Encounter*, 234.

31. Nhat Hanh, *Going Home*, 164.

32. Nhat Hanh, *Living Buddha, Living Christ*, 91.

33. Ibid.

34. Ibid., 67.

35. *Eckhart*, #13a: p. 110.

36. Dalai Lama, *Good Heart*, 68.

37. Nhat Hanh, *Living Buddha, Living Christ*, 78.

38. *Gethsemani Encounter*, 133.

Chapter 9: The Tree of the Cross

1. Meister Eckhart, OP, *Meister Eckhart: Sermons and Treatises*, 3 vols., ed. and trans. Maurice O'C. Walshe (Shaftesbury: Element Books, 1979), #24a: p. 188.

2. Meister Eckhart, OP, *The Book of Divine Comfort*, in *Meister Eckhart: Sermons and Treatises*, ed. and trans. Walshe, 3:89.

3. Meister Eckhart, *On Detachment*, in *Meister Eckhart*, ed. and trans. Walshe, 3:120-21.

4. *Eckhart*, #55: p. 78.

5. Thich Nhat Hanh, *Living Buddha, Living Christ* (New York: Riverhead Books, 1995), 117.

6. *Gateless Gate*, trans. and commentary by Zen Master Koun Yamada (Tucson: University of Arizona Press, 1979), 31. Mumon, for whom the *Mumonkan*, or *Gateless Gate*, is named, was the fifteenth successor of Master Rinzai and also the eighth successor of the Yogi school of Zen. His teachings have influenced both the Rinzai and Soto schools of Zen.

7. *Eckhart*, see #7: p. 66 and #88: p. 283.

8. *Eckhart*, #11: p. 98.

9. Oscar A. Romero, from a homily preached on February 24, 1980, *Día a Día con Monseñor Romero* (San Salvador: Arzobispado de San Salvador, 1999), 365.

10. *Eckhart*, #82: p. 245.

11. Nhat Hanh, *Living Buddha, Living Christ*, 157.

12. *Gateless Gate*, 31.

13. Nhat Hanh, *Living Buddha, Living Christ*, 152-53.

14. Ibid., 153.

15. David Steindl-Rast, OSB, in the Foreword to *Living Buddha, Living Christ*, xvii-xviii.

16. Thich Nhat Hanh, *Going Home: Jesus and Buddha as Brothers* (New York: Riverhead Books, 1999), 46.

17. D. T. Suzuki, *Mysticism: Christian and Buddhist* (New York: Harper and Row, 1957), 145.

18. His Holiness Pope John Paul II, *Solicitudo Rei Socialis*, cited in *The New Dictionary of Catholic Social Thought* (Collegeville, Minn.: Liturgical Press, 1994), 909.

19. Ibid., #40, p. 916.

20. Nhat Hanh, *Going Home*, 36-37.

21. Thomas K. Tewell, "The Cross is Empty!" *The Living Pulpit* (Jan.-Mar. 2002): 48.

22. Ibid.

23. Ruben Habito, *Living Zen, Loving God* (Boston: Wisdom Publications, 2004), 83-84.

24. Beatrice Bruteau, *Radical Optimism* (New York: Crossroad, 1993), 98-99.

25. *Eckhart*, #25b: p. 194.

26. Nhat Hanh, *Going Home*, 32.

27. Ibid., 37.

28. *The Gethsemani Encounter: A Dialogue on the Spiritual Life by Buddhist and Christian Monastics*, ed. Donald Mitchell and James Wiseman, OSB (New York: Continuum, 1997), 232.

29. Archbishop Oscar A. Romero, *The Church Is All of You*, ed. James R. Brockman, SJ (Minneapolis: Winston Press, 1984), 55. From a homily on January 1, 1979.

30. Ibid., 91. Homily of July 22, 1979.

31. Ibid., 100. Homily of November 11, 1979.

32. Ibid., 110. Homily of March 24, 1980.

33. *Ahimsa* is the practice of active nonviolence, as taught by Mahatma Gandhi.

34. Nhat Hanh, *Going Home*, 161.

35. *Zazen* is sitting meditation in the Zen Buddhist tradition. The Zen meditation hall in question was at Takamori in Japan, under the spiritual guidance of Father Oshida, OP.

36. I borrow the phrase "gentle mirror" from the writings of St. Catherine of Siena, *The Dialogue*, trans. and intro. Suzanne Noffke, OP (New York: Paulist Press, 1980), no. 13, p. 167.

37. During the writing of this chapter (June 2004), His Holiness Pope John Paul II made a public confession of repentance for the Catholic Church's participation in the Inquisition. Such gestures are necessary if we are to heal the abuses of the past.

38. *Santo Domingo: Conclusions*, Message of the IV Conference to the Peoples of Latin America and the Caribbean, IV General Conference of the Latin American Bishops (October 12-28, 1992), #3.

Chapter 10: Love in Full Bloom

1. Meister Eckhart, OP, *The Book of Divine Comfort*, in *Meister Eckhart: Sermons and Treatises*, 3 vols., ed. and trans. Maurice O'C. Walshe, (Shaftesbury: Element Books, 1979), 3:95.

2. Thich Nhat Hanh, *Living Buddha, Living Christ* (New York: Riverhead Books, 1995), 3.

3. Ibid., 3-4.

4. Ibid., 72.

5. Meister Eckhart, OP, *Meister Eckhart: Sermons and Treatises*, 3 vols., ed. and trans. Maurice O'C. Walshe (Shaftesbury: Element Books, 1979), #13a: p. 110.

6. His Holiness the Dalai Lama, *The Good Heart: A Buddhist Perspective on the Teachings of Jesus* (Boston: Wisdom Publications, 1996), 49.

7. See ch. 2, n. 2 above.

8. Thich Nhat Hanh, *Going Home: Jesus and Buddha as Brothers* (New York: Riverhead Books, 1999), 161.

9. *Eckhart*, #9: pp. 86-87.

10. *Eckhart*, #66: p. 146.

11. *Eckhart*, #69: p. 167.

12. Thich Nhat Hanh, "Liberation from Suffering," *The Mindfulness Bell* no. 19 (May-August 1977): 1-3.

13. Ibid., 1.

14. Meister Eckhart, *The Talks of Instruction*, in *Meister Eckhart: Sermons and Treatises*, ed. and trans. Walshe, 3:12.

15. Ibid.

16. *Eckhart*, #11: pp. 93, 95-96.

17. *Eckhart*, #43: p. 4.

18. Eckhart, *Divine Comfort*, in *Meister Eckhart*, ed. and trans. Walshe, 3:71.

19. Ibid., 64-65. The masculine pronouns have been changed to be more inclusive.

20. Ibid., 65.

21. Nhat Hanh, *Living Buddha, Living Christ*, 49.

22. Julian of Norwich, *Julian of Norwich: Showings*, trans. Edmund Colledge, OSA, and James Walsh, SJ (New York: Paulist Press, 1978), p. 225.

23. Ibid.

24. Nhat Hanh, *Going Home*, 165-66.

25. Thich Nhat Hanh, "The Four Immeasureable Minds," *The Mindfulness Bell* no.18 (January-April 1997): 5.

26. Dalai Lama, *The Good Heart*, 67-68.

27. Nhat Hanh, *Living Buddha, Living Christ*, 84-85.

28. D. T. Suzuki, *Mysticism: Christian and Buddhist* (New York: Harper & Row, 1957), 150.

29. Ibid., 150-51.

30. Thomas Merton, *The Asian Journal of Thomas Merton* (New York: New Directions Books, 1973), 233-36.

31. Ibid., 257.

32. Ibid.

33. Ibid., 236.

Conclusion: A Journey and a Begging Bowl

1. Thomas Merton, *Thoughts in Solitude* (Boston: Shambhala, 1993), 89.

2. Ruben Habito, "The Zen Ox-Herding Pictures," *Maria Kannon Zen Journal* 5, no. 2 (1996): 5.

3. Thich Nhat Hanh, *Going Home: Jesus and Buddha as Brothers* (New York: Riverhead Books, 1999), 41-42.